Christ in a Pluralistic Age

Books by JOHN B. COBB, JR.
Published by The Westminster Press

Christ in a Pluralistic Age

Liberal Christianity at the Crossroads

The Theology of Altizer:
  Critique and Response (Ed.)

God and the World

The Structure of Christian Existence

A Christian Natural Theology:
  Based on the Thought of Alfred North Whitehead

Living Options in Protestant Theology:
  A Survey of Methods

Varieties of Protestantism

Christ in a Pluralistic Age

by JOHN B. COBB, JR.

THE WESTMINSTER PRESS
PHILADELPHIA

BOOK DESIGN BY DOROTHY E. JONES

PUBLISHED BY THE WESTMINSTER PRESS®
PHILADELPHIA, PENNSYLVANIA

PRINTED IN THE UNITED STATES OF AMERICA
9 8 7 6 5 4 3 2

Library of Congress Cataloging in Publication Data

Cobb, John B
    Christ in a pluralistic age.

    Includes bibliographical references and index.
    1. Jesus Christ—Person and offices. I. Title.
BT202.C62   232   74-820
ISBN 0-664-24522-6 (pbk.)

In grateful memory of
Ernest Cadman Colwell
to whose scholarly and professional encouragement
and persistent and penetrating study
of Jesus I owe so much

CONTENTS

FOREWORD

The Alumni Association and the Board of Trustees of the Austin Presbyterian Theological Seminary established a lectureship in 1945 to bring to the seminary campus each year a distinguished scholar to address an annual midwinter convocation of ministers, students, and laity on some phase of Christian thought.

The Thomas White Currie Bible Class of Highland Park Presbyterian Church of Dallas, Texas, in 1950 undertook the support of this lectureship in memory of the late Dr. Thomas White Currie, founder of the class and president of the seminary from 1921 to 1943.

This volume arises from the lectures that Dr. Cobb delivered in the winter of 1972. We are proud to have sponsored his lectures and to have given him occasion to publish this volume.

PRESCOTT H. WILLIAMS, JR.
President
Austin Presbyterian Theological Seminary
Austin, Texas

PREFACE

This book expresses the results of a long process of change within myself to which others have contributed in many ways. It is impossible even to list all of those to whom I am indebted. A decade ago I argued that Christology is possible only where the notions of God and man have been clarified. Accordingly I proceeded in three books to work out my understanding on this subject: *A Christian Natural Theology*, *The Structure of Christian Existence*, and *God and the World*. I still believe that to speak of God as having become incarnated in a human being presupposes that we know something of what we mean by the terms "God" and "human being." It also presupposes that what we mean allows for the notion of incarnation. I am fundamentally indebted to Alfred North Whitehead for my understanding of all this; and for my understanding of Whitehead and his importance for Christian thought, I am indebted especially to my teacher Charles Hartshorne.

But during most of the time I was writing those books, the Christology I envisioned was little more than a Jesusology. The questions I had in mind were how God could be affirmed to have been incarnate in Jesus and how this historical figure is present and effective in our world. I resisted the use of "Christ" as a name for that which the Christian worships, believing that this use confused the Jesus in whom God was distinctively present with God himself. The distinctions within the Trinity seemed to me more a source of confusion for theology than a help. Also, I thought that Christology could be largely worked out without relation to hope for the future. On these points my thought has changed and, I trust, advanced, but I realize that it is still in flux and that this book is more a progress report than a finished Christology.

The most potent influences upon my Christological reflections through this decade have been Wolfhart Pannenberg and Thomas Altizer. Pannenberg compelled me more and more to recognize that historical Christianity is bound up with hope and that this is not a feature of our tradition that we can shed. On the contrary, now more than ever hope is essential to meaning, and we can no longer rely on an unconscious carry-over from the days when hope was effectively articulated. I have resisted Pannenberg's own image of hope, and am still troubled where he seems secure. But this book in its present form cannot be understood apart from the long inner struggle with the orientation toward the future to which Pannenberg has given the most systematic, intelligible, and scholarly form. I have also perceived in Pannenberg an ideal integration of scholarship and imaginative, constructive thinking. But I experience this more as judgment than as stimulus, for I have no hope of emulating him in this.

Thomas Altizer has long represented to me a quite alien way of theological thinking in which I have recognized a power that my own work lacked. He works as an idealist in the realm of images. I have worked as a realist and a naturalist in the attempt to achieve conceptual clarity about the actual structures of the world. I have recognized that it was the idealist and not the realist who spoke to the reality of our time. This has perplexed and disturbed me, but for many years I could see no way of overcoming my limitation. Two events have particularly helped me. First, Altizer himself stepped across the divide in an article in which he interpreted Whitehead in terms of Christian images.[1] This showed me that the association of traditional images with a philosophical conceptuality was neither arbitrary nor unfruitful.

The other contribution was from the side of a Whiteheadian. William Beardslee in *A House for Hope* suggested that Christ should be understood in technical Whiteheadian terms as a "proposition."[2] Through this I found a way from the philosophical conceptuality in which I was immersed to the world of images. I have not used the technical term "proposition" in the

book, but my identification of Christ as an image and my
account of the ontological status of the image in Chapter 3 are
dependent upon Beardslee's insight.

Both Altizer and Pannenberg are Hegelians. It is not surprising, therefore, that I detect a certain Hegelian dialectic in my
own developing vision and work. I will leave it to readers to find
it for themselves in the body of the book, but it may help to
summarize what has been said above in several dialectical
schemata. The thesis of the realist concern for accurate desig-
nation of actual structures and the antithesis of the idealist
interest in lived meanings have led me to the synthesis of
images understood as the union of actuality and possibility. The
thesis of the fullness and richness of orthodox Christianity and
the antithesis of the honesty and responsibility of modernism
have led me to the post-modern pluralistic method. The thesis
of affirming a single truth, characteristic of both orthodoxy and
modernism, and the antithesis of pluralistic relativism, have led
me to affirm Christ as the process itself through which these
movements occur.

Pannenberg, Altizer, and Beardslee have all made more
specific contributions to the book as well. So have a host of
others: Hunter Beaumont, Dieter Betz, Delwin Brown, Clifford
Cobb, Lewis Ford, David Griffin, David Lull, Ekkehard Mühlen-
berg, Schubert Ogden, Dan Rhoades, Frederick Sontag, Jack
Verheyden, and Robert Voelkel are conspicuous examples. I
owe a special debt to Paul van Buren, whose negative criticism
of a portion of an earlier version of the manuscript caused me,
with the help of some of those just mentioned, to reconsider the
whole, withdraw it from publication, delete most of what he had
read, reorganize, rethink, and rewrite. The present book has
many limitations, and it does not go far toward meeting van
Buren's particular objections. But it is a substantially better
book because of this process.

That this book has been written at all is partly due to the
opportunity to give the Currie Lectures at Austin Presbyterian
Theological Seminary in the winter of 1972. Those lectures
have now been expanded, revised, and reworked several times,
before taking on the form in which they are offered here. Much
of the material in Chapter 12, "The City of God," appeared in an
article by the author, entitled "The Christian, the Future, and
Paolo Soleri," in *The Christian Century*, Oct. 30, 1974. I did

most of the work on this book while on sabbatical in Honolulu, and I am indebted to the pluralistic context of Hawaii and specifically to the Church of the Crossroads, whose members struggle seriously with the question of faithfulness in that context. My assistants Joseph Deegan and Ernest Simmons and my wife helped ready the manuscript for the publisher. Joseph Deegan also prepared the Index. The School of Theology at Claremont and its administration, by the generous allowance of time and by practical assistance, as well as by the general atmosphere of the school, makes possible the undertaking of projects of this sort.

                                                                    J.B.C., JR.

INTRODUCTION

For Christian believers and even for Christendom as a whole Christ has been the central image of saving power in the present as well as in both past and future. The decline of that image outside the church's most interior life is an event of vast spiritual importance for the entire world. This event can be interpreted by Christians as expressing a new separation of faith from its false confusion with the world, but this interpretation is belied by the increasing discomfort with the Christ image even in the church. Another interpretation is that ours is a post-Christian age, in which Christianity is an anachronism. But there is too much vitality in Christian life and thought for this easy dismissal. In some way the power that was once present in the image seems present still in both the church and the world.

Can Christ be alive when his image has passed from our basic vision? This book is an affirmative answer to that question. It undertakes to identify Christ within the concrete actuality of our history and our time. To do this requires some preliminary definition of "Christ" to give direction to the inquiry, but such a definition must be a formal one leaving open the actual contemporary meaning of Christ. In this formal sense "Christ" names what is experienced as supremely important when this is bound up with Jesus. Those who experience what is supremely important as bound up with Jesus are Christians. Materially, Christians have experienced the supremely important reality bound up with Jesus in diverse ways, such as the giving of life, the overcoming of evil, the forgiving of sin, and the transforming of the world.

Two related factors of modern experience, the profane consciousness and pluralism, have played a dominant role in obscuring Christ. First, the profane consciousness drove the sacred Christ out of the world into a special and vanishing sphere. For it, what was supremely important in the world seemed to be disassociated from the efficacy of Jesus. Since "Christ" is meaningful only for those who find what is most important for them to be bound up with Jesus, Christ could be addressed only in the worship of the Christian community.

Since World War I, initiated by aspects of Karl Barth's theology, thematically developed in different ways by such thinkers as Rudolf Bultmann, Reinhold Niebuhr, and Friedrich Gogarten, and profoundly symbolized by Dietrich Bonhoeffer, a creative response was made by Protestant theology to this threat to Christ. It recognized that much of what is supremely important for the Christian is indeed found in the profane world, but it showed also that the movement toward the appreciation of this world and the principle of action within it are bound up with Jesus and his influence.

The second major factor that has obscured Christ is pluralism. The fact that Christianity is one way in the midst of other ways has always been apparent, but the common response has been that Christianity is the one right or true way. Other ways are seen either as evil or as anticipations of that which is perfected in the Christian one. In either of these cases the conviction is unchallenged that "Christ" names the reality that is in fact supremely important for all, whether or not it is recognized as such. This conviction remained intact for most of those Christians who responded creatively to the challenge of the profane consciousness. Pluralism was not recognized at a level significant for Christology.

But today Christians can no longer view the other great Ways of mankind in this negative or condescending fashion. The traditional Ways of the Far East, for example, are not only recognized as having their own integrity and impressive achievements but also as offering much that Christians find sorely lacking in themselves. It is impossible to dismiss the Zen master as a benighted pagan, and "Buddha" must be recognized as rightly naming that reality which is for vast numbers of people supremely important.

One Christian response is to assert that Christ and Buddha are but two names for the same reality. In this way serious disruption or traditional Christology is avoided. "Christ" continues to name that which is supremely important for all, and Christians continue to acknowledge that for them this reality is found uniquely in Jesus. They add that God has worked in other communities through other persons and images, so that mutual respect should now replace efforts at mutual conversion. But this response is unrealistic. What is supremely important to the Buddhist is not what appears supremely important to the Christian. "Christ" and "Buddha" do not name the same reality. Christians must come to understand Christ in a world in which they deeply appreciate and respect those who do not find Christ to be what is supremely important to them.

The pressing danger of the acceptance of this deeper level of pluralism is an unqualified relativism. Relativism in a very important sense is simply true. All our explicit beliefs and attitudes are historically, culturally, and biographically conditioned. But this need not entail that all beliefs and attitudes are equally true or desirable. It is not enough to recognize that different communities hold different views and that all are to be equally tolerated. Christians cannot continue to be Christians without believing that for them Christ is truly supremely important. But this leads to an opposite danger. If Christ is supremely important for Christians and if Buddha is supremely important for Buddhists, and if Christ and Buddha are different, then it seems that Christians must close themselves to the full meaning of the Buddhist claim, and vice versa, and that the thrust toward openness, inclusiveness, and universality that is present in both Christ and Buddha must be thwarted for the sake of mutual toleration. But when Christ becomes a principle of closedness, exclusiveness, and limitation, he ceases to be what is most important for the Christian and the appropriate expression of the efficacy of Jesus. In short, what would then be called Christ is in fact the Antichrist.

A third response to the awareness of pluralism is to set aside the image of Christ. In many contexts within and without the church the name "Christ" is repressive. It is bound up with the sacred, from which people are rightly striving to become free; with the absolutization of particulars that they are rightly seeking to relativize; and with the history of Christian colonialism, against which the Third World inwardly as well as outwardly rightly revolts. Therefore, in many spheres of public discourse, the word should be avoided. Sometimes we can speak instead of the ultimate, or of the divine spirit. In some contexts technical philosophical words will help. Sometimes we must use language that does not have the note of transcendence at all. There is no deception in this, for our task is to find the image that best communicates what we mean to those to whom we speak, and often, "Christ" is not now that image. But it is not the case that by abandoning distinctive Christian terminology we can find common ground with the other great Ways. The diversity goes much deeper, and although some unnecessary obstacles to mutual appreciation may be removed by terminological change, no other image is identical with Christ, and theology itself cannot abandon its concern for just that image. In faithfulness to the image, theology must undertake to free it from its oppressive elements to become again the focus of liberating power.

David L. Miller has recently deepened for us the issue of pluralism by identifying it as polytheism.[1] Miller has less in mind the religions of the Orient and their claim upon us than the inner breakdown of the Christian effort to achieve a single center of meaning and existence in terms of which the many centers of meaning and existence are ordered. He acknowledges that we must live from one center at a time, but he urges that we recognize that there are many centers and that we not hold as an ideal that all be subordinated to one. He associates each center with a particular story capable of giving meaning to life but incapable of subsuming all stories. He sees that theology has dealt with this problem by abandoning stories and seeking the ultimate unity in a static metaphysical principle, but precisely by this move it rendered God abstract and ensured his death.

In the present book, pluralism is treated primarily with reference to the variety of great traditions and the diverse claims and opportunities they embody for us. Buddhism is chosen as a particularly important example of the kind of tradition in the face of which Christian theology should reconceive Christ. Miller treats pluralism as the polytheism of competing centers of meaning and existence in our individual lives. He sees in prephilosophical Greek mythology a more appropriate imagery for our religious imagination. The difference is real, but the challenge to theology is much the same. Christ claims universality, whereas pluralism and polytheism deny that any form of saving reality can have universal validity. Much that we have meant by Christ in the past, when we did not acknowledge pluralism, becomes destructive in our new situation. If Christ means the absolutization of one pattern of life against others or of one potential center of meaning and existence against others, then Christ is, as Miller shows, in opposition to our real need today. But Miller's response to this situation, simply calling for the recognition and acceptance of polytheism, is not the only one or the most creative. It is but an instance of that process in which our imagination and life orientation can be transformed by lucidity of vision and openness to what we see. It will not be the final step of that process. It is that process itself, and not that for which it calls at any moment, around which life can best be organized. In this book that process is called creative transformation. Christ, as the image of creative transformation, can provide a unity within which the many centers of meaning and existence can be appreciated and encouraged and through which openness to the other great Ways of mankind can lead to a deepening of Christian existence.

This proposal can be clarified in relation to a well-known formulation of Paul Tillich. He pointed out that the human problem has been experienced variously in different periods of Christian history, and that accordingly the meaning of Christ as the answer also changes. "While the norm for the early Greek church was the liberation of finite man from death and error by the incarnation of immortal life and eternal truth, for the Roman church it was salvation from guilt and disruption by the actual and sacramental sacrifice of the God-man. For modern Protestantism it was the picture of the 'synoptic' Jesus, representing the personal and social ideal of human existence; and for recent Protestantism it has been the prophetic message of the Kingdom of God in the Old and New Testaments."[2] These are all contrasted by Tillich with Luther's doctrine of justification by faith and his own idea of the New Being in Jesus as the Christ that overcomes "disruption, conflict, self-destruction, meaninglessness and despair in all realms of life." [3]

The process of change does not end with Tillich, and indeed the process is accelerated. Today the basic human question is no longer exclusively or primarily existential. We find ourselves together on a limited and endangered planet we have learned to think of as Spaceship Earth. At the moment of our recognition of how great is the threat our own actions pose to that spaceship, we also see more clearly than ever before how deep are the divisions that separate our communities from one another, how confused and confusing are the voices that would direct our management of the spaceship, how widespread is the sense of impotence and futility, and how lacking we are collectively in relevant, creative vision. The question the Christian hears in this situation is whether there is a Way through the chaos of our time so that we can be brought together with others rather than try to run roughshod over them. This book proposes that for us Christ is the Way that excludes no Ways. Tillich by no means intended to deny continuity and unity to Christ. No more do I. He believed that the New Being is the answer in every human situation. Similarly, to understand Christ as creative transformation illuminates also the creative transformation of Christ himself through which he answers the changing needs of human history without ceasing to be one and the same Christ.

An account of Christ can move forward from the prophetic expectation of Christ, through Jesus himself and his immediate effects, to the widening appropriation of his work down to the present. It can also begin with the present situation, tentatively discerning Christ within it and then grounding its conjecture by relating what it takes to be Christ to Jesus and Christian history. Each approach needs the other. The historical approach, unless guided by a keen sense of present experience, can lead to making a past epoch normative or can so trace the history of Christ as to miss those threads most important for our time. The approach from the present backward, when not richly informed with historical understanding, is in danger of identifying our present problem in a way that is not truly shaped by Jesus and his efficacy and of distorting Christian history to make it support substantially un-Christian theories. The ideal solution is a Christology in which historical wisdom and aliveness to present issues fructify each other.

Unfortunately my own historical knowledge is too limited to enable me to strive for this ideal. It seems more honest, therefore, to display in the structure of this book more nearly the form of my own reflection. In scattered investigation of the meaning of Christ in Christian history I have found clues to how Christians should now move forward in a pluralistic context. I have been convinced that these clues fit with major aspects of that understanding of Jesus and his efficacy which has emerged in recent study. And I have struggled to find through the resultant understanding of Christ the kind of hope that can undergird and direct our efforts. Accordingly, the argument moves from present to past to future.

The chapters that develop this argument make no pretense of constituting a complete Christology or even a comprehensive study of the aspects of Christology they treat. They express the results of a series of forays into interrelated topics. The results, in my experience, have been mutually supportive and illuminating. I hope that the book as a whole will give substance to a realistic understanding of the work of Christ in our time. But a full-fledged Christology would have to supplement, integrate, and transform these essays.

A milestone in my own understanding was my encounter with André Malraux's work in art history.[4] Malraux is a perceptive student of the Christ image in Western art and of its disappearance. In his account Western art triumphs over Christ; for Christ is bound to particularity, whereas Western art finally embraces all art. This struck me as highly suggestive of the course that Christian thought at its best is now taking. It seemed to me that if Malraux's account is accurate—and I find it convincing—art's move to universality was not a betrayal of the Christ it had once celebrated but a deeper appropriation of his meaning. I believe that Malraux's own insights into what has happened support this judgment, but he does not share it. Chapter 1 summarizes the results of my encounter with Malraux. It proposes that in the creative transformation of styles that is the history of art the Christian may discern Christ.

Malraux sees modern art as opposed to Christ because he believes that Christianity can never transcend its particularity as art has done. It is bound to the relativities of history and is therefore no longer in principle a living faith. But against Malraux it should be recognized that Christians find universality internal to their faith. This tension allows us to accept the historical relativization of beliefs, images, and practices as part of an ongoing community of faith. It is true that the celebration of Christian origins, which art could transcend, is experienced as essential to Christian faith, and this makes the achievement of universality far more difficult for Christianity than for art. But Chapter 2 shows that creative theology has moved along lines not unlike those followed by creative art. Even now theology is struggling to complete the task to which this book as well is dedicated. Precisely through deepening its central conviction of incarnation, Christian faith moves toward its own transformation through openness to all faiths. The creative transformation of theology that leads toward universality can responsibly be identified as Christ.

The remaining chapters of the book expand the justification of this proposal as to where we find Christ today. Chapter 3 deals philosophically with creative transformation to show that it is indeed the universal presence of the transcendent Logos. Chapter 4 describes the importance of rightly naming the process.

Since Christians can only name Christ in responsible relation to Jesus, Part Two examines Jesus and his effects in the world to determine how they are related to the creative transformation described in Part One. The conclusion is that both encounter with the words of Jesus and incorporation into the field of his influence effect creative transformation in the hearer. Further, the evidence of history indicates that what is identified as the Logos in Part One was distinctively embodied in Jesus. The resultant doctrine of Jesus as Christ or the full incarnation of the Logos is compared with the official teaching of the church as summed up in its creeds.

"Christ" cannot name the process that has been described if the process leads to nothing. If there is no hope, then all that has been said becomes pointless. Christ is essentially bound up with hope. Part Three explores four images of hope that can be claimed as Christian and that have some possibility of effectiveness in our world. The final chapter draws them together and shows that "Christ" also names the Christian hope. Part Three is especially tentative in its proposals. There is no shared image of hope in the Christian community today. The only images that have power are highly personal ones fashioned by individuals in the teeth of the prevailing lack of hope. What can be hoped for from an exploration and unification of some of these images is to strengthen the hope that a new image of Christ as our hope can emerge in power.

The book embraces an approach and an attitude that require explanation. My conviction is that the best explanation of any phenomenon is the one that does most justice to its own spontaneous self-interpretation. The best explanation of the sense of freedom is to show that we are free. The best explanation of the sense of moral obligation is to show that we are morally obligated. The best explanation for the mystic's belief that union with God has occurred is to show how union with God occurs. The best explanation of the Buddhist experience of no-self is to show that an existence as no-self is possible. Of course the world is full of deluded people. But, especially in the interpretation of those who have shaped the insights, imagination, and vision of humanity, delusion should be affirmed only as a last resort.[5]

This principle runs counter to the dominant modern one. The dominant principle is that the best explanation of any phenomenon is one that displays it as an instance of a more general type of phenomenon that is already understood. This leads to familiar patterns of reductionism. Their power is not to be questioned, but their limits become more and more apparent. The difference is one of tendency. No one is a consistent reductionist. Further, reductionists recognize that their understanding of the basic principles from which all phenomena are to be explained must be changed and developed in the process of expanding the power of the reduction. But the tendency is to attend to those phenomena that can be made to fit the existing first principles and to force those principles as far as possible on phenomena that appear inexplicable by them.

It is still clearer that the other approach—I will call it "post-modern"—can only be a matter of tendency. No one can simply interpret every phenomenon on its own terms. To try to do so would require the learning of many separate disconnected languages. The unity of the human person would be lost. But the tendency is constantly to check one's inclination to see the new phenomenon as nothing but an instance of what is already known and to allow it instead to appear in its distinctiveness for what it is. The effort to integrate it into a comprehensive view is postponed.

The different tendencies can be seen to be at work in the history of religions. In the eighteenth century the modern approach was controlling. All religions were understood to be expressions of natural religion distorted by superstition and priestcraft. In the nineteenth century this naïve view was quickly superseded, but there was still much interest in the religious *a priori* or the common essence in terms of which all the particular religions could be understood. Only gradually was this superseded by the effort to understand each phenomenon on its own terms. In this post-modern approach one allows oneself to be drawn as deeply as possible into the alien world of experience and thought. The interpretation of what is there found in terms that are acceptable or even intelligible in other universes of discourse is postponed.

The postponement cannot be permanent. Questions of truth and error, of authenticity and delusion, do arise. Also, even the most thoroughgoing proponents of the post-modern approach intend to contribute from their new understanding to others who do not make the full journey. Those who most deeply grasp the alien phenomena best realize the difficulty of communicating about them. The conceptualities that are available in our own culture are permeated either with the tendencies of modernist reductionism or with those of distinctively Western religion, especially Christianity. Only a new language will serve.

Where the modern mind is unchallenged, theology has been forced to engage in special pleading in order to give an account of Christian faith. It has understood itself as a confession of faith and it has justified its affirmations without regard to the kind of evidence and argumentation that is acceptable to the modern mind. That has been a necessary ploy. But where the post-modern mind establishes itself, this ploy is neither necessary nor acceptable. Christian phenomena, including the phenomenon of faith, can be understood in their own terms without appeal to faith as a source of special knowledge. The results are that many traditional Christian beliefs, practices, and experiences can be reaffirmed, but now in such a way that their truth and reality do not oppose the truth and reality of what is affirmed in the study of other traditions. This affirmation of the reality of highly diverse experiences and the truth of highly diverse convictions is essential to pluralism.

This reaffirmation of traditional Christian beliefs in a pluralistic context is characteristic of the chapters that follow. The attempt is made, however, to go one step beyond this toward their interpretation. For this purpose I have employed a conceptuality derived from Alfred North Whitehead. There are indications that persons from other traditions, especially Asian ones, find Whitehead's conceptuality fruitful for the nonreductionist interpretation of their worlds of thought and experience.[6] If so, an important step can be taken to realize the potential of the emerging pluralism.

This book will not be understood unless the reader perceives that the results reached by this approach are quite different from both traditional theology and the modernist alternatives. For example, in the chapters that follow, the incarnation of the Logos in Jesus is affirmed literally and seriously, as by traditional theology. When we allow the phenomena to speak for themselves, this interpretation follows. But this distinctive structure of Jesus' existence is now recognized as one of the many structures of existence that have appeared in human history. The supernaturalist and exclusivist implications that the tradition drew from its correct starting point are rejected.

This position pleases neither the orthodox nor the liberal. As a first attempt to develop the implications of this post-modern approach for the understanding of our own tradition, it may be wide of the mark. But I do not apologize for the offense to either orthodox or liberal. We must move ahead in a pluralistic spirit, and the results of the interiorization of this post-modern approach will relativize and supersede the alternatives of the recent past. We will oppose the tendencies to which we have been driven by modernism to reduce Christianity to a single essence, whether of experience, belief, or structure of existence,[7] and will treat many topics that have been virtually taboo in liberal circles. We will thus recover much of the rich complexity and diversity of meaning in the orthodox traditions. But all that we recover will be understood through-and-through historically and therefore relativized. I am far more confident that this is the way ahead than I am of the accuracy of the particular results attained in this book.

PART ONE
Christ as the Logos

CHAPTER 1

Christ as Creative Transformation in Art

The meaning and reality of Christ in any age is not settled by definition or even by dogmatic pronouncements of bishops in council. Unless the definition clarifies or helps to shape the actual image of Christ of the time, it is an artificial gesture. Further, the present meaning of Christ is not settled by past uses. "Christ" does not mean today what it meant in the first or thirteenth centuries, but its meaning today grows out of what it meant in those periods. In short, the image of Christ has a history, and its present meaning is inseparable from that history.

The meaning of Christ is bound up with Jesus. One major dimension of the role and effect of Jesus in history is his shaping of language and vision. A comprehensive account of his role in this respect would be a particular kind of history of Christianity and Christendom that would include political, social, and economic history as well as science, religion, and art.

This comprehensive task is far beyond the capacity of this writer or the scope of this book. Yet a theory as to what such a study would reveal underlies the structure of the book. This theory has developed in interaction with the perceptive and convincing interpretation of Christ in art offered by André Malraux in *The Voices of Silence* and *The Metamorphosis of the Gods*. Our theory is that as Christ disappeared from the content of Western art he became, under other names, its acknowledged inner principle.

The purpose of this chapter, then, is to wrest from the work of an art historian who sees Christ as having disappeared from Western art the evidence that Christ is the power that is expressed through it. Since there are other interpretations of the history of art, and since there are other segments of history in which Christ has disappeared from public view, this chapter can only be a sample study representing a type of theological endeavor that is important for our time. But since the visual arts are a sensitive measure of culture and a significantly creative element within it, and since Malraux is an art historian with a rare theological sensitivity, success in this venture should lend an initial plausibility to a bold theory that will be further supported in later chapters.

There is an additional reason for selecting Malraux for this foray into the Christological interpretation of culture. This book deals with Christ in an age of pluralism. One main theme of Malraux is how Western art broke out of self-absolutization and embraced pluralism. The problem for Christianity is analogous to that faced and solved by Western art. If so, both the recent history of art and Malraux's interpretation of it are particularly instructive for the Christian theologian.

Malraux recognizes that, for art, the ability to appreciate more than one style is a quite recent achievement. "No real pluralism in art was known in Europe until the simultaneous acceptance of the Northern and Mediterranean traditions which took place, not in the Renaissance, but when the supremacy of Rome was challenged by a coalition of Venice, Spain and the North during the nineteenth century." [1] The ability to appreciate many of the non-European arts is still more recent. "Before the coming of modern art no one *saw* a Khmer head, still less a Polynesian sculpture, for the good reason that no one looked at them. Just as in the twelfth century no one looked at Greek art, or in the seventeenth century at Medieval art." [2]

Malraux believes that a comparable internalization of pluralism is impossible for Christians. For him there is a fundamental conflict between modern art and Christianity as well as any other religion. Modern art has been informed by the historical consciousness through which it is able to transcend its immersion in any particular style toward an appreciation of all great styles. But this consciousness, Malraux believes, is fatal to religions. He says: "The rise to power of history, which began with the decline of Christendom and even of Christianity, is due neither to modern science nor to historical research into the lives of Christ and Buddha, but to the fact that history pigeon-holes each religion within a temporal context, thus depriving it of its value as an absolute. . . . This concept of religion as an absolute had ruled out the possibility of any mutual understanding on a deeper, universal level." [3]

The thesis of this book is that Christ is no more bound to any particular system of religious belief and practice than is the creative power of art to any particular style, and the preliminary thesis of this chapter is that Christ himself is the creative power of art. This means that the supremely important reality, which is bound up with Jesus, is also the principle of all true art. To argue this, or at least to show that Malraux's writings bear unintended witness to its truth, the chapter is divided into two parts. First, Malraux's account of the history of Christ in art is summarized to show how as Christ disappears from the content of art the artist increasingly serves inwardly the power that the visible image objectively represented. Second, the argument is developed that Malraux's account of what has happened since the disappearance of Christ from the content of art witnesses to the continuing power of Christ in a new form as that which has brought art to universality.

To begin, we shall summarize Malraux's account of the history of Christ in art under three themes, showing how (1) the Christ image was progressively enfleshed or incarnated; (2) human beings were progressively personalized; and (3) the artist was progressively individualized.

1. Although official church teaching strove to maintain a balance between the human and the divine in Jesus, it did not succeed in imposing this balance on the artistic imagination. Christianity spread in the Roman Empire at a time when the sacred, whose dominance had been broken by the Greeks, was returning. The arts of the crumbling empire from Egypt to Gaul broke with the classical representation of the human figure and resumed the archaic symbolization of the sacred. Christianity competed not with classical humanism in the portrayal of the human but with the religions of Asia in the symbolization of the sacred.

In the Christian imagination of Byzantium, God the Father

was the sacred mystery rather than the one whom Jesus had addressed intimately as "Abba." Christ was the omnipotent pantocrator, ruler and judge of all things, omniscient, immutable, and severely just. Even on the cross he was impassible in his transcendence of human suffering. Thus Byzantine art glorified "the monophysitism that Byzantium repudiated in its dogmas; never has any Christian art treated Christ so clearly as a manifestation of God himself." [4]

In the West, also, even after the break with Byzantium, the influence of Augustine ensured that the imagination was dominated by God the Father, and Christ was largely assimilated to his image. However, the emphasis was not so much on the divine aloofness and inscrutability as it had been in Byzantium. Even "before the year one thousand, there had emerged in France, in Spain, and in the Rhineland certain tendencies towards humanization very different from the Byzantine formalism." [5]

In spite of these tendencies the Christ who dominated the Romanesque cathedrals was still not Jesus but God. Yet gradually, because God's immanence was insistently affirmed, "Christ's presence on earth was likewise affirmed; immanent in all created things and accessible to all mankind." [6] This Christ remained sacred, but "no other art in any other civilization ever caused the sacred to embody so much of the human and so fully expressed the sacred through the human." [7]

As Romanesque gave way to Gothic art, this unity of the sacred and the human fell apart. The sacred was separated from Christ, who became more and more the human Jesus. In Malraux's striking words, "Western Christianity was now to celebrate with noble works of art the metamorphosis of the Logos into Jesus." [8] Furthermore, it was this humanized Christ, envisioned as a benevolent king, who dominated the Gothic imagination, while the Father as sacred power receded.

In the fourteenth century a further step was taken. The victorious, kingly, idealized Christ gave way to the Christ who suffered and died. He was portrayed not only as hanging on the cross but as suffering agony there. The serene and beautiful features of the thirteenth century were now contorted in death. Christ's passion dominated the imagination. "It was almost as if He had just died, a second time." [9]

The events of Jesus' life were progressively transposed from the idealized world of the thirteenth-century imagination to the human world. In the fifteenth century, religious scenes for the first time included representations of human time, and the scenes of Jesus' life were increasingly introduced into the artist's own world. "In Flanders the sacred figures had for backgrounds Gothic towns, not fabulous cities, and it was there that finally the world of men replaced the world of God." [10] It was now the actual, everyday world in which incarnation and redemption occurred, rather than either a sacred or an imagined one. Christ had become Jesus, and Jesus had become a man among men.

2. The progressive incarnation of the divine was accompanied by increased personalization and individualization of the human. This appears in the representation of human beings in religious art and the emergence of secular art. Thus the history of Christ is at the same time a history of human self-understanding.

Whereas Byzantine art is an overcoming of the humanistic elements of classical art, the West entered a new period of humanism in the thirteenth century. However, this Christian humanism was quite different from the classical one. In it men and women became individualized, personalized, or ensouled. Malraux shows this especially in his account of portraits. These were lacking in Greece, where artists "moved on from abstract to idealized figures without an intermediate stage of portraiture." [11] In Rome, portraits were common, but Roman portraits "were primarily character studies. . . . A classical face, even if it be not a god's face, may bear the stamp of any experience—except life." [12] In the Christian West, "starting off from abstract or symbolical forms (the Christs on Romanesque tympana, the animals symbolizing the Evangelists), art was now progressing, by way of the saints, toward the widest possible diversity and discarding the abstract in proportion as it humanized it; was passing on from St. Mark's lion to St. Mark himself. . . . Gothic Christianity . . . idealizes *only* the individual." [13] It presents the individual in terms of his biography, in terms of the "imprint of his private drama on every man's face." [14]

The Christian individualism reflected in this Gothic portraiture broke up the unity of the cathedral. By the fourteenth century "that collective devotion of which the cathedral was the grandiose expression was giving place to a new relationship between man and the divine; Christ no longer spoke to men at large, but to the *individual believer*." [15] This individualism in turn paved the way for secular portraits.

Through most of the fourteenth century, although there had been many statues of secular personages, they were all connected with the world of God.[16] But quite suddenly at the end of that century, statues of secular figures were made for the château as well as the cathedral. The fifteenth-century Flemish painters also began to paint portraits separated from their connection with sacred figures, although imbued with a "distinctive spirituality." [17] The intrinsic interest once reserved for the divine was now directed to the individual personality as well.

3. Changes in the Christ image and in the understanding of human beings were accompanied on the artist's part by a new understanding of himself as an individual. "The atelier now became the headquarters of a Master, not of the foreman of a team of workers, and sculpture was ceasing to be anonymous. The sculptor now sought in himself alone the inspiration he had formerly derived from the cathedral. . . . He made the discovery of a new mysterious, personal power." [18] Art was born—the world of statues and paintings. And now into that world he could pour not only divine and secular figures, fiction and reality, but also figures from his dreams. The autonomous power of art as such was being realized.

Whereas heretofore art had always been expected to represent its object, whether sacred, imaginary, or worldly, the autonomy of art now made possible the gradual dominance of the artist over his subject matter. "It was Hals who inaugurated—timidly, yet with a touch of bravado to begin with—that conflict between the painter and his model which characterized modern art. . . . Hals' brushstroke does not exalt his model, but transmutes him into painting." [19]

The humanization of Christ, the individualization of human beings, and the emergence of the artist as the creator of his world did not put an end to Christian art. Much of the great art of the sixteenth and seventeenth centuries is explicitly Christian in theme as well as spirit. In the greatest art Christ, the world, and the artist came into new relations of union and conflict.

The private piety that had replaced the public faith of the thirteenth century left wide scope for artistic expression. The believing painter now struggled to find God. God meant for El Greco "not what he meant to the Chartres sculptors to whom he was *given,* but what he meant to votaries of the religious sects—to the saints and heresiarchs of the age: a Visitant, known in secret." [20] El Greco's struggle is manifest in the series of paintings culminating in *Toledo in a Thunderstorm:* "He began by placing the donors underneath his Christ; later, on one side only of the Cross—while on the other side one saw Toledo. Then the donors disappeared altogether. And, lastly Christ too disappeared. Only Toledo remains. . . . From now on, whether portrayed or not, Christ is immanent in all his art; indeed He has become the driving force behind it." [21]

The piety of Rembrandt was, if possible, still more intensely inward and personal. "In his parleyings with the angel who alternately overwhelmed him and abandoned him only two figures existed on earth, Christ and himself—and the man confronting Christ was not Mijnheer Rembrandt Harmenzoon of Amsterdam but an embodiment of all that suffering humanity, to which Christ's message was addressed." [22] For him as for some of the work of Michelangelo and El Greco "the spectator has ceased to count." [23]

After Rembrandt, the Christ image moved to the periphery of the great art of the West. Occasional paintings represent scenes from his life. More often there are scenes of ordinary life in which elements of the Christ image—poverty, weakness, compassion, suffering—qualify some human character as a Christ figure. But even this is on the periphery of the advance of art.

We now turn to the second major task of this chapter. This is to show that Malraux's account of the history of art justifies the claim that when the visual figure of Christ disappeared from painting and sculpture he became the recognized power of that Western art which accepted and interiorized pluralism. Translated into the formal definition of Christ proposed at the beginning of the Introduction, this would mean that the reality which is supremely important to Christians becomes the explicit principle of Western art. But can that power be recognized as bound up with Jesus and his efficacy?

As we have seen, Malraux traces the visual representation of this power from the Byzantine cosmocrator to the tortured figures of the crucified. His account also moves us farther toward the recognition that as this power ceased to receive distinctive pictorial representation it increasingly functioned in a more interior way in art itself. We have seen that he shows, first, that Christ became Jesus and Jesus became a man among men. That means that Christ is found in the present in the real, contemporary, everyday world. He describes, second, how individual personality shared with Christ in detailed attention and received from him a distinctive spirituality. The locus of ultimate significance that had once been beyond the world or only in special sacred places within it came to be found in individual personality. He explains, third, how artists shared in this process of individualization through union with what had been recognized as Christ and gained thereby a new consciousness of creative power. They became conscious transformers of the world. In Rembrandt, the artist became the humanity that struggles with the claim of Christ. In El Greco, when Christ disappears from the painting, he becomes "the driving force behind it."

Our task now is to show from Malraux's account that the growth of the artistic consciousness of transforming the world and the artist's sense of serving art at the cost of personal suffering justify the assertion that for modern art, as for El Greco, the Christ who has disappeared from its subject matter has become the driving force behind it. The conditions for this assertion are as follows. (1) It can be justified only if the development in Western art requires that what happened after Hals, El Greco, and Rembrandt be viewed as in continuity with what occurred in them. This continuous development must have carried through the tendency to view all humanity as Christified, in the sense of being inherently worthy of attention, and the tendency to see the particular individuality of persons, and especially of artists themselves, as bearers of a sacred meaning and responsibility. (2) It can be justified only if art is not viewed as absolute or as serving a power unique to itself but rather is seen as only one vehicle of service or embodiment of a power of universal importance and relevance. I will discuss these two conditions in order.

1. Malraux's whole presentation offers the strongest evidence

of the continuity of Western art. There are repeated transformations, but no new beginning comparable to that of Western art in relation to classical or Byzantine art. Each style, indeed, is a transmutation of the forms of the style that preceded it. No other art has ever proceeded through so many profound alterations. But when earlier periods are rediscovered and become sources of fresh inspiration, as when in the high Renaissance classical statuary was enthusiastically admired, this was not the initiation of a new departure or return to classical style. It was a further development of trends already fully established in Gothic art. Similarly Malraux sees the anticipated movement from and beyond modern art as a continuation of the whole process he has traced from the Romanesque humanization of the sacred to Picasso's constructivism. He does not anticipate a new beginning or transformation from without; rather, he anticipates a further development of a Western art that has now become universal. "The first culture to include the whole world's art, this culture of ours, which will certainly transform modern art (by which until now it was given its lead), does not stand for an invasion but for one of the crowning victories of the West. Whether we desire it or not, Western man will light his path only by the torch he carries, even if it burns his hands." [24]

The direction of modern art continues that which was begun in the medieval period. The greatest art of the West is an intensification and completion of those features imparted to it through the Gothic incarnation and crucifixion of Christ. Malraux sees that the individualization begun in the fourteenth century progressively detached the artist not only from the dominance of Christian images but also from society. Social value ceased to be given. The spirit of inquiry became dominant.[25]

Not only did art become autonomous, it also arrogated to itself more and more the absoluteness that once belonged to Christ. In a society that has no common structure of value "there *is* a fundamental value of modern art. . . . Its annexation of the visible world was but a preliminary move, and it stands for that immemorial impulse of creative art: the desire to build up a world apart and self-contained, existing in its own right: A desire which, for the first time in the history of art, has become the be-all and the end-all of the artist." [26] Art is thus "not a religion but a faith . . . the negation of the tainted world." [27]

"From the Romantic period onward art became more and more the object of a cult. . . . The artist's personal life has come to be regarded as the mere vehicle of his art. Such men as Velázquez and Leonardo who painted only when commissioned were very different from Cézanne for whom painting was a *vocation*." [28] "Once a mere collection, the art museum is by way of becoming a sort of shrine, the only one of the modern age." [29]

2. It is clear, then, that the movements associated with the visually represented incarnation and crucifixion of Christ continued in modern art. Art became increasingly autonomous and the sacredness that once attached to the visible Christ progressively defined the creative principle of art itself. In this way the power that can transform, redeem, unify, and order moved in a continuous process from a transcendent world into the inner being of artists themselves.

But before Christians can identify the creative principle of art with Christ, we must ascertain whether this principle is only a particular power of transformation, redemption, unification, and order, to be distinguished from other operations in other dimensions of human existence. For if so, Christ could not be identified with this power without dividing Christ against himself and thus destroying him. If to name this power "Christ" would be to deny that Christ is present in science, philosophy, and above all, in the Christian community, the Christian could not make this identification.

This is not an easy question, for it does seem that the autonomy of modern art has led to its absolutization. However, the absolutization that is found in art requires fuller consideration before it is attacked as idolatrous. The modern art that most fully participates in this absolutization is precisely the art that has relativized itself by bringing into view the whole of world art. "And art which found its values in itself alone . . . resuscitated . . . values foreign to its own; . . . Manet and Braque . . . acted as interpreters of the language in which the Sumerians, the pre-Columbians and the great Buddhist arts address us." [30] Thus modern art has unified all art not by absolutizing its own style, still less its own products, but "by substituting art's *specific* value for the values to which hitherto art had been subordinated." [31]

What now is this specific value of art? Clearly it is not the value of any particular subject matter or style or relation of the artist to his work. It is instead what all great styles have in common. "Every great style of the past impresses us as being a special interpretation of the world, but this collective conquest is obviously a sum total of the individual conquests that have gone to its making. Always these are victorious over forms, achieved by means of forms. . . . Once we realize how all-important is the significance of styles, we understand why every artist of genius . . . becomes a transformer of the meaning of the world, which he masters by reducing it to forms he has selected or invented. . . . And he attains this mastery not through his visual experience of the world itself, but by a victory over one of the forms of an immediate predecessor that he has taken over and transmuted in the crucible of genius." [32]

In modern art for the first time this specific value of art becomes freely manifest. It rejects "*all* values that are not purely those of painting." [33] "Artists had decided that henceforth painting was to dominate its subject matter instead of being dominated by it." [34] Just for this reason, every great style of the past can be appreciated and encompassed. In this process, however, the meaning of the effigies, statues, and paintings of the past is transmuted. They no longer bear their original sacred meaning. They are set alongside the work of the modern artist and are thereby transformed into works of art.

Thus modern art has destroyed every fixed value and every established order, even its own. Every particular meaning that has been associated with Christianity and with Christ, as similarly every particular meaning of every other culture, has been relativized. There can no longer be a Buddhist or Hindu or pagan or Marxist art. Art by its nature must now relativize the forms that would express the distinctive values of each tradition. Equally there can be no Christian art in that sense. Still the art that overcomes all traditions, including Christianity, is the art in which the consequences of Christ's history in art are most fully expressed.

The absolute of modern art, therefore, is not itself a style. It is, rather, artistic creativity as such through which the world of meaning is repeatedly transmuted by new forms. Even so, an idolatrous element remains. This art seems to separate itself as absolute from the other spheres of life and thereby denies value to them. It splits off the world of the artist from the world of

politics, business, family, and piety and even from the worlds of
science and philosophy. The Christian must reject this separation of art as absolute from the rest of life for the same essential
reason that Malraux rejects the church's absolutization of a
particular tradition.

However, Malraux's presentation again gives confidence that
art will transcend its present form in service of its absolute. He
knows that modern art, too, in its specificity will be transcended. "Victorious as it is, our modern art fears it may not
outlast its victory without undergoing a metamorphosis." [35]
Furthermore, Malraux senses that the direction of change may
relativize painting as such. He sees that in Picasso and Miró a
passionate constructivism leads the artists to grope "for some
pictorial outlet other than the easel picture." [36] And Malraux
himself further relativizes the absolute value of art; for he
recognizes that the specific value of art as mastering and
transforming the world through new visual forms is analogous
to the specific value of philosophy and science. These in a
similar way master and transform the meaning of the world
through concepts and laws.[37]

These suggestions in Malraux are receiving significant vindication in the decades since he wrote *The Voices of Silence*.[38]
Painters themselves are engaged in the deabsolutization and
demystification of painting. They are fast destroying the boundaries that divide their art from sculpture and even architecture.
They are destroying also the boundaries that separate it from
the rest of life. The creative transformation that is art and the
creative transformation that is life are increasingly recognized
in their identity. The remaining absolute is to be found in
creative transformation as such.

Before Christ can be fully recognized as the moving principle
of our art one more change is needed. The autonomy of the
individual must be transcended. The rise of this autonomy
accompanied the incarnation and death of the Christ image. It
was an autonomy over against the sacred, against all imposed
values, and eventually against all control by the forms of the
visible, natural world. Artists became creators of forms out of
their own inner resources. The power of creation became the
artist's own individual possession, owed to nothing and to no
one.

Malraux notes that this extreme individualism is a transitional phenomenon. The triumph of the individual "is coming to look to us as precarious as it is spectacular." [39] He rightly sees that "it is quite possible that the successor of the art we call 'modern' will be still more individualist," [40] but the individualist spirit turns its questioning finally on itself as well. "The same conquest of the outside world that brought in our modern individualism, so different from that of the Renaissance, is by way of relativizing the individual. It is plain to see that man's faculty of transformation, which began by remaking of the natural world, has ended by calling man himself in question." [41]

The argument of this chapter has been developed in dialogue with Malraux's history of Christ in art. It will now be summarized. "Christ" is understood as the power of transformation, redemption, unification, and order as that power has been apprehended through Jesus and his historical effects. The grasp of this power in Christendom can be traced in part through the visual representation of Christ. Here there is a striking movement from radical transcendence through incarnation to crucifixion and assimilation with suffering humanity. This move expresses the increasing efficacy of the story of Jesus in shaping the image of Christ. As this supremely important power is experienced in an increasingly incarnate form, human beings realize their own individual significance as agents of the transformation of the world. In an especially vivid way artists come to understand themselves as bearers and servants of this power. When they do so, they recognize that the art of other times and places also unconsciously served the same power and can therefore be appreciated and appropriated as art. That is, the differentiation of the power of transformation from every particular expression of that power enabled the artist to internalize the pluralism of artistic styles. The recognition that this power is not the power of art alone but of all life leads the artist to demystify art and destroy the boundaries between it and creative activity in general. It is now time for the Christian boldly to name as Christ what has for so long been separated from that name. When that is done, theology will have a clue as to how in faithfulness to Christ it can internalize the pluralism which is its present context.

CHAPTER 2

Christ as Creative Transformation in Theology

Malraux traced the disappearance of the visual figure of Christ from Western art. He showed that as the figure disappeared there continued the creative transformation of styles for which the reality expressed by the figure had been responsible. Eventually this creative transformation itself was recognized as the specific value of art. Only then did it become possible for Western art to see the essential genius of art in all styles and thus to become truly catholic. Chapter 1 argued that the power of creative transformation manifest especially in Western art is the continuation of the effects of Jesus in the Western experience.

There is nothing new in seeing a theological significance in the creative principle that is the essence of art. Nicolas Berdyaev wrote: "Creativeness in art, like every other form of creative activity, consists in triumph over given, determined, concrete life, it is a victory over the world. . . . Creative power anticipates the transfiguration of the world. This is the meaning of art, of art of any kind. And creative power has an eschatological element in it. It is an end of this world and beginning of the new world. . . . Creation is a divine-human work." [1] And John Dixon shows that our time has witnessed the fullest expression of art as creativeness. "The achievement of the twentieth century is constructive, the creating of a type of object and a type of making that had not existed before. This was a liberation of man from a kind of oppression of his imagination and represents clearly man himself the creator. . . . This liberation of creativity had consequences beyond this kind of making. Man was liberated into creativity." [2]

We have taken a further bold step, in proposing the name of Christ for the eschatological divine-human work of which Berdyaev speaks and the creativity into which Dixon shows that twentieth-century art is liberated. The justification provided in the previous chapter was that this creative transformation is continuous with the Christ image represented in the visual figures of the artist both historically and substantively. But more justification is needed, and the remainder of the book undertakes to offer it by unfolding the understanding of Christ that is involved.

This chapter begins this process by arguing that the recent history of theology warrants the understanding of Christ as creative transformation. It is appropriate to name as Christ the process whereby the Christ figure was displaced and a true pluralism was attained in Western art only if this meaning of Christ is supported by that discipline which is particularly responsible for explicit reflection about Christ. The thesis is that Christ names the creative transformation of theology by objective study which has broken the correlation of faith and the sacred and made pluralism possible. We will consider theology in terms of (1) its interpretation of other religions and (2) its relation to the history of religions. We will then treat (3) the justification of naming as Christ the process of creative transformation of theology effected in this relation, and we will conclude with a discussion of (4) how Christian pluralism can avoid debilitating relativism while leaving open the question of how other traditions, such as Buddhism, can also appropriate pluralism apart from Christ.

1. Christian attitudes toward other religious traditions have varied from early times. At first they were shaped chiefly in relation to Judaism, Greco-Roman cults, and Greek philosophy. Islam later played a large role. Some Christians saw these other traditions as preparation for the gospel while some viewed them as demonic. The absolute claim of Christ to be the one bearer of the only salvation was unquestioned. In the Reformation the claim was hardened further against Jews and Muslims and the pretensions of philosophy.

In the seventeenth century, deists invented the notion of a

pure and true natural religion by which all positive religions are to be judged.[3] They varied in their appraisals of Christianity, but, in spite of their intentions, they failed to pave the way for any real acceptance of non-Western religion. Their natural religion was a rationalized version of Christianity. This movement reached its culmination, breaking its own bounds, in Immanuel Kant's *Religion Within the Limits of Reason Alone.*

By the beginning of the nineteenth century, Christian thinkers began to deal more seriously with other religions, including Asian ones. Roughly during the same period that modern art was learning to appropriate non-European arts, Christian theologians were beginning to appreciate non-European Ways. Their new understanding of Eastern culture led to a deeper recognition that Christianity is one Way among others, that others have positive value, and that Christian self-understanding must be forged in this context.

The first major Christian thinker to interpret Christianity as one religion among others was Friedrich Schleiermacher. His interest was chiefly in the relation of Christianity to Judaism and Islam and to their polytheistic predecessors, but he took some account also of the religions of the East. He found that an advance in the history of religions from idol worship to polytheism occurred in both Greece and India.[4] But neither moved on to monotheism, which is clearly superior in that in it "all religious affections express the dependence of everything finite upon the Supreme and Infinite Being."[5] This step has been taken only in Judaism, Islam, and Christianity, and it is to the explanation of Christian superiority to the other monotheistic faiths that Schleiermacher devotes his major attention.

The Eastern traditions are taken more seriously by G. W. F. Hegel. Hegel inherited from Kant the understanding that the experienced world is structured by the human Mind or Spirit. For neither Kant nor Hegel did this mean that individuals choose how to structure their worlds. For both men, the agent of this structuring is Mind or Spirit as such, not the individual person. But for Hegel, Spirit realized itself progressively in history through those who conform their merely private concerns to its claims. Indeed, history is the self-development of Spirit. Its "goal of attainment is Spirit in its *completeness,* in its essential nature, i.e., Freedom."[6] Hence "Universal History exhibits *gradations* in the development of that principle whose substantial purport is the consciousness of Freedom." [7]

This history begins in the Far East, in China; it proceeds through India to Persia, Greece, and Rome, and reaches its consummation in the German people. The idea of incarnation that appears with Christianity is completed in the actuality of the Spirit in the Protestant German states of Hegel's time. There the idea of freedom is fulfilled in the union of objective freedom and subjective freedom, which is the coincidence of the rational laws of society with individual obedience to reason.

Both Schleiermacher and Hegel give a positive place to Eastern traditions. The issue for them is not that of the truth of one religion and the falsity of others, but of the stage of development and finally, in Schleiermacher's words, of "the exclusive superiority" of Christianity.[8] This prepared the way for serious attention by Christians to the religions of the East. It did not, of course, constitute a pluralistic stance or open Christians to the inner appropriation of the distinctive achievements of the East.

Partly in reaction against Schleiermacher and Hegel, Arthur Schopenhauer, through his antipathy to Christianity, attained a deeper grasp of the real relations of East and West. He saw that the issues between the monotheistic and the Indian religions involve two basically opposed attitudes toward the world. "The fundamental characteristics of the Jewish religion are realism and optimism, views of the world which are closely allied; they form, in fact, the conditions of theism. For theism looks upon the material world as absolutely real, and regards life as a pleasant gift bestowed upon us. On the other hand, the fundamental characteristics of the Brahman and Buddhist religions are idealism and pessimism, which look upon the existence of the world as in the nature of a dream, and life as the result of our sins." [9]

Schopenhauer thus saw that Indian religion constitutes a radical challenge to Christianity rather than a lower stage of a development leading toward it. His own decision was emphatically against Christianity because of its optimism, its anthropocentric indifference to the suffering of animals, and its confusion of history and doctrine. His position was no more pluralistic than that of those who pronounced Christianity exclusively superior; but the presence within the Western tradition of an insightful advocate of Indian religion helped initiate the slow movement toward pluralism.

Christian theology in the context of the history of religions reached its highest flowering in the early twentieth century in the work of Rudolf Otto. Otto penetrated deeply into the meaning and nature of religion and saw with imaginative appreciation the manifold ways in which it came to expression. More than any predecessor, and better than most successors, he developed his categories from the study of the history of religions in general instead of by generalization of Christian experience.[10] He was able to employ these categories in his theological interpretation of Christianity as well.[11] The task he undertook, however, was an enormous one, and theologically he was not himself ready for a complete pluralism. In order to show the unity of all religions, he exaggerated the centrality to each of that element of the numinous which he found common to all. Since it was still important for him to show the superiority or finality of Christianity, his interpretation of the numinous was skewed in favor of the form it took in Christianity. At the same time his interpretation of Christianity was also flawed.

Otto carried to its fullest perfection the typological approach of Schleiermacher. His contemporary, Ernst Troeltsch, went beyond him by building on the historical approach of Hegel. This allowed for a deeper appreciation of the diversity of religions, whose commonality he found only in their bearing of the universal Spirit—not in a common essence.

Troeltsch undertook to display the superiority of Christianity as Hegel had done in the context of his vastly greater knowledge of the actual history of religions. In his book *The Absoluteness of Christianity* he argued that Christianity through its understanding of revelation was uniquely independent of every particular culture and therefore the one truly universal religion. But he continued to wrestle with the issues of relativity. His great work *The Social Teaching of the Christian Churches* forced him to recognize that Christianity, too, is a "purely historical, individual, relative phenomenon, which could, as we actually find it, only have arisen in the territory of classical culture, and among the Latin and Germanic races." [12] He also found that the religions of Asia were far more capable of transcending particular cultural contexts than he had supposed. Hence he finally acknowledged the relativity of the higher religions, including Christianity, as varied expressions of one Divine Life. Christianity is best for the heirs of Western civilization, but Hinduism and Buddhism best meet the needs of the cultures they have shaped.

Unfortunately, Troeltsch did not recognize this acknowledgment of relativity as a creative breakthrough of Christian faith itself. Instead, he felt partly defeated and withdrew from full identification with the theological task. It was left to H. Richard Niebuhr to show that the kind of relativity acknowledged by Troeltsch is to be affirmed by Christians as precisely what their faith requires. Christians are called to confess what they have received through their tradition. They are not called to make claims of superiority. They are to share with others while asking others to share with them.[13]

Most Christians, however, continued to believe, as does Malraux, that their faith requires the absolutization of the particular in their history rather than its confession as particular. In the years following World War I, this absolutization of the particular was vigorously renewed. Troeltsch had shown that the identification of Christianity as a religion and of religion as a part of culture led inevitably to historicism or relativism. Insofar as Christianity is a religion, this result was accepted by Karl Barth, the leading theologian of the new movement. But Christianity, when it is true to itself, Barth said, is not a religion but faith in Christ, the unique and particular incarnation of God. That incarnation, as opposed to Troeltsch's universal immanent Spirit, is the absolute. All else is relative.

Barth opened the way to comparative religions and gave the discipline a free hand. But it was free precisely because what it treated was not theologically important. Hence the actual effect of his teaching was to strengthen the tendency of Christian thinkers to study and reaffirm their own tradition, ignoring the emerging awareness of the claims of other traditions that had become important in the nineteenth century and the early part of the twentieth century.

2. Since World War I leading Christian thinkers have believed, as a result of Barth's imposing achievement, that they must choose between theology on the one side and the objective

study of religion as a phenomenon on the other. Theology has been understood to be the articulation of Christian faith from within. It deals confessionally with its own content, leaving other subject matters, including religions, undiscussed. History of religions, on the other hand, was assigned the objective approach. Sometimes it has been viewed as the encompassing rubric for all objective study of religion, sometimes as one of these studies alongside sociology and psychology.

In any choice between theology and the history of religions it has been widely believed that faith calls for the former. Theology often struggles to maintain an unbroken relationship to the formative events of Christianity. It tries to bear witness to the sacrality of those events, of some aspect of them, or of some features of their reception. Thus theology has continued the correlation of faith and the sacred which has characterized Christianity as well as other major traditional Ways.

History of religions in the inclusive sense of objective study of religions breaks that correlation. It is concerned with the sacred as a type of phenomenon. The sacred is what is sacred for others, not for the student. Even if the methodology of study includes empathetic identification with the stance of the believer, the conscious adoption of that approach destroys the sacrality of what is apprehended within it. The historian of religion as such is not a believer in this traditional sense. In the last resort the sacred is relativized and therefore introduced into the profane world.

History of religions in this sense has helped to erode the power of the sacred in its traditional forms. Above all, "God" has ceased to function effectively as the name of the sacred. Those, such as Gerhard Ebeling, who are most concerned that "God" be used only when there is ultimate seriousness of personal involvement find it increasingly difficult to speak of God. Others talk more comfortably of how the word should be employed precisely because they treat it as a concept separated from the sacred it has formerly named. This is clearest among those who speak lightly of "God talk." The "death of God" theologians, on the other hand, combined ultimate personal seriousness with the continuing identification of "God" and that which is sacred, but they did so only by their negations.

Other traditional Christian language has retained its association with the sacred longer. "Christ" and "Word" and "Kingdom of God," for example, still carry remnants of their earlier sacred meaning. For others, especially among Lutheran theologians, "faith" has become the final bastion of the sacred, the one reality they can assert as beyond location in the profane world.[14] In Bultmann and Ebeling, for example, "faith" points to that state of being which transcends its own analysis by psychology and sociology and calls up a sense of ultimacy that eludes those disciplines. But the process of desacralization does not stop there. What Christians mean by "faith" must be laid alongside what Martin Heidegger means by "authentic existence," what Buddhists mean by "enlightenment," what Abraham Maslow means by "peak experiences," and what others mean by wholeness, release, or fulfillment. In the critical comparison of these ideals for existence, the sacredness of each is broken.

The question for the Christian is how to understand this phenomenon of the desacralization of all received words and images. Does it mean the end of Christian faith? Can Christianity be viewed now only as one human movement among others from a perspective that is grounded outside of it? If objective study of Christianity desacralizes and relativizes that to which Christians are committed, is the only alternative for Christians to turn our backs on the history of religions and reaffirm the absoluteness of our faith?

This book is written in the conviction that the answer to all these questions is No. Christian faith can continue, but for it to continue as a creative rather than obstructive force, it must accept and affirm the break in its relation to traditional language and beliefs that their objective study necessarily entails. Christian faith can reestablish itself now only as the basis for the objective study that breaks the correlation of faith and the sacred.

Thus far, however, objective study is still felt largely as a threat to faith rather than as its expression, and indeed it seems too often to function in this way. A recent illustration is the valuable study *My Brother Paul,* by Richard Rubenstein. Rubenstein vividly grasps that "the conflict between faith and history cannot be dismissed lightly. The objective historian is compelled to place the affirmations of faith in the context of the social and cultural movements out of which they arose. In the light of objective history, no religious position can be privileged. The same relativizing tendency is also manifest in the sociology

of religion." [15] Rubenstein's book presents Paul appreciatively
and with deep understanding. It recognizes Paul's great historical contribution and even suggests his contemporary relevance.
But the normative perspective is Freudian theory. The value of
Paul and other significant religious figures is interpreted in
terms of stages "on the road to psychological man, which
culminated in the psychoanalytic revolution." [16] Hence his book
is not offered as a contribution to Christian theology, despite its
interest and value for Christians. Instead it appropriates Paul
from the perspective of psychological man who "represents a
type of demystified consciousness that neither Paul nor the
rabbis could have anticipated." [17]

Much of the same content could have been presented in
another way. It would be possible to appropriate the demystified consciousness of psychological man from a perspective
recognized as derived from Paul instead of appropriating Paul
from the perspective of that consciousness. Rubenstein even
hints at that possibility when he notes the indebtedness of depth
psychology to Paul.[18] Given this recognition, a Christian theologian might present depth psychology as an important step in the
continuing influence of Paul on Western history rather than as
the definite culmination in terms of which all other events are
normatively understood. Instead of taking Freudianism as a
kind of science that stands above historical events and makes
their deeper understanding possible, one can see it as another
historically conditioned phenomenon that must be relativized in
its turn by this perspective. The contribution of depth psychology to the understanding of Paul as well as of Freud would by
no means be denied by such an approach, and many of
Rubenstein's brilliant insights could be incorporated.

Such study of Paul would still objectify and distance its
object, thus breaking the correlation of a faith stance and the
sacredness of what is studied. But the decision to study
objectively and the categories, Freudian or other, with which
the study was pursued would be experienced as the appropriate
expression of Paul's own influence and meaning for us. In that
case the book would express Christian faith as it functions
through and beyond the historical or objectifying study of
religion, and it would embody that new form of Christian
theology which has long been struggling to be born.

There is no reason why Rubenstein should have written a

theological book instead of this psychoanalytic one. He identifies himself as a psychological man and not as a Christian. The point of these comments is that a Christian study need not be less critical, detached, or objective. Indeed, one might argue that the quasi-absolutization and sacralization of Freud's perspective in Rubenstein's book limits its objectivity. For example, Rubenstein's insistence that for Paul the end sought was "the objectless state of quiescence out of which we have come" [19] seems more determined by Freudian theory than by Pauline texts, and this possible distortion might be corrected by a more self-critical approach. Hence a theological treatment based on a truly contemporary, and therefore broken or desacralized, relation to Paul can be at least as objective as a Freudian one. The distinction is that the theological approach locates itself in a history that continues to be normatively affected by the liberating effects of Paul's teaching instead of a history that is normatively determined by Freud.

A generation ago it was popular to argue that since everyone occupied some position, no special defense was required for confessing the Christian one. That argument usually intended to justify continuation of the traditional correlation of faith and the sacred in which it believed. That is not what is being defended here. Instead, it is assumed that the study of the many faith stances correlated with the many forms of the sacred has permanently eroded them all. The question is not one of justifying any of them. The relativizing consequences of the historical (psychological or sociological) approach is to be fully accepted, but it can be accepted by the Christian, as H. Richard Niebuhr showed, not with resignation, but with affirmation. Further, the historical approach, which erodes the correlation of faith with a sacred object, also requires reflection on the perspective from which the erosion occurs. It is important that the thought of Freud, for example, not become the new absolute or sacred but itself be brought under the eroding power of responsible criticism. Part of that self-criticism is historical understanding. If through historical understanding we come to see what we are doing as the appropriate continuation of Christian tradition, that is not to return to an earlier form of Christian faith which resists the eroding effects of the history of religion. It is to enter into a new form of faith which affirms that history.

Historians of religion may object that this location of our
present responsible reflection in either the Freudian perspective
or the course of Christian history is still too narrow. They may
call us to locate ourselves in global history, breaking out of all
provincial standpoints. This is important, but the exact significance of this critique of provincialism requires clarification
through the following questions. Through what history have we
come to the conviction that we should transcend our particular
history toward a global one? Who produced the discipline of
history of religions? Why do we suppose that objectivity and
universality are important values over against self-justification
and exclusivism? Honest answers to these questions must
recognize the peculiar role of the Christian tradition in shaping
the standpoint that aims to criticize itself through the history of
religions.

3. In considering Malraux's history of art, we argued that the
process that relativized the Christ figure and then omitted it
altogether was itself the power represented by the Christ figure,
namely, Christ himself. In this chapter we have traced the
process through which traditional theology, with its correlation
of the theologians' faith with their sacred object, has produced
and been superseded by the history of religions that relativizes
every sacred form. We now ask whether this process, too, so
often opposed for its supposed faithlessness to Christ, is in fact
itself Christ.

Against an affirmative answer it is asserted that "Christ" has
named God, who is sacred, absolute, and transcendent, whereas
it is here proposed that the word name an immanent process of
relativizing every given object or claim. "Christ" has been the
symbol of Christian exclusive superiority, whereas the word is
here appealed to as identifying the principle of critical overcoming of any such exclusiveness.

There is historical justification for these protests, but it is an
ironic history that justifies them. "Christ" names the divine
reality as that reality is held to have been present and manifest
in Jesus, who is accordingly called Christ. Hence one would, in
Jaroslav Pelikan's words, "expect that the Christian definition
of the deity of God would be regulated by the content of the
divine as revealed in [Jesus] Christ. In fact, however, the early
Christian picture of God was controlled by the self-evident

axiom, accepted by all, of the absoluteness and the impassibility of the divine nature. Nowhere in all of Christian doctrine was that axiom more influential than in Christology, with the result that the content of the divine as revealed in Christ was itself regulated by the axiomatically given definition of the deity of God." [20] This meant also that in the image of Christ the paradoxical power manifest in the cross was replaced by the conventional power of compulsion and control manifest in worldly rule, now projected on the cosmos. Church teaching established God as absolute, impassible, eternal, immutable, transcendent, omnipotent, omniscient, and demanding of perfect obedience; and it established Christ as God.

The history of theology can be read as a long struggle between two tendencies: on the one hand, the trend toward assimilation of what is manifest in Jesus to the prior understanding of deity; and, on the other hand, the effort to maintain what is distinctive in the manifestation. Chapter 1 showed how in the history of art Christ was first identified with the transcendent power of God, then was detached from God the Father, became more fully Jesus, and then disappeared into suffering humanity. In the history of art God the Father seemed quietly to evaporate from the scene, but in the history of theology as a propositional discipline, this could not occur. In the eighteenth and nineteenth centuries God and Jesus were drawn apart, with God removed to the transcendent metaphysical realm and Jesus brought fully into that of history. "Christ" became little more than an honorific title for Jesus. God disappeared from science and history, as he had from art, but theology remained bound to this language. Among liberal theologians some identified God with the Hegelian *Geist*. Others tried to allow the New Testament understanding of God as the Father of Jesus to shape their images. At the beginning of this century Adolf von Harnack summarized the gospel in terms of the message of Jesus as "God the Father and the infinite value of the human soul." [21] But even this fatherly God remained "above," and despite Harnack's popularity, this imagery had no strong purchase on the modern sensibility.

The renewal of the Christ image as something more than a name for the historical Jesus was due chiefly to Karl Barth. Barth began his reaction against liberal theology by reemphasizing the transcendence and sovereignty of God and renewing the identity of Christ with God. The historical Jesus was declared to be only the historian's Jesus and of no interest to faith. Thus, as with the dominant orthodox tradition, Jesus was once more assimilated to a Christ who was assimilated to deity as understood apart from Jesus. But Barth recognized that since Christ was God, God was Christ, and he took seriously his own pronouncement that God made himself known in Christ and only in Christ. He therefore began to rethink God in terms of what is revealed in Jesus.

Dietrich Bonhoeffer carried through this renewed incarnation of God. In the notes jotted down in prison for his never-written book, Bonhoeffer wrestled with the question, "What do we mean by 'God'?" His answer brought "God" into closest relation with "Christ"—in turn, closely identified with Jesus. Bonhoeffer wrote: "What do we mean by 'God'? Not in the first place an abstract belief in his omnipotence, etc. That is not a genuine experience of God, but a partial extension of the world. Encounter with Jesus Christ, implying a complete orientation of human being in the experience of Jesus as one whose only concern is for others. This concern of Jesus for others is the experience of transcendence. This freedom from self, maintained to the point of death, the sole ground of his omnipotence, omniscience and ubiquity. Faith is participation in this Being of Jesus (incarnation, cross and resurrection). Our relation to God not a religious relationship to a supreme Being, absolute in power and goodness, which is a spurious conception of transcendence, but a new life for others, through participation in the Being of God. The transcendence consists not in tasks beyond our scope and power, but in the nearest thing to hand. God in human form, not, as in other religions, in animal form—the monstrous, chaotic, remote and terrifying—nor yet in abstract form—the absolute, metaphysical, infinite, etc.—nor yet in the Greek divine-human of autonomous man, but man existing for others, and hence the Crucified. A life based on the transcendent." [22]

In Bonhoeffer's last reflections God became that Christ who in art much earlier had become identified with suffering humanity. In the years since Bonhoeffer wrote, the identification of deity with the suffering Christ has become normative for theology, and the theologies of hope and liberation have been especially effective in pointing to the identification of Christ with the oppressed and dispossessed. These are most clearly defined as those who are economically, socially, and politically exploited and abused. Identification with suffering is not a merely psychological matter, however. The cross is not the symbol of suffering as such but of redemptive suffering. Christ is not to be seen in the miserable as such but in every impulse within them and within others to overcome that misery. He appears in the creative transformation of consciousness from hopeless resignation to the demand for justice. He appears especially in sustained and effective efforts to transform the structures that produce misery.

Further, oppression and misery are not limited to particular classes. Women have come to a new consciousness of their oppression, and in the process of a powerful surge of self-liberation they have raised the consciousness of men as to how we too are oppressed. Even the rich are oppressed by their wealth and the powerful by their authority. And we now recognize with Paul that the whole creation groans in travail waiting for liberation. The drive toward redemption is universal, and Christ appears in the creative transformation of all life everywhere.

Finally, we now realize that no new order into which liberation might lead us would be free of new forms of oppression. Utopia does not lie ahead as an actual future. Whatever we accomplish, the need for liberation will continue. In the unending drive toward liberation, yesterday, today, and tomorrow, we discern Christ.

This recognition of Christ in the liberation movements of our time is now widespread. It is also widely recognized that these movements are essentially transformations of consciousness and understanding which then express themselves in new organization and overt action. To identify Christ with these movements is to see Christ as the creative transformation of thought and imagination even more than of economic and political structures. The mass transformation of thought and imagination is possible only as new understanding of traditions has been achieved and the relation to established sacred forms has been broken. The process of liberation from the past as bondage and its transformation into a resource for creative novelty is fundamental to all liberation. To see Christ in the movements of social, political, economic, ethnic, national, and

sexual liberation of our time is to recognize him in the process
of creative transformation of basic understanding and of the
theology in which that is expressed. Christ's work in theology is
analogous to that in art: He breaks the relation to himself as
objectified figure and becomes the principle of liberation at
work in theology itself. Thereby he liberates theology for
pluralism as well.

4. To pass through the history of religions and to internalize it
is a necessary but not sufficient condition of pluralism. It is
necessary because only thereby is the relation of theology to its
traditional sacred form sufficiently broken to allow for the
appreciation and acceptance of other forms of the sacred. But it
is not sufficient, since the history of religions may absolutize a
favored conceptuality that is alien to the perspectives of the
traditions studied. For example, Rubenstein could study Gautama and Confucius as well as Paul from the perspective of
Freudian theory, illuminating their lives and thought, but he
would not thereby become a pluralist. Only what he studied
would be relativized; the Freudian perspective would remain
absolute. Pluralism requires that the student of religion recognize the inherent power and validity of each tradition in its own
terms. The plurality of faiths must be studied in such a way that
their own modes of understanding, including their understanding of one another and of Freudian theory, be acknowledged as
warranted. This requires a relativization of the perspective of
the student as well.

The apparent danger of pluralism is that it leads to a
debilitating relativism. If pluralism relativizes all traditions, it
seems to imply that because they are equally good our own
choice of values or meanings is arbitrary. Choice becomes
either, as with Sartre, an arbitrary creation of values, or as with
much positivism, an empty gesture. In neither case can it be the
appropriate response to the actual situation. Morality is undercut.

When Christians name Christ as the transforming power that
relativizes every position, we counter this kind of relativism.
But pluralism does relativize all settled and formal norms. To
accept pluralism is to see that our received Christian ethics, for
example, even in its most general and convincing principles, is

but one system among others produced under historically conditioned circumstances. It does not bind us, and therefore it does not give us definitive guidance. The threat of relativism is the most critical issue the Christian pluralist has to face.

This was not the problem in the early Christian community. Nevertheless, there are clues in the New Testament understanding of Christ that are relevant. The New Testament Christ does not embody a system of values. The New Testament does not offer an ethical code. Christ is a reality in terms of which one is called and empowered to act responsibly. Responsible action in the light of Christ ordinarily conforms to some generally recognized principle of morality, but the need is to discern the call of Christ in each particular situation. That is not decided by appeal to any established principle. It is to be determined in openness to the meaning of Christ for that situation. Where cultural values differ, there will be a difference of meaning. But the meaning will not be settled by the cultural values alone; for Christ has his own meaning. He is the not-yet-realized transforming the givenness of the past from a burden into a potentiality for new creation. Christ always means, regardless of what the cultural values are, that they must be relativized without being abrogated; that the believer lives toward the future rather than attempting to defend, repeat, or destroy the past; that each should be open to the neighbor, in whom also one meets the claim of Christ; and that the good in what is now happening is to be completed and fulfilled.

To give up all commitment to established beliefs and patterns of morality is possible for Christians without relativism. We live from and for the new. This does not mean, of course, that we favor change for the sake of change. Most of what is called change is simply the rearrangement of what is given, the return to earlier forms, or even the abandonment of the achievements of the past without compensating advantage. To destroy life on the planet would produce a different situation from the one we now enjoy, but it would not produce a significantly new one. It would wipe out the achievements of true novelty through millennia and destroy even the places at which novelty can now have effective entry into the world. To identify Christ with the new is to see the new as unrealized potentiality for transforming the world without destroying it. The new builds upon the old and transfuses it with meaning it could not have apart from the new. The new not only frees us from the old but also frees us for it. It establishes the world as it transforms it.

When Christ is known as this process of creative transformation and when faith is wholeheartedly directed to him, pluralism can be inwardly appropriated without relativism. But against this it may be objected that since creative transformation is not affirmed and reverenced in all traditions, unqualified faith in it is incompatible with pluralism. To serve Christ in this sense would seem to prejudge the case against those who do not orient themselves to the process of creative transformation.

The questions raised here are complex, but the objection expresses a misunderstanding of pluralism. Pluralism cannot be indifference. To affirm pluralism is to affirm as necessary and valuable what many traditions strongly oppose. It is to affirm universal openness and inward appropriation of other traditions, whereas these attitudes are rare in the history of religions. To be a pluralist is not to be neutral with respect to all values. Further, the high appraisal of pluralism does not spring rootless from nowhere. It can only arise in the actual world and its actual traditions of thought and feeling. For the Christian it can arise only through a deepening of the understanding of Christ.

This leaves open the question whether and how the inner appropriation of pluralism can arise in other traditions. A leading Buddhist scholar, Masao Abe, believes that "the dynamic relativism of *nirvana* may provide a spiritual foundation for the formation of the rapidly approaching One World in which the co-existence of a variety of contrasting values and ways of life is indispensable." [23] He explains that "the Buddhist position, founded in *nirvana,* is a 'positionless position' in the sense that, being itself empty, it lets every position stand and work just as it is. . . . Buddhism . . . recognizes the relative truths which they contain. . . . Buddhism starts to work critically and creatively *through* this basic recognition of the relative truths contained in other positions, hoping for productive dialogue and cooperation with other faiths." [24]

If Christ as creative transformation is the principle of Christian pluralism, and if nirvana as the positionless position is the principle of Buddhist pluralism, then what of the new pluralism of principles? We are not ready to answer that question.

Perhaps the ultimate duality of principles cannot be overcome; but perhaps nirvana can be creatively transformed; or perhaps Christ will be absorbed into the positionless position. For now, both Christians and Buddhists have reason to trust the process, and that suffices.

The argument of this chapter has been that Christ is not to be identified with any given form established by past doctrine but instead with the creative transformation of theology that has broken our relationship to every established form. The transformation of theology has come about chiefly through the rise of objective study of Christian history and experience as this is viewed in the global history of religions. We find Christ today as the principle of affirmation of the resultant pluralism, and hence we can internalize this pluralism as the present expression of our own faith.

CHAPTER 3

Creative Transformation as the Logos

In Chapter 1 it was shown that in Malraux's reading of the history of art the redirection of commitment from particular styles to the creative transformation that produces all styles made possible the pluralistic inclusion of all art in Western art. In Chapter 2 it was shown that a similar redirection is occurring in theology through the historical study of all religions and the interiorization of pluralism. In the case of art, it was shown that by Malraux's own account the progressive incarnation of Christ in the artistic imagination initiated the process that eventuated in this transference of commitment. The whole process can be interpreted as a completion of this incarnation. Hence it was proposed that the creative transformation which functions as the center of the artist's life as artist is Christ. Theology knows that it must serve Christ, but it is only now learning that it does so by allowing itself to be creatively transformed by those disciplines which relativize and desacralize every form in which Christ has previously been known.

This account of Christ in art and theology cannot stand alone. Christ is indissolubly bound up with Jesus, and in Part Two this relationship will be treated. Christ is also indissolubly bound up with hope, and Part Three treats their relationship. In addition, there are questions about the meaning and reality of Christ that can only be treated philosophically. The discussion of these questions is necessarily more abstract than most of the rest of the book. This chapter discusses four such questions, as follows.

First, Christ cannot be viewed by Christians as creative transformation in art and theology unless the ontological status thereby attributed to Christ is satisfactorily explained. Christians cannot live by abstract concepts on the one side or worship a multiplicity of events on the other. But Christ cannot simply designate some one event or entity. The proposal made here is that Christ is an image, and the ontological status and existential function of images is examined.

Second, the locus of Christ must be clarified. If Christ is creative transformation in art and theology, he is not only that. Malraux recognizes the same reality in philosophy and science, and post-modern art is further relativizing art by overcoming the boundaries that separate it from life. Theology could never be satisfied to find Christ only or primarily in its own history. The Christ it serves is the Lord and Savior both of the public world and of individual persons in the inwardness of their experience. Christ cannot be creative transformation in art and theology and something quite different in nature and in individual existence. If creative transformation is Christ, it must be discernible in all life. To establish the universality of Christ, there is offered an analysis of the relation of past and future in the basic process of all becoming as illustrated in a moment of human experience.

Third, Christ cannot be identified with an immanent aspect of events unless he is also transcendent. The polarity of immanence and transcendence is shown to be a common characteristic of all events, but its special application to Christ must be clarified. Reflection on the Logos helps to bring out this characeristic of Christ. Christ is the incarnation of the Logos, or the Logos as incarnate.

Fourth, deeply entrenched habits of thought oppose the acceptance of the actuality and efficacy of the immanent-transcendent Christ. These are closely bound up with the often unconscious assumption that we are related to what transcends us only through our sense experience. This assumption is critically exposed as false to experience and as seriously distorting in its consequences for all thought and especially for theology.

1. "Christ" is first of all, and most certainly, a word. As a word it is a mark on a piece of paper or a sound in the ear. But,

like all words, it is much more than that; it has meaning. It receives its meaning from a changing matrix of language and experience in an ongoing community of discourse. In recent years much attention has rightly been directed to the use of language and its function in social relations. The discussion of Christ up to this point has largely presupposed this context of interpretation.

But there is another dimension of meaning that has been less considered in recent discussion. This is the traditional referential one. Although there are forms of language in which this dimension is of minor importance, "Christ" functions importantly within a community of discourse only if it is tacitly assumed that it refers beyond the language and what the language effects to a power or reality that can be distinguished from human language and has reality even when not named. But it is not immediately evident what kind of referent "Christ" has.

Some words designate particular things or persons. The demonstratives "this" and "that," in contexts that specify their referents, approach a purely designative meaning. Proper names in some circumstances can be similarly designative. For example, in a crowded room in an employment office, a clerk unacquainted with those present may read out a list of names of those who should report to an employer.

Some words sometimes stand for concepts. A concept is an abstraction or a pure potentiality. Triangularity, virtue, democracy, redness, and pridefulness can name concepts when the context indicates that these are to be considered in themselves and not in their actual embodiment in the world. Science and philosophy concern themselves chiefly with concepts. But in ordinary language few words identify either entities in abstraction from concepts or concepts in abstraction from entities. Most words in most contexts name entities as qualified actually or possibly by concepts or name concepts as actually or possibly ingredient in entities. Indeed, this is still much too simple an account. Most words in most contexts designate sets of entities as qualified by sets of concepts, with the boundaries of neither set clearly determined. In the face of such confusion and vagueness, the dominant tendency in mathematics, science, and philosophy has been to achieve clarity by precise definitions. That by which things can be defined is called essence.

The discovery of essences and their interconnections was the great achievement of Greek thought. Without it, science would be impossible.

Literature in general has accepted the vagueness of language. In the clusters of ill-defined meanings to which most words refer, it has recognized that by which people actually understand their world and communicate with one another. Successful writers live and feel deeply into these meanings of words. In the process they see more clearly the connections that exist among them. They also sense that the meanings are capable of change and development, and they become the bearers or agents of the history of meanings through their shaping of language.

Although the referents of few words are strictly limited to entities or concepts, many are sufficiently bound to one or another of these as to be little distorted when studied in that way. Others have as their referents vast and changing clusters of meanings that unite entities and concepts. These words name images, and it is these images by which life is chiefly ordered and energy given direction. The great religious words in all traditions name images. "Christ" names an image. The unity of entity and concept that "Christ" names is creative transformation—or Christ.

Theology stands on the boundary between philosophy and literature. It has the responsibility to nurture the images of its tradition. Such nurture can neither keep the images forever static nor allow them to develop unchecked. The task of the theologians is to distinguish the responsible and appropriate development of images from their perversion. To achieve this they must pursue clarity with the philosophers, while recognizing that this clarity must serve the images rather than displace them with concepts.

Both philosophy and literature are in danger of obscuring the designative side of images. The essences that philosophy seeks are concepts, and it is with respect to these that a measure of clarity can be achieved. The tendency is that actual entities be understood in terms of actuality and "entitativeness" as concepts, rather than in the concrete particularity of being. The being of entities repeatedly eludes the philosopher's grasp. Literary images contain this elusive reference to the actual world, but there too it is in danger. The temptation of writers is to allow the free play of their imagination to associate the imprecise concepts involved in the image without checking them against the actual entities also designated in the image. Life in the midst of images tends to become dissociated from the actual facts of the world and to overlay those facts with a vision that both illumines and obscures them.

Theology must resist this tendency in both philosophy and literature. Christ is not a concept or fluid nexus of concepts. "Christ" does not designate Jesus as such but refers to Jesus in a particular way, namely, as the incarnation of the divine. It does not designate deity as such but refers to deity experienced as graciously incarnate in the world. To abstract the designative element from the conceptual would be to distort the meaning of "Christ" beyond Christian usage. But to abstract the conceptual meaning from the designative one is equally unacceptable. The responsible development of the conceptual side of the meaning must be checked by repeated reference to both history and ontology.

The argument in Chapter 1 was that while the visual picture of Jesus and of deity disappeared from art, the cluster of meanings whose history could be traced through the art continued to evolve. They no longer suggested to the artist or the viewer the words "Jesus" and "God." They were indeed little named. But Malraux names them as the specific value of art, and his account of that specific value can be summed up as creative transformation of style. The emergent style takes the past style up into itself and is thus continuous with it, but it gives new life to the old style precisely by its transformation. This creative transformation of style has a religious dimension and the artist may relate to it as servant. When it is seen that this divine power served by the artist is a continuous development from the image that was once pictorially represented as the divine Jesus or as the Christian God, now internalized into the artist's own work, creative transformation, it can be named Christ. The analogous argument for naming as Christ creative transformation as it has operated in theology need not be repeated. But it must be shown that creative transformation is an actual fact, not only in these two traditions but in all life.

2. In every event innumerable strands of influence come to bear and are integrated into a new unity. If this were all,

however, there would be no reason to speak of creative transformation. Each experience, and therefore also the reshaping of the world, would be nothing more than the rearrangement of elements of the past. Indeed, these elements would be rearranging themselves, for no other factor would be involved than their own intrinsic force. Experience would be the passive effect of these causes; the present would be the impotent consequence of the past; complete metaphysical determinism would be the final truth; and creativity would be an illusion.

But a system of thought that declares what appears as real to be an illusion does not deserve immediate assent. Alternatives should first be explored to determine whether the appearance can be saved. The major option is to suppose that each experience is open to unrealized potentiality as well as to realized actuality, to the future as well as to the past, to the "not yet" as well as to the "has been." The relationship between the influence of the past and the lure of the future has been a major theme of Western thought.

In traditional Aristotelian terms, efficient causality was supplemented by final causality or teleology. In that context an adequate explanation of what occurred required both an account of the antecedent conditions that led up to it and an account of the purpose that directed it. Modern science progressively displaced explanation in terms of final cause or purpose by explanation in terms of efficient cause—i.e.,the way the past conditions necessitated a particular outcome. Down through the nineteenth century, intellectual progress was measured by the gain of the explanatory power of the resultant mechanistic model of reality. To many it seemed that the Darwinian explanation of the human race incorporated mankind within this model and showed that even the human subjective experience of purpose would finally be seen as an illusory product of deterministic forces. To a large extent the scientific program of the twentieth century continues in this direction.

Nevertheless, the tide has turned. Obviously there can be no return to the easy teleological explanations of the past. But the scientific advance has displayed the limits of the categories of science in such a way as to reopen questions that were discouraged, if not forbidden, by the earlier stage of the scientific program.

The more advanced forms of science have now abolished efficient causality from their purview as fully as final causality. Thus the model of the past exhaustively shaping the present, fundamental to earlier scientific thought, no longer receives specific support. Mathematical formulas of enormous predictive power now constitute the highest achievements of science. In Aristotelian terms, formal causes have succeeded efficient causes as the mode of scientific explanation.

Although materialistic and mechanical models continue to work well in relation to the ordinary objects of sense perception, especially the inanimate ones, it is now recognized that even these objects are composed of myriads of entities to which such models have very limited application. The world of subatomic particles continues to unfold depth upon mysterious depth. The mathematical formulas of exact science are now seen as statements of statistical probability, and the idea of laws of efficient causation determining the behavior of the ultimate individual is outdated.

Even when events of ordinary proportions are in view, and when explanation in terms of antecedent conditions or efficient causation is appropriately sought, what is explained is never the event as such in its concrete actuality and particularity. Explanation is always of a type of event or an aspect of an event. In principle as well as in practical fact, no event, however simple, can be exhaustively analyzed into aspects that can be explained in this way.

These familiar truths do not imply that science is now open to the reintroduction of the once-banished explanation by purposes or final causes. Such explanation is more remote than ever from the interests of most scientists. But it is now clear that the ideally complete scientific explanation does not account for the behavior or experience of individual actual entities. Philosophy can follow science in this respect, or it can reopen the question of the explanation of the individual. If it takes the latter course, it should seek an account that correlates with what science shows about the efficient causal determination of aspects of individuals and statistical laws about them. But there is no justification for the lingering supposition that the findings of science, or even its program, require the reduction of purposive phenomena to nonpurposive ones.

Purposive phenomena are those which appear to be oriented to the future. Hence the same point can be put in another way. There is no longer any reason to attempt to reduce future-orientation to the efficient causality of the past. The possibility should be left open that such reduction is possible; that, for example, a human experience is *only* a vector resultant of the past events that influence it. But that should be recognized as only one hypothesis alongside others and subject to the test of phenomenological analysis. In that test it does not fare well. The evidence is strong that present purpose affects the way in which past influences are weighted and adjusted.

It is true that present purpose grows out of past conditions. Hence, to a large extent purposes can be explained by their efficient causes. But it is equally true that in the concrete actuality of each momentary experience the meaning and effectiveness of past conditions are determined by the present purpose. Efficient causation and final causation interact in such a way that neither is wholly independent of the other or wholly dependent on the other.

Purpose is sometimes directed toward distant goals. But it is more fruitful to think of it in its universal immediate aspects. There is in every momentary experience the aim to be and the aim to be in a particular way that is as satisfying as the circumstances allow. That aim is fundamental to the becoming of the experience. In many experiences the aim at satisfaction is an aim to break new ground, to go beyond repetition of the past; in other words, to grow by the inclusion of possibilities that have not been actualized in the past. Finally, in some experiences, the satisfaction toward which energy is directed is one that has in view a wider future, the welfare of others as well as one's own.

In this sense, each momentary experience can be seen as the meeting place of past actuality experienced as the demand for some measure of conformation and certain unrealized possibilities experienced as worthy of actualization. The aim at becoming—and at becoming in such a way as to achieve some optimum of satisfaction, immediately and also for the sake of a wider future—is a factor in human experience that should not be reduced to the conformal pressures of the past. It is the principle of novelty, spontaneity, growth, and self-transcendence. It is that element in experience by which a continuing restlessness is introduced into the human race, a refusal of mere acquiescence in the given.

The effort to display novelty in its distinctness from what is given from the past has the danger of implying a dualistic opposition. One might suppose that the more the past is effectively reenacted in an event, the less novelty there would be, or that the more novelty was present, the less room there would be for the contributions of the past. But the actual relation is just the reverse of this. Only as novelty enters creatively into an event can the many strands of potential contributions of the past be jointly realized.

A simple example will clarify this point. If I hold a particular opinion and encounter a conflicting one, one opinion may simply assert itself against the other. The latter is then rendered ineffective and inoperative. But if a new idea or point of view emerges in my experience, then I may be able to understand and appropriate both opinions without being bound to either. In this case my thought will be creatively transformed by that novelty specifically relevant to my given situation in just that way which enables me to maintain the greatest possible continuity with the past, that is, a continuity with both opinions.

3. That creative transformation is a reality in experience is no longer an eccentric doctrine. It is widely accepted by the emerging post-modern mind. The account of the aim toward the new in the preceding section follows Whitehead's doctrine of the "initial aim." [1] But both in its description of experience and in its ascription of transcendence to the new it shares in a growing consensus.

Psychology in its humanistic forms has broken with the dominant reductionism of the past. It can speak of growth as advance into the new. Among recent humanistic Marxists, Ernst Bloch has provided a highly congenial account of the role of the new in the creative transformation of life and history. Heinrich Barth, in an essay cited with approval by his brother Karl, defined "existence" as "the concrete decision for a possibility which experiences its realization in this decision." [2] Christian existentialists such as Rudolf Bultmann have closely associated God with openness to the future. Catholic theology, especially under the influence of Pierre Teilhard de Chardin, has come to emphasize the unrealized future as the locus of God's agency in the present. More recently Jürgen Moltmann's theology of hope has located the future as the mode of God's transcendence for many Protestant theologians. Wolfhart Pannenberg has provided the most penetrating analysis of how human life is shaped and constituted by an anticipation of ultimate fulfillment, which he identifies as the Power of the Future, or God.

The basic point was beautifully made by Nicolas Berdyaev:

> The creative act is by its very nature ecstatic; it involves movement out beyond the boundaries; there is an act of transcendence in it. Creativeness is not an immanent process, nor susceptible of explanation in terms of immanence. There is always more in it than in any of the causes by which it is sought to explain creative power; that is to say, the forcing of a way through within the realm of fettering determinism. Creative activity will not come to terms with the given state of the world, it desires another. The creative act always calls up the image of something different; it imagines something higher, better and more beautiful than this—than the "given." This evoking of the image of something different, something better and more beautiful, is a mysterious power in man and it cannot be explained by the action of the world environment.[3]

Although there is consensus that the effective new is transcendent in some sense, there is confusion as to the ontological status of such transcendence. How can what is found in the analysis of experience genuinely transcend the experience? Before Christians can confidently name what creatively transforms the given as Christ, there must be more clarity about its transcendence.

In Christian tradition the transcendent reality that in its incarnate form is named Christ is called the Logos. Christ is the Logos as incarnate. The Logos is the cosmic principle of order, the ground of meaning, and the source of purpose. Whitehead has called this transcendent source of the aim at the new the principle of concretion, the principle of limitation, the organ of novelty, the lure for feeling, the eternal urge of desire, the divine Eros, and God in his Primordial Nature. His clarification of the nature of this Reality underlies what follows.

The word "Logos" is Greek. It would be convenient to translate it in what follows in the usual way as "Word." Unfortunately, Word, in spite of its capitalization, is bound up in contemporary hearing with language, and language is understood quite concretely and exclusively as human language. Gerhard Ebeling, for example, follows these associations in his argument that the Word of God cannot but be a particular event of human speaking, that is, assurance-giving speech. This understanding of Logos as human language is also dominantly characteristic of New Testament usage, but there it operates against a richer background of Hellenistic thought that makes it possible to think of Jesus himself, and not his words alone, as the Logos made flesh. In the influential Prologue to the Fourth Gospel the Logos names the preexistent divine reality that enters the world decisively in Jesus, and thus the idea of Logos was a bridge to the Hellenistic thought of deity as the universal principle of meaning and order. This ontological and cosmological status of the Logos, adopted by the fathers of the church, is far removed from that of human language, although human thought and speech are made possible by it and give expression to it. It is this inclusive meaning of Logos, pointing to that which transcends humanity but expresses itself through creatures, which is adopted in this book. The Logos in its transcendence is timeless and infinite, but in its incarnation or immanence it is always a specific force for just that creative transformation which is possible and optimal in each situation. In its timeless and infinite form it contains the principle of its differentiated relevance to each situation as it arises.

The idea of the immanence of a transcendent reality has been widely regarded as a special theological mystery associated with Christian dogma about Jesus. In fact, however, the immanence of the transcendent Logos is but a special case of causal efficacy in general. A cause both transcends its effect and is immanent within it. If it is transcendent only, it has no efficacy. If it is immanent only, it is a mere aspect of the supposed effect and not a cause. The past can have efficacy in the present only if it is both transcendent of the present and immanent to it. Once this general point is grasped, a context is available for understanding how the Logos can be genuinely present or embodied in the events of the world without ceasing to be genuinely transcendent.

The idea of the presence or embodiment of one entity in another is impossible to formulate clearly when the entities involved are thought of as substances. Common sense insists that two things cannot occupy the same space at the same time. If the things under consideration are like stones and tables, this is true. As long as the basic model of reality in terms of which God and human beings are conceived is derived from stones and tables, God cannot occupy at the same time the space occupied by a man or woman. Understood as substances, they must each be self-identical through time and externally related to one another. A stone can be placed on a table, and a piece of it can even be driven into the table. But in order for part of the stone to occupy the space of part of the table, it must displace some of the wood.

Substantialist thinking remains widespread even when it is explicitly disavowed. However, today the thinker is not restricted to ideas of relation derived from the relations of supposed substances. There are also relations between human experiences, especially between successive momentary experiences in a person's life. Each of these experiences is a dynamic event in which many elements from the past are brought into creative synthesis. As soon as this synthesis is achieved it passes and offers itself as datum for new creative syntheses.

Each of these momentary experiences can be analyzed into all the past entities or events which it incorporates into its final synthesis. A human experience incorporates elements from predecessor experiences of the same person, other elements provided by the brain, and, through the brain, elements from other parts of the body and the larger world. There is evidence that human experience also contains elements derived from the experience of other persons in more direct ways as well. Since these many elements are integrated into a single new synthesis, the fuller analysis must include the stages of the process of integration in which many elements from the past are also rejected. In this process there emerge as new elements the private feeling or emotion of the new experience and its creative imagination and reason.

Two successive moments of such experience are now under consideration. How is the first of these related to the second? How is one momentary experience of a woman, in which—for example—she starts to formulate a syllable, related to the next, in which she completes that syllable? The two are, of course, distinct. The former is past when the latter occurs. In this sense they are external to each other. But in a much more significant sense, the former is internal to the latter.

In the case of two substances, they must be conceived as having their essential being first and then coming into relation subsequently. The relation is external to their being. But in the case of the two experiences, the second cannot come into being except as a process of reactualizing and completing the first. The syllable begun in the first moment demands completion in the second. The second momentary experience has no essential being that does not include the effective presence within it of the first. The presence of the first is constitutive of the second. The second embodies the first. In this very general sense every experience incarnates all the entities that it includes. The idea of genuine presence of one entity in another, the lack of which has made many difficulties for theology, is fundamental and fully intelligible when the model is taken from experience instead of material objects. For most theology the idea of God's presence has necessarily been viewed as a radical exception to the way in which entities in general are related to each other. When entities are conceived as experiential events rather than as substances, however, no such exception is needed.

The aim at unrealized possibilities, or the not-yet, is the presence in experience of that which is not derived from the past world. What is present in this case, too, is also transcendent. The unrealized possibilities that present themselves as lures for aims do not exist only in their effective entertainment in the appetitions of a single occasion of experience. They are felt as potentialities that, as potentials, are real in themselves, whether or not they are actualized in the world. They are lures to action, thus exercising their own persuasive agency upon the world.

But potentiality conceived in itself is infinite and unordered. If it were felt in this sense only, it would provide no actual direction to the world. Merely disjointed potentiality would have no relevance to events. If it were effective in some way, it could lead only to chaos. To be open to such potentiality, if that were a meaningful notion at all, would be demonic and destructive.

What is in fact experienced vividly in the artistic act is not the encounter with sheer indeterminate potentiality but the relevance to what is given of particular new possibilities of form. Through these the given order can be preserved, transformed, and transcended. A particular possibility, often beyond conscious awareness and understanding, grasps the act and expresses itself through it. Similarly, it is not every not-yet, but a particular not-yet that embodies itself in imaginative anticipation. In short, there is a given order of possibility that constitutes ever-new potentialities as relevant lures in the ongoing process of human experience. Through the given ordering of novelty there is achieved the possibility of a novel order that continues and preserves the past while going beyond it. The Logos is, therefore, not simply the sum of random purposes, anticipations, and novelties of experience. It is the ordered givenness of relevant potentiality. Ultimately it is the transcendent ordering from which derive the novel order and the ordered novelty in the world.

Whereas this shows that the Logos is a transcendent ground of order, it leaves open the question of a second principle of order, a competing Logos. The Logos as described is the order of unrealized potentiality making possible by its immanence the realization of novel order. But there is also an order in the past, given world. What is the status or principle of this order, the order that science investigates?

Against the view of natural law as imposed, static order, we can see today that the order in the given world is statistically descriptive of its dominant patterns and tendencies. It is the common product of myriads of similar events in their interactions and as they effect the becoming of new events. There are not the events and in addition the laws to which these conform. There are only conformations to dominant patterns of antecedent events.

Furthermore, the order in the past world derives from the ordering power of the Logos. Past events as such are not now affected by the Logos, but in their own past becoming the Logos played the role it now plays in the present event. Every event inherits dominant patterns from the past, but insofar as those patterns are not eternal, all arose originally in the response of many events to the possibilities of order derived from the Logos.

Finally, apart from the effectiveness of the Logos in introducing novelty, order decays. That is, to whatever extent events come into being simply in conformity to the pressures of the past, they are governed by entropy. There would, of course, be an order also in a universe in which entropy had run its full course, but it would be only a statistical order. Events would not be ordered to ends. In comparison with the order that is present in a single living cell, it would be a poor order indeed. The Logos as the power of creative transformation is therefore the one principle of all significant order. Against it there is inertia, but this functions only in the context of the order of the Logos.

The Logos is immanent in all things as the initial phase of their subjective aim, that is, as their fundamental impulse toward actualization. In simple events this is the center or principle in terms of which the event is actualized, and in these instances there is little difference between the divine impulse and the final actualization. In the events that make up ordinary physical objects, the aim in each moment is at little more than repetition or reenactment of what has been in the immediate past. But in living persons a new feature appears: The initial aim is at a relevant novelty rather than at reenactment. The novelty that is aimed at is one that allows maximum incorporation of elements from the past in a new synthesis. This novelty must struggle for actualization against habit, anxiety, and defensiveness. To whatever extent the new aim is successful, to that extent there is creative transformation. This creative transformation is Christ.

Christ is thus the immanence or incarnation of the Logos in the world of living things and especially of human beings. Since there is no sharp line between the living and the nonliving, there is no need to stress this limitation of creative transformation or Christ to the sphere of life. If creative transformation could not work in the sphere of the inorganic, life could never have emerged. In that emergence Christ can be discerned. But since within the scope of our ordinary time-scales creative transformation in the inorganic world is negligible, Christ means predominantly the immanence of the Logos in the living sphere, and it is especially among human beings that he is to be found.

"Christ" is therefore a name for the Logos. No statement can be made about Christ that is not true of the Logos. But "Christ" does not simply designate the Logos as God as the principle of order and novelty. It refers to the Logos *as* incarnate, hence *as* the process of creative transformation in and of the world. Of course, what is incarnate is the transcendent Logos; so it is not false to attribute to Christ the transcendent characteristics of deity as well, but Christ as an image does not focus on deity in abstraction from the world but as incarnate in the world, that is, as creative transformation. But just as "Christ" does not mean the Logos as such but the Logos as incarnate, so also creative transformation is named Christ only by those who recognize in it the incarnation of the Logos. It is creative transformation *as* the incarnation of the Logos.

The Logos makes possible free decision as well, which can curtail its effectiveness. But since this too is derived from the Logos it is not a competing principle of order. Hence the Logos as the principle of novelty is the only ground of order. All authentic thinking and speaking embodies this creative transformation as does all sensitivity of feeling and free imagination. Indeed life itself is the continuing expression of the Logos as creative transformation. When creative transformation ceases, the organism dies and its body decays. There can only be advance into novelty or else erosion of what has been attained.

In concluding this section we must restate succinctly the identity and difference of Christ and Logos. The Logos is an eternal aspect of deity transcending every actual world as the principle of possibility and of the relevance of that possibility. But the Logos is at the same time immanent or incarnate in the world. Only as incarnate does it exercise any effect. As incarnate, its effect is decisive. In Whitehead's words, "The world lives by its incarnation of God."[4] God or the Logos as incarnate is Christ.

4. The implication of this analysis is that God as Logos is effectively, if unconsciously, present and felt in all events. The Logos is truly incarnate in the world. Christ is a reality in the world. This idea has deep roots in Christian rhetoric and liturgy, but it has fared poorly in philosophy and theology. Even when the reality of the divine is strongly affirmed, notions of how it is inwardly effective as Christ are hard to find.

In part the obstacle has been that substantialist modes of thought have blocked understanding of divine immanence. The discussion in section 3 was intended to overcome this barrier. But there is another obstacle to realistic thinking about Christ.

In the dominant Western view all experience arises through

the senses, and God is not an object of sense experience. These
assumptions have led to three ways of thinking of the relation of
God to experience. The first proposes that God is known only
by inference. God is not experienced at all but inferred from the
evidence of the senses. The mind deduces God's reality from the
being, the order, the novelty, the value, or the contingency of
what is known through the senses.

A second group accepts this consequence of the basic
assumptions of the West for all purposes except in regard to the
knowledge of God. In addition to inferential knowledge, or
instead of it, there is a unique form of knowledge derived from
the unique experience of God. Usually this is understood to be
mystical experience, and it is ordinarily regarded as something
very special and very rare.

A third group identifies God as Being as such instead of a
Being.[5] In this view, God is not experienced as an existent thing
or Supreme Being would be experienced, but in and through all
ordinary experience. God is the being of all the things that are,
and God is experienced to whatever extent we experience the
being of things in distinction from the particular forms of their
existence. As expressed and embodied in creatures God is the
Logos, and hence in this view the Logos functions as the
immanence of the transcendent.

Clearly the third position is most satisfactory in clarifying the
way in which the transcendent is immanent. But it too has its
limitations. It cannot give an account of the particularity of the
divine efficacy in the world. If God is Being, and if the Logos is
expressive Being, then the Logos is present and effective in the
world to whatever extent the world has being. The efforts of
theologians who think of God in this way to speak of his
purposes and agency display the inherent tension of their
thought of the God beyond the God of Biblical faith with the
Biblical understanding of God as historically and personally
active.[6]

If we are to understand how God can be effectively immanent
in the world in a way that gives direction to worldly affairs and
personal response, God must be understood neither as an
inference from the world known in sense experience, nor as an
object of rare mystical experience, nor as the Being of all things.
A different conceptuality or model is required. To develop such
a model, it is necessary to reject the fundamental dogma of

Western epistemology, that is, the primacy of sense experience. Against this it must be argued that sense experience is only one special form of experience. It is not primitive, as is supposed, but derivative from a prior form of experience.

Whitehead has been especially helpful in placing sense experience in proper perspective. There is no doubt of its importance. It is the source of the animal's most accurate knowledge of the environment that is crucial to its survival. For this reason, evolutionary selection has led to its dominance of conscious experience. When philosophers seek clear and distinct ideas, they find these in and derived from sense experience, especially sight and touch.

Nevertheless, even the most ordinary conscious experience testifies to other dimensions of experience. No one is without some sense of temporal passage. The present experience realizes that it arises from experiences that are now past. This awareness of the distinction of past and present occurs even when there are no conscious memories. The phenomenon of memory further accentuates and raises into clearer consciousness this mode of nonsensory experience.

That memory is nonsensory is not always recognized, because much of what is remembered has sensory content. Hume even denied that memory is nonsensory, distinguishing memory from present sensory experience only by the lack of vivacity of the sensory images that are presented. But analysis of experience does not support that view. Memory is a way in which *past* experience affects present experience, and however dominant the sensory element may have been in that past experience, the relation of the two experiences is not a sensory one. I do not now see the past experience of seeing. The past experience of seeing causes images to arise in my present experience in a way that may affect the eyes, but the present experience of the past experience is not mediated by the eyes.

Furthermore, memory is not an isolated case of nonsensory experience. We are aware also of the derivation of present experience from our bodies, especially—but not exclusively—from our sense organs. This relation, on which sense experience depends, is not itself sensory. In consciousness this relation lacks vividness, and it can easily be overlooked, as it has been in the dominant philosophical traditions. But physiology demonstrates its importance. For ordinary sense experience to occur, numerous events must take place in the body. The relation between these events and conscious experience is not a sensory one.

Whereas in clear consciousness vision appears to give direct awareness of events located at a distance from the body, actually those events influence us only, or chiefly, through the mediation of many others. Visual experience is directly related to, and derivative from, the events in the brain. Whether these are rightly interpreted as indirectly deriving from events in the external world where sight projects them depends—among other things—on the healthy functioning of the body.

In sum, although sensory experience dominates consciousness, the primary elements and relations shaping the whole experience are nonsensory. Sense experience is a special result of nonsensory events and by no means exhausts the content of experience. This is true even if no credence is given to the impressive evidence for what is usually called extrasensory perception. Hence the fact that God is not experienced through the sense organs and is not like the objects of sense perception does not count against his being a real factor in experience. We are free to follow the evidence of history and Christian experience in affirming and serving the indwelling Christ.

The four philosophical topics discussed in this chapter are closely related. "Christ" is not the name simply of Jesus or of God. Yet "Christ" is not a figment of imagination. "Christ" points to a reality that exists whether we recognize it or not, but it points to this reality as experienced and known in Christian history. The reality known in Christian history is recognized as present, if unacknowledged, everywhere. For the Christian, Christ is visible also where he is denied.

Creative transformation is discoverable in nature, in history, and in personal experience. In this sense Christ is fully immanent. But the exclusive alternatives of immanent and transcendent reflect a dualistic mode of thinking that is antithetical to Christian understanding. Christ is not simply identical with each and every instance of creative transformation. Christ is also that in reality by virtue of which each of these instances occurs. As such he transcends all instances. Indeed, Christ is but an illustration of the principle that everything experienced is both immanent in the experience and transcendent of it in the sense of being given to it. This mode of thinking, appropriate to the incarnation, requires us to break from the widespread notion that sense perception of the contemporary world is the basic paradigm of relatedness or experience. We have seen that the philosophy of Whitehead is particularly helpful in offering an alternative analysis and model.

CHAPTER 4

The Logos as Christ

The Logos has operated anonymously in art and theology. It functions cosmically whether or not it is recognized or named in any way. Hence it may seem that recognition and naming are not important. But although the Logos has not ceased to work in theology when it is not rightly identified, blindness to it endangers its work and leads to false commitments and misdirected energy. And although as cosmic principle it does not depend for its existence on human recognition, such recognition is important for its maximal effectiveness in human affairs and through them for the whole future of our planet.

Most human conceptualities have tended to deny or obscure the work of the Logos. In modern culture we have often been encouraged to understand existence as simply determined by the past and to suppose that everything in our experience is mediated by the senses. Either of these beliefs leads to a mode of self-understanding that has no place for the principle of novelty. Lack of recognition does not make the Logos disappear, and many features of ordinary language and common sense continue to bear witness to it. But its operations are not brought into clear consciousness; attention is not focused upon them; and their effectiveness is hampered.

An example of the effect of a conceptuality can be seen in Freudianism. Since we in this country have only recently emerged from a Freudian epoch, this is an important example for us. Freud interpreted ethical experience as superego. He interpreted aspiration as libido. The former he understood as internalization of social demands; the latter, as sexual energy. There is no question but that Freud's interpretation brought to light much that was hidden, and there is no possibility of returning to a pre-Freudian consciousness. But, as many psychologists recognize, when all goal orientation is viewed under these headings, attention is directed away from disciplined imagination, creative personal growth through appropriation of changing ideals, and even kindness. Clearly it is important that the Logos be named in order that the principle of creativity and growth be recognized.

How the Logos is named is equally important. Accordingly this chapter considers (1) the importance of naming the Logos in its immanence or incarnation as Christ. Only so is its character as dynamic, trustworthy love brought to effective realization. It then discusses (2) the implication for the relation of faith and reason of the recognition that Christ is the Logos: namely, that true faith and true reason are identical.

1. "Conscience," in many of its uses, when not confused with the Freudian superego, refers to what Whitehead calls the "initial aim." The designative reference of "Christ" is also to this aim. Both terms have positive, normative connotations within the Christian community. If we clarify the differences between the two images, the importance of retaining and stressing the image of Christ will become evident.

First, conscience suggests an inner possession or given aspect of the self, whereas Christ suggests the presence of an other. In actuality, every element ingredient in a momentary experience is the presence of an other. That other is either an actual entity or a possibility. An experience constitutes itself in its uniqueness out of these elements of actuality and possibility into a new actuality. But elements in the experience bear weaker or stronger testimony to their external origins, and the awareness of these origins is affected by the way they are understood and named. As we use words we can think of ourselves either as "knowing" them or as "recalling" them. Only in the latter case is the fact brought into focus that the ability to use the word originated in an earlier experience. Similarly the derivation of the initial aim from beyond itself is brought into awareness when it is named Christ but not when it is named conscience.

Secondly, even when conscience is distinguished from the superego's introjection of social mores, it connotes a static grasp of principles. Therefore, when attention is directed to the initial aim as conscience, formal patterns are brought into view. Conscience is correlative with just distribution of goods, faithfulness to commitments, appropriate response to kindness, seeking the inclusive good, and submission of opinions to testing; for the initial aim of human occasions consistently directs in these ways. But Christ points away from static principles to a dynamic and concrete reality. The aim that directs toward optimal satisfaction is never in fact directed toward general principles as such. In each moment it is directed at that specific actualization which is the best outcome for the given situation.

Thirdly, when the initial aim is interpreted as conscience, it is assumed to be conscious or immediately accessible to consciousness. Conscience is associated with knowledge of what is right and wrong. But much human anguish derives from confusion and uncertainty, and the resolution of such uncertainty by the application of formal principles is problematic in its results. The reality is that these principles can at best only help to discriminate the urge to optimal actualization from the many other lures and promptings that together with it stand at the fringes of awareness. This situation is better described as the mysterious presence of Christ than as the possession of conscience. What is needed is sensitive openness to Christ rather than lucid grasp and rigid application of the formal principles of conscience.

But the importance of naming the incarnate Logos "Christ" runs deeper still, for even where the power of the Logos as creative transformation is recognized, it can be rejected as enemy. Indeed the Logos is threatening to any given world, for it functions to transcend and transform it. That means that the given, familiar forms are subordinate to new ones, that established habits of mind are undercut, that revered teaching is relativized, that moral practices which have allowed a secure conscience are rendered questionable. In short, the function of the Logos is to introduce tension between what has been and what might be and continuously to challenge and upset the established order for the sake of the new.

The dominant wisdom of the race has seen novelty as threat

rather than opportunity. It has preferred to sustain the order given in the past than to pioneer new forms of order. It has projected the established order back upon sacred origins. The norm of its thought and action has been faithfulness to those origins. Its highest truth is the wisdom of the ancestors.

To name the Logos "Christ" is to express and to elicit trust. It is to promise that the unknown into which we are called is life rather than death. In short, it is to call for and make possible radical conversion from bondage to the past to openness to the future. This is to say that to name the Logos "Christ" is to recognize that the cosmic Logos is love. This is not an easy recognition. We experience the Logos as demanding of us that we give up what we ourselves love, our security in our own achievements. It forces us to recognize that in fact these are not our own achievements at all but achievements of the Logos in which we have actively participated. We want to rest in them and stabilize them. The Logos makes us restless and condemns our desire for stability. In short we experience the Logos as judgment. But when we name it Christ we recognize that the judgment is for our sake, that what it condemns in us is that in us which would destroy us, that what it demands of us is what it gives us.

Not only is the Logos itself love but the creative transformation which is its work in us is human love. That also is not immediately apparent; for love as creative transformation is not emotion, or sentiment, or moral virtue. It is a way in which the process of becoming is formed or structured. But this ontological character of love is not strange to the Christian; for Christian love has never been an expendable addition to an already formed being. Love is not Christian if it is not constitutive of existence.

The meaning of love for Christians has been determined by Jesus. Through him we are called to a concern for others that is not governed by their attractiveness, their capacity to reciprocate, or any need on the part of the one who loves. It expresses itself particularly toward the weak and oppressed. It extends to the enemy and the persecutor. To love in this sense is to constitute ourselves in each moment in relation to the future of the other as well as to our own future. Christians know, in naming the Logos "Christ," that the divine has constituted itself toward the world once and for all as love. That act of God allows us in some small measure to participate in this structure of becoming.

This kind of love, *agapē*, has been the primary ideal in the Christian tradition, but it is not the only form of love embodied in Jesus. Jesus also displayed compassion. This has often been understood only as the tone of feeling that accompanies *agapē*, as self-constitution toward the inclusive future, but it too has a structural and constitutive character that is more quickly heard in the word "empathy." Although Christian love includes both forms, and can inclusively be named as *agapē*, it will be better for a while to lift up empathy alongside *agapē*, understood in the narrower sense that has been dominant in the past.

Empathy is feeling with others, viewing the situation as they do, allowing one's feelings to conform to theirs. This is not merely a means of being motivated to acts expressive of love. It is in itself an important act of love; for to feel oneself understood by another is already to be helped, quite apart from further assistance that may be given by the empathetic person. Further, empathy is not a subjective feeling or emotion only. It is a mode of self-constitution that includes the past of the other. Christians know that this kind of love also is constitutive of the very being of God and, knowing ourselves to be loved in this way, in some small measure we can participate in this structure of becoming.

Love for the Christian is also directed to God. The objective actuality of God's love for us creates in us the possibility, and in some measure even the actuality, of that love. To seek truth and affirm life is to love God, and no one can live without some openness to truth and life. But when God is not known, or is experienced as threat, existence is a living death that shuns truth and life. That God is the lover of the world is the good news that gives life by freeing the world to love God, and therefore also itself. This love of God, like the love of the neighbor, is not emotion, or sentiment, or moral virtue, although—as with all forms of love—these will accompany it. It is primarily self-constitution in openness and responsiveness to God.

This threefold structure of love—toward the future, toward the past, and toward God—is identical with the creative transformation described philosophically in the preceding chapter. The Logos is immanent in the new possibilities that emerge in each moment. Those possibilities are ordered in relevance to the particularity of each situation, but they are lures to the expansion of horizons of concern toward truth and the future of others. The more responsive the occasion is to the relevant novelty the more of the past it can include within itself. The love of God, which always entails the love of truth, expands the scope of the past and the future which we love. When the Logos is known as Christ, creative transformation is recognized as love.

Naming the Logos as Christ implies that the meanings of "Logos" and "Christ" are not identical. They designate the same actuality, but whereas "Logos" is primarily designative, "Christ" is an image. "Christ" names the Logos as incarnate, and if it were shown that in fact the Logos is not incarnate, then we could not name it Christ. Similarly "Christ" names the Logos as dynamic, trustworthy, loving. If the Logos were shown not to be dynamic, trustworthy, or loving, then the name "Christ" could not be used.

There is a more subtle point. "Christ" names the Logos as that by which Christians orient themselves, that to which they commit themselves. Wholly abstracted from this existential dimension, the Logos is not Christ at all in actuality, although it would remain a potentiality for becoming Christ. Yet Christians can name as Christ the unrecognized or misunderstood working of the Logos in the world if they thereby mean to identify what they name with what they intend to serve. In this sense Christians can name as Christ creative transformation in art, in persons of other faiths, and in the planetary biosphere.

2. To recognize that Christ is the Logos also affects the meaning of faith. Faith in Christ is faith in the Logos. To affirm that is to move toward a new understanding of the relation of faith and reason. Faith has meant and rightly means many things. Sometimes it means a vision of reality or a structure of existence. Sometimes it refers specifically to the Christian vision of reality or the Christian structure of existence. Receptivity to the personal presence of Jesus is faith, as is the assuredness of the one who knows himself or herself justified. Faith in a different sense is "the substance of things hoped for." Faith as confidence in the future grounds meaning in the present and is intimately related to faith as the Christian vision of

reality and the Christian structure of existence. In other contexts faith is used to mean faithfulness, life-affirmation, confidence, commitment, trust, and ultimate concern. Indeed, an exhaustive list of meanings is impossible. Sometimes faith is treated as a genus of which Christian faith is one species. Sometimes faith is seen instead as that which is unique to Christianity. Sometimes it is defined as a relation to another; sometimes, as a property of the individual. As long as no one of these meanings of faith is exalted into the one thing required in an absolutist and particularizing sense, a pluralistic approach should be open to accepting them all and sorting out their complex interconnections with one another and their varying relations with Christ and with other religious traditions.

Still faith is too important a theme of Christianity to be left simply in this relativistic sea. Recognizing that any definition has an arbitrary element, but guided by the historical importance and changing content of faith, we can establish that a central and normative theological meaning of faith is "the appropriate, primal response to what the divine is and does."

This definition focuses upon the correlation of faith and the divine, and it displays faith as fundamental to Christianity as well as to Judaism and Islam. It neither limits faith to its Christian form nor establishes faith as a universal characteristic of human beings, religious or otherwise. The various roles of faith in primitive and Asian religions should be determined by careful investigation. It appears that the relation of the Shin Buddhist to Amida Buddha is faith in this sense, despite the reluctance to speak of Amida as "God." This definition allows for great diversity of judgment as to what the appropriate, primal response to the divine may be and for the possibility that it may differ markedly from time to time. On the other hand, it excludes from faith nonrelational aspects of human existence as well as relations to other people, causes, and institutions, although faith in other senses can refer to these. It leaves open the question of the importance or possibility of faith in a pluralistic context.

In the Old Testament the appropriate, primal response to God was trust in God's faithfulness and obedience to divine requirements. This correlated with the structure of personal existence centering in the will. A person as will can commit life to the covenant with God, orienting it around God's promises and acting to fulfill the divine commandments.

These elements continue in the New Testament, but in the distinctive Christian structure of existence the self distinguishes itself from the process of willing, objectifies it, and thereby becomes transcendent over it. In this way trust and obedience as characteristic acts of will are relativized. The response to God of the self-transcending self or spirit cannot be exhaustively or even primarily expressed in the "works" that are the offering of the will. Hence in this new context faith and works, even the work of trusting, must be distinguished and finally juxtaposed. When this distinction is made, it is faith, the appropriate primal response to what God is and does, which is primary and decisive and not works, the appropriate expression of that response at the level of the will.

The appropriate primal response at the level of spirit is openness to Christ as the new and always coming divine reality. Christian faith is a living from the not-yet and thus a continuous relativizing of what is past and accomplished. Expectancy, openness to the future, and freedom from the past are marks of the newly appropriate, primal response to God. Faith is life in Christ.

What now is the relation of this faith to reason? Some think of the problem of faith and reason as a formal one and suppose that when faith is removed the problem is solved. But a solution of that kind is not possible. When reason is formally opposed to faith, it is regarded as having unconditional objectivity, neutrality, and detachment from precommitment. Reason is thought to point to what is accessible to every person who is willing to be honest and open and to free himself or herself from prejudice. But the course of modern thought has increasingly shown that reason in this sense can generate no content. The effort of philosophy to restrict itself to reason has led to its redefinition as analysis. What is analyzed may be language or phenomena, but in either case philosophy is dependent on what is nonrationally given and can do nothing more than clarify this. Any effort to go beyond what is given loses the cherished objectivity and neutrality.

Even in pure analysis neutrality is not really achieved. First, there is the question of what is given. For some, the answer is ordinary language. But ordinary language is a very complex affair, and every analysis that employs it and operates upon it is selective. The principle of selection is never completely objective. Secondly, what one finds in ordinary language and the tools one brings to bear upon it always presuppose some latent understanding of reality and of the relation of language to it. The traditional ontological issues do not disappear just because they are not directly faced, as is indicated by the recent reappearance of metaphysical discussions in the work of P. F. Strawson, Wilfrid Sellars, and other analytic philosophers.

The fullest effort to achieve pure rationality in this sense takes the further step of abandoning ordinary language in favor of artificial languages. At this point philosophy becomes mathematics. But even in mathematics pure reason operates only within axiomatic systems, and complete axiomatization is impossible. The attempt to achieve pure rationality leads away from the empirical world and from all questions of human importance, but even in its chosen sphere of abstraction, it fails.

This, of course, is not what has been meant by reason in the major philosophical traditions of the past, where reason was thought to be able to grasp reality. We are now aware that each way reality has been grasped by reason has been conditioned by culture as a historical actuality as well as by the personal experience of the philosopher. In most instances religion has played an important role in the shaping of that historical actuality, so that what is grasped by reason is influenced by religion. But even if the culture is not religious, it remains a way of organizing and interpreting meaningful reality. This can be criticized, tested, and refined, and in this process reason plays a relatively objective role. But some vision of reality must be given to the one who engages in this process of reformulation. Such a vision of reality is one of the meanings of "faith." Everyone without exception has such a faith, for life is impossible without some meaningful, primal organization of the stimuli that affect the physical organism. This organization must be both perceptual and valuational, and in human beings it is always also linguistic and therefore implicitly conceptual. The major religiocultural traditions of mankind correspond to basic faiths in this sense. Reason functions within all of them, and in some respects its functioning is common to them; for, there are formal patterns exemplified in reason wherever it is found. But that does not mean that reason can replace or do without the visions of reality within which it operates.

Whether or not they are consciously and explicitly committed to the visions of reality out of which they live, people may fail to recognize that they have any faith at all in this sense. That only means that they suppose that their way of experiencing the world, conditioned by their particular history, is not conditioned at all. They do not confess that they have been brought by their experience to perceive reality in a particular way, and they announce instead that reality simply is the way they perceive it to be, as if anyone who did not agree were blind, ignorant, or stupid. This leads to rationalistic dogmatism, which is as much to be avoided as is ecclesiastical authoritarianism.

Faith as vision of reality is the indispensable context for reason, but if any one vision of reality is absolutized or sacralized, it inhibits the fullest development and use of reason. Every vision of reality, including the one proposed and employed in this book, should be subject to the eroding and transforming consequences of unfettered rational inquiry. To whatever extent faith is identified or bound up with a vision of reality, the faith that supports the pluralistic consciousness must oppose its own sacralization.

For the most part, faith and reason have not functioned chiefly at the formal level. Their concrete meanings stem from the events of Christian history. Christendom has inherited traditions from both Israel and Hellenism. Its loyalty to its Jewish heritage, embodied in the Bible, is named faith, and its loyalty to its Greek heritage, given climactic expression in Plato and Aristotle, is named reason. Despite continuing tensions, the church has welded these two elements into an effective unity. But when faith is understood as faithfulness to a particular cultural heritage in a world in which it is now possible to learn from many such heritages, it must not be absolutized or sacralized.

Modern science arose out of the matrix of the Christian synthesis of Jewish and Greek themes, but it rapidly outgrew that matrix and created a vision of its own. This embodied the critical spirit, which it thematized and to which it gave methodological rigor. But science also constructed a closed universe from which many of the concerns of both Jew and Greek were excluded. Reason became science, its methods, assumptions, and conclusions. Faith became all forms of apprehending levels or dimensions of reality that were excluded from reason. Reason as science claimed all nature as its sphere. Faith was driven to speak of a supernatural realm. As long as faith is identified in this way as grounds of affirming a reality not accessible to science and juxtaposed to the methodology of science, it can at best be but a fragmentary approach to truth. Fortunately this view of science is crumbling and with it is crumbling the supernaturalist orientation of faith and its objects.

There is another concrete use of faith in juxtaposition to reason that receives its most dramatic illustration when primitive and traditional cultures encounter more advanced ones. What has heretofore been unquestionable becomes problematic. The given sacred loses its sacrality. The critical faculty is awakened and corrodes the ancient certainties. In too many instances the results are chiefly negative. Here reason represents the destructive novelty and faith, the tradition on which it operates.

This encounter of cultures is an extreme instance of what occurs continually in any dynamic civilization. Tradition always meets criticism. The best of the past is confronted by possibilities that are in some measure antithetical to it. Thus faith represents loyalty and commitment to the established values, and reason represents the principle of criticism and creativeness that transforms and transcends what is given. The results of reason's victory are often destructive, and our sympathies are understandably directed to those who seek to preserve an established and once functional way against the corrosive acids of change.

Even so, despite the grave risks that destruction of the old may fail to lead to a better new, Christians cannot allow the sacralization of faith in this sense. Indeed, we must judge this faith as idolatrous. The preservation of elements from the past in a new structure is a laudable and even necessary undertaking when it is done in the context of openness to the new. But it is reason, and not faith in this idolatrous sense, with which Christians identify, while recognizing that much of Christianity, as indeed of all religions and of all secular movements as well, has been idolatrous. It is easier to celebrate and emulate past achievements than to venture forward into uncharted seas.

This understanding of faith and reason opens up the one possibility for the full overcoming of their antithesis. If faith is the primal, appropriate response to God, and if God is the Logos that calls men and women into the open future, then faith is reason in its struggle with all idolatries.[1] This reason is by the same token more inclusive than any of the meanings of reason considered heretofore. It is not abstract and dispassionate analysis alone, although it includes that. It is not the Greek heritage and temper in distinction from the heritage and temper of other cultures, although it owes much to Greece. It is not science as method, vision, or doctrine, although today it is deeply affected by that. It is the grasp of novel images, ideas, and meanings in their tension with and fructification of the achievements of the past and the willingness to submit itself continuously to further testing. It is participation in creative transformation. As such, this reason is the appropriate, primal response to the Logos, and the Logos is Christ.

The reason which is faith is disciplined imagination. It is not the mere application of existing methods and criteria, for it is that which creates methods and criteria and then modifies and transcends those which it has created. It functions in the spheres both of abstract speculation and of the most intimate moral experience.

Reason in the sphere of morality involves imaginatively viewing the situation from a perspective that transcends the given, private one. It gropes toward disinterestedness and universality. It involves also imagination of the experience of others and of different modes of relating between persons and between human beings and other creatures. Thus it continuously challenges both the personal prejudices and preferences of the reasoner and also the received moral code. It is faith in the life-giving Logos that moves within us as that faith appreciates, but transcends bondage to both self and law.

Reason in the sphere of speculation is no less of the essence of faith. Whitehead had remarkable penetration into the connection between speculative reason and the religious spirit. "Reason which is speculative questions the methods, refusing to let them rest. The passionate demand for freedom of thought is a tribute to the deep connection of the speculative Reason with religious intuitions. The Stoics emphasized this right of the religious spirit to face the infinitude of things, with such

understanding as it might. In the first period when the speculative Reason emerged as a distinguishable force, it appeared in
the guise of sporadic inspirations. Seers, prophets, men with a
new secret, appeared. They brought to the world fire, or
salvation, or release, or moral insight. Their common character
was to be bearers of some imaginative novelty, relevant and yet
transcending traditional ways." [2]

But practical and speculative imagination are truly reason
only as they are disciplined, only as the novelty they grasp is
truly relevant novelty capable of the creative transformation of
the given. The development of the requisite discipline is itself a
central act of reason as disciplined imagination. The Logos is
the ordering of potentiality in its relevance to the ever-changing
world. Christ is that ordered novelty insofar as it is incarnate in
the world. The appropriate response, whether called faith or
reason, is the actualization of the proffered potentiality, thus
sharing in the deepening of the incarnation.

PART TWO
Christ as Jesus

CHAPTER 5

Jesus' Words
and Christ

Part One dealt with Christ as the Logos incarnate in the world as creative transformation. Chapters 1 and 2 illustrated this incarnation in the history of art and of theology. Chapter 3 clarified its ontological status, and Chapter 4 drew important implications of this way of understanding Christ. The point of Part One as a whole is to guide Christian imagination and commitment in the present toward a wholehearted identification with the divine process that is now creatively transforming us. Christians must go beyond the division of their loyalties: between truth and particularistic doctrines; between the needs of the world and of particular institutions; between the present claims of creative process and a particular historical figure. We can do so only if we know that, without qualification, Christ is to be found on the side of truth, the world, and creative process.

However, "Christ" names also, and more certainly, the singular figure of a Nazarene carpenter. Unless the power of creative transformation discerned in art and theology is also the power that was present in him and that continues to operate through his word, the affirmations of Part One cannot stand. Part Two examines the relation between what is known of Jesus and the creative transformation that has been named Christ.

Most of our knowledge of Jesus is of his influence. The Christian community and its Scriptures have been bearers of much of that influence, but it has been felt in every corner of the world and pervades our language and modes of thought. Because of him and the faith he elicited, the vision of reality that arose in Israel under the influence of the prophets creatively transformed the Greco-Roman mind and provided the foundation of the Western civilization that is now becoming global. The importance and distinctiveness of this event are well stated by the historian of technology, Lynn White, Jr.:

> The Semitization of the Greco-Roman *oikumene,* which was accomplished in the fourth century by the victory of Christianity, marks the most drastic change of world view, both among intellectuals and among the common people, that, before our own time, has ever been experienced by a major culture. In China the indigenous Confucian-Taoist symbiosis was supplemented, not displaced, by Indic Buddhism. In India itself, Vedic Brahmanism slowly broadened and diversified to engulf all rivals except the Islamic intrusion that was totally unassimilable and which produced two societies in tragic confrontation. The Muslim annexation of the southern shores of the Mediterranean had no such result because, as Dante rightly saw it (Inferno 28.22–31), Muhammed was a Judeo-Christian schismatic, not the founder of a new religion. In the regions thus overrun, the faith of the *Koran* confirmed basic Jewish views of the nature of time, the cosmos, and destiny which had already been spread at all levels of society by Christianity, Judaism's daughter.[1]

The Czech Marxist philosopher, Milan Machoveč, is another witness to the historical importance of Jesus. In *Jesus für Atheisten* he recognizes the centrality of Jesus for all Western history, not least for that of Marxism, and he sees Jesus as having continuing meaning and relevance in our own time. In his view "the Old Testament prophets have shown mankind the dimension of the future and thereby grounded the dynamic, first of Western history and perhaps even of the future history of mankind. (Today through Marxism the dynamically conceived universalism penetrates also the great lands of the East, which did not know it until recently.) Jesus gives to the dimension of the future the authentically human character, in that he took from it strangeness, apocalyptic, fantasy, and thereby freed it from the prison of metaphysics."[2]

This historical importance of Jesus leads us to ask how he has affected others and can affect us today. The quotations from Lynn White and Milan Machoveč rightly point to Jesus as the one through whom the insights and vision of Jewish prophetism transformed the West and now the East as well. The understanding of Jesus also shaped the imagination of Christendom.

The image of Christ that was treated in Part One is inseparable from him and must be tested in relation to him. Among other ways Jesus has affected history, two are selected for special attention in this part: his message and his objective efficacy. Our reliable knowledge of Jesus today is chiefly of his message. This chapter summarizes it on the basis of comparing the results attained by four historians, examines the effect it is capable of having today when it is truly heard, and relates that effect to what, in Part One, was named Christ. The conclusion is that the encounter with Jesus' words even today is an experience of creative transformation, or, otherwise stated, that Jesus' words can be the occasion for the deepening of the incarnation or the fuller realization of Christ. But the encounter with Jesus' teaching has been only one side of the way in which Jesus was known and his saving power experienced in the church. Equally important has been the sense of his objective efficacy for those who believe in him. Chapter 6 considers Paul's understanding of this efficacy, summed up in his understanding of being-in-Christ. Chapters 5 and 6, therefore, add to the general historical role of Jesus in the spread of Jewish thought and life more specific functions he has played in the realization of Christ among those who hear and believe.

The remarkable efficacy of the work of Jesus leads to questions as to who he was and what distinctive character should be attributed to his person. These questions are intensified when we realize that both in the ancient church and for us today the efficacy of his work not only leads to questions about his person but also is dependent in large measure on the answers given to those questions. Chapter 7 offers a transition from the two chapters on Jesus' work to the subsequent discussion of his person in Chapter 8. The evidence of his authoritative manner of teaching is taken as the particular key to consideration of how he resembles us and how he differs from us. The conclusion is tested to determine how it fits with the work of Jesus described in Chapters 5 and 6.

Since the early church also wrestled with the question of the structure of Jesus' existence and since its formulations are taken as normative in large sections of the church, it is important to understand just what these formulations say. Chapter 9 summarizes the history of creedal controversy to clarify the conceptual meaning of the resulting creeds. Finally, in Chapter 10 the proposal about the structure of Jesus' existence worked out in Chapter 8 is compared with these official statements of the early church.

Through most of Christian history the results of the councils have acted as filters through which the New Testament record of Jesus is encountered. The New Testament record in its turn already was a highly interpretative expression of the experience with Christ in the early community. But beginning with the Enlightenment, leading thinkers in the West attempted to disengage the human historical Jesus from this matrix of beliefs about him. In the latter part of the eighteenth century they initiated a quest of the historical Jesus that absorbed the energies of some of the finest Christian thinkers. During the nineteenth century the pendulum swung widely. Some believed that the Gospels provide accurate information about what was seen and heard, requiring only that the events reported be so explained as to be credible and acceptable (Paulus). Others concluded that the story of Jesus must be read as a product of the mythical imagination of a later community (Bauer).

At the beginning of the twentieth century, Albert Schweitzer summed up the alternatives as thoroughgoing skepticism and thoroughgoing eschatology. Either we have no materials from which to gain an understanding of Jesus, or else Jesus was an eschatological extremist whose world of ethical and religious thought is utterly remote. Schweitzer opted for the second alternative and still found it worthwhile to submit to the challenge to struggle with him. Schweitzer saw it as the Christian's task to Christianize the inevitable world affirmation of modern times "by the personal rejection of the word which is preached in the sayings of Jesus." [3]

These disturbing results of the quest led theologians to reconsider the significance of historical study for the faith of the church. If the picture of Jesus produced by the historian does not connect with the believer's experience of Jesus as the Christ, what does this mean? Martin Kähler, Søren Kierkegaard, and, most influentially, Karl Barth declared that faith in Jesus as the Christ has its own grounding independent of these results. From this point of view the quest had shown that a reliable life of Jesus could not be reconstructed, and theological reflection showed that any such undertaking is irrelevant to faith. Meanwhile, historical study left Schweitzer's alternatives behind. Form criticism, joined later by redaction criticism, showed that the Gospels as we have them are products of long traditions. We cannot reconstruct a picture of Jesus, as Schweitzer had done, from the final texts of Matthew and Mark. But we do not have to accept extreme skeptical conclusions; for by working back to older layers of tradition we can arrive at reliable information about Jesus. There are sayings which, freed from subsequent interpretations, can be responsibly attributed to Jesus himself.

The greatest New Testament scholar of our century, Rudolf Bultmann, accepted the position of Barth that faith is in no way affected by or even interested in the historian's results about Jesus. Nevertheless, he continued as historian to study the sayings and mission of Jesus and to present Jesus in a way that displayed his human-historical importance. The meaning he found in Jesus' message closely resembled the meaning of the gospel itself, and some of his students affirmed that in Jesus' teaching too the gospel is to be found. They inaugurated a new quest of the historical Jesus, undertaking to present Jesus in his decisive importance for faith. This meant that Jesus' message was presented as a call to Christian faith parallel with that in the proclamation of the early church. Thus faith and history were reunited.

Much of the best work on the historical Jesus has been done in this context of faith. The eyes of the believer probe deeply, and believing historians have shown that they do not betray their historical responsibility in the process of expressing their results as important for faith. Nevertheless, a special factor of selection, emphasis, and interpretation is intentionally introduced when the historian interprets Jesus for the sake of faith, and there are equally scholarly accounts of Jesus that are detached from this purpose. For the purpose of gaining an independent judgment of Jesus' relation to Christ as incarnate Logos, the latter are preferable.

The separation of historical reconstruction from concern for faith does not avoid the problem that the results are relative to the historian's special interest and bias. That tends to be the case in all historical writing. That tendency can be checked only by the awareness of the problem on the part of the historian and the reader and by the critical interaction of historians with varying points of view. Accordingly, I will compare four books

about Jesus that result from varied approaches to him. Their
agreements will serve to show the remarkable degree of consensus that historical study has at last achieved.

The first selection is Bultmann's own *Jesus and the Word*.
This has become a classic of modern scholarship. Bultmann
approaches Jesus with the concerns of an existentialist and
pictures Jesus as calling for decision. But in Bultmann's view
that decision is not the decision of Christian faith. His concern
in this book is to make clear just what the decision is to which
this particular Jewish figure calls us without regard to the role
Jesus plays in Christianity.

Among those of Bultmann's pupils who refused to make this
sharp distinction, the initial interest in faith gave way progressively to the renewal of more objective historical inquiry. The
resultant aim at detached inquiry is fully explicit in the work of
Norman Perrin, a pupil of Joachim Jeremias who increasingly
associated himself with the post-Bultmann group. Accordingly,
the second selection for this chapter is Perrin's book *Rediscovering the Teaching of Jesus*.[4] Perrin carefully explains the now
widely accepted methods of form criticism and then proceeds to
apply them to identifying the authentic sayings of Jesus. Unlike
Bultmann, for whom the historically accurate explanation of the
thought of a great man is a challenge to our present existence,
Perrin attempts to avoid modernization and to expound the
meaning of Jesus' message for his own hearers without regard
to its present implications. The latter he reserves for a separate
chapter.

Perrin, like Bultmann, stands in the German tradition of New
Testament scholarship. There is no question that this is the
dominant tradition and that all New Testament scholars must
take it heavily into account. Still there have been partly
independent traditions in the English-speaking world. In the
United States the Chicago school was one such tradition, in
which freshness of approach was combined with the drive for
optimal objectivity. Ernest Cadman Colwell has embodied that
tradition in its last years. His deceptively simple book, *Jesus
and the Gospel*,[5] sums up his insights and will be the third
selection.

Although Bultmann, Perrin, and Colwell seek to learn who
Jesus really was rather than to support a preestablished faith,
they are all Christians, and there has been a dearth of scholarly

study of Jesus by adherents of other traditions. We are fortunate, therefore, to have the recent book by Machoveč to use as the fourth selection.[6] Machoveč's work is neither more nor less pure in its historical objectivity than the others. His interpretation is influenced by Marxism in much the same way that Bultmann's is indebted to existentialism.

All four historians agree that the proclamation of Jesus centers on the Kingdom of God. Jesus means by the Kingdom a historical occurrence rather than an always existing state of affairs or a dimension of universal reality. This proclamation of a new age did not distinguish Jesus from other Jews of his time. His distinctiveness lay in his understanding of the Kingdom and the meaning of its coming.

All our sources stress that for Jesus the coming of the Kingdom makes necessary a decision now. In Machoveč's words, Jesus "was a compelling proclaimer *of the immediate claim on man* from the standpoint of the 'Age to come.'"[7] Jesus' parables emphasize the urgency of decision. The coming of the Kingdom reverses the normal expectations and evaluations of life. The penitent tax collector is justified rather than the righteous Pharisee. The laborers who work an hour are rewarded just as those who work all day. Harlots precede the virtuous into the Kingdom.

All agree that the call of the Kingdom comes to men and women as individuals. Each can and must decide for himself and herself. No outward condition finally compels or prevents one. Jesus' parables focus attention on preparation, decision, and immediate response.

Machoveč stresses that although the change required of each human being is individual and personal, one is not called to passive waiting or escape into inwardness.[8] Similarly the requirement to refrain from revenge does not call for acquiescence in injustice and evil but the desire to bring also the sinner into the Kingdom. Colwell stresses that even the solution to all social problems of poverty and injustice will leave untouched a deeper evil. "The triumph over covetousness, over materialism as the end-all of human achievement—this will be the last victory."[9]

Bultmann writes that "the requirement for conduct toward others may . . . be epitomized in the commandment of love."[10] But he notes "that neither Jesus nor his church thought the command of love was a new requirement." [11] Jesus' emphasis was not on love in general but on the extravagant type of love required by the coming Kingdom. Perrin, concentrating on the parables of Jesus, writes little of love, but in his exposition of such parables as the prodigal son and the good Samaritan he shows that Jesus depicts a new quality of love that breaks out of established bounds. Machoveč also sees that Jesus' message is not a repetition of the traditional requirement of love but its radicalization in terms of love of the enemy. For Machoveč this can only be understood eschatologically, as viewing everyone through the "prism of the Kingdom." [12]

Colwell recognizes that the Kingdom, as the will of God, calls for extravagant love. But his special emphasis is upon humility as the fundamental response. He stresses that this was Jesus' own stance. He "actually called himself servant, minister, and slave." [13] It was also the norm in terms of which he judged the responses of others.[14]

Machoveč, writing as an atheist for atheists, says little of Jesus' teaching about God. Bultmann and Perrin agree that Jesus did not teach a new doctrine of God. He taught instead the "Jewish conception of God in its purity and consistency." [15] But by intensifying the authentic Jewish teaching Jesus changed it. This is especially clear in his emphasis on God's grace and forgiveness.

Bultmann summarizes the Jewish view of Jesus' time as follows: "In Judaism God overlooks the sins of the religious, and this is God's grace; God condemns the completely sinful and godless, and therefore the religious man feels himself fundamentally good." [16] Perrin elaborates the distinction among the classes of people in their relation to God's grace. The Jews thought "in terms of three groups of 'sinners': Jews who could turn to their heavenly father in penitence and hope; Gentile sinners for whom hope was dubious, most Jews regarding them as beyond the pale of God's mercy; and Jews who had made themselves as Gentiles, for whom penitence was, if not impossible, certainly almost insurmountably difficult." [17] The latter included tax collectors and harlots.

Jesus so understood the claim of God for obedience that all pretense to righteousness was undercut. Repentance was a necessity for everyone. At the same time he understood God as ready without limit to accept the penitent. This is expressed in his declaration that precisely the tax collectors and harlots are the first to receive forgiveness.

Perrin derives from the scholarly work of Jeremias a related but different point about Jesus' understanding of God. "Jesus addressed God as *abba* and taught his disciples to do so." [18] *Abba* is the word for father used by a child. It compares with the "papa" of earlier generations or today's "daddy." Used of God, it expresses a sense of assured intimacy alien to Judaism and to the later church alike.

Colwell gathers up Jesus' themes of God's grace, forgiveness, and availability in a still more radical formulation.

> In his deeds and words we meet a God who does not condescend, who does not need to lay aside his divinity to meet man in history, who can actually accept sinners as friends, who is separated from man only by man's pride and resistance, who runs to meet the returning delinquent teen-ager, who delights to give good things to men, who above everything else gives love, richly, inexhaustibly, beyond our deserving or our hope, even if it means he must be nailed to a cross! [19]

There are also some points important for this statement of Jesus' message on which there is a difference, at least of emphasis, among the four authors. Bultmann understands Jesus as looking to the imminent future for the coming of the Kingdom. Colwell sees Jesus as affirming it as already beginning. The "straight and simple meaning" of the parables of the mustard seed and the yeast "is that the work Jesus was doing did not look like a royal kingdom. It was not adorned with 'the power and the glory.' But it was the Kingdom all the same." [20] Perrin, too, stresses that Jesus saw the Kingdom as already present in his ministry and table fellowship. Machoveč holds that such a controversy is "grounded in the lack of understanding precisely for the essence of all eschatological thought." [21]

The difference is not extreme. Bultmann and Machoveč agree with Perrin's statement about Jesus that, in contrast to apocalyptic preachers, "although he spoke of the future, he neither gave specific form to his future expectation (beyond the general one of vindication and implied judgment), nor did he express it in terms of a specific time element." [22] But whereas Bultmann stresses the discontinuity in Jesus' understanding between the present and the new age, Perrin stresses the continuity. In his

view Jesus saw an immediate connection between what was
happening in his ministry and what was yet to come. "Extraor-
dinarily significant . . . is the way in which elements of the
disciples' experience in the present form an integral part of
the teaching concerning the future. The disciples experience the
Kingdom of God in their present; they are taught to pray: 'Thy
Kingdom come.' They gather together in the table-fellowship of
the Kingdom; they are reminded that this is an anticipation of
the table-fellowship in the Kingdom. The whole tenor of the
teaching of Jesus at this point is that the experience of the
present is an anticipation of the future. Further, the experience
of the present is a guarantee of the future." [23] Machoveč, on the
other hand, speaks of "the entirely distinctive penetration of the
present with the future by consistently eschatological men, to
whom Jesus unquestionably belongs." [24]

A similar tension is present in the discussion of Jesus'
teaching on faith. Perrin agrees with Bultmann's observation
that Jesus spoke of faith "only with reference to definite actual
situations in connection with miracles and with prayer." [25] But
Bultmann is concerned to make clear that the faith of which
Jesus spoke differs from that written of by Paul and John. The
latter speak of "the obedience of men under God's redeeming
revelation," [26] which Bultmann believes to have been given only
with the Easter occurrence. Perrin does not deny that there are
differences, but they would have to be worked out in other
terms. In his formulation the faith to which Jesus called men
was "recognition and response to the challenge of his proclamation—recognition that God was, indeed, active as king in his
ministry, and in a specific event, occasion or incident for the
individual concerned, and response in terms of absolute trust
and complete obedience." [27]

Neither Machoveč nor Colwell enters directly into this discussion. Machoveč tends to support Bultmann by making the point
that the first disciples did not believe "in Jesus" but were
directed by him to believe "in the gospel," in the message of the
coming Age and its claim on all.[28] For him the contrast favors
Jesus and makes questionable the later faith of the church.
Colwell, on the other hand, joins Perrin in appreciating the
continuities between Jesus' message and the thought of the
church.[29] Further, he insists that the encounter with Jesus'

deeds and words mediated by historical study is important for Christian faith.[30]

All four authors present Jesus as—in the language of this book—creatively transforming the Judaism of his day. On the one side, the content of his teaching is Jewish through and through. The concepts he employed were for the most part widely used in his day. There is hardly an authentic saying for which illuminating parallels cannot be found in other Jewish sources. On the other side, the parallels are rarely exact. Jesus radicalized and transformed the meaning of the ideas he adopted from others and presented them in such a way that their concrete significance both for him and for his hearers was new.

This means that we can discern Christ, the power of creative transformation, in Jesus. But to say only this, while important, would fall short of what Christians have meant by naming Jesus the Christ. It would leave open the possibility that Jesus is to be seen alongside hundreds of other creative transformers who have fashioned our history. If Jesus is in a more significant sense the Christ, his efficacy must include the advancement of creative transformation of others. Our question is now whether Jesus' message in its creative transformation of Judaism has authority for us today. Does it rightly claim our repeated attention? Does it function to elicit creative transformation in us?

Jesus' authority resembles that of the philosopher or the mystic whose disciplines of thought and contemplation have led to perception not readily available to others. But it is distinct from theirs. Unlike the words of the philosopher, Jesus' words "are not formularized thought. They are descriptions of direct insights." [31] Unlike the words of the mystic, Jesus' words are of the everyday world. Jesus unveils us to ourselves by placing us in a quite unaccustomed perspective. His authority resides first in the actual effect of his words and actions. If the hearers of the word do not see what they are being directed toward, they will have no reason to acknowledge its authority.

The parable of the Pharisee and the publican will serve as an illustration. It is a simple story about everyday occurrences in the world of Jesus' hearers. The Pharisee expresses gratitude that he is able to lead a virtuous life and not fall into the grossly vicious behavior of the publican. The publican just cries out for help. The punch line, now all too familiar, is that it is the publican who is accepted by God. For an effective translation into the contemporary situation the story would have to be told about a popular hero and a traitor, or more concretely, in a given community, one of those most respected and one of those most condemned, perhaps Ralph Nader and John Ehrlichman.[32] The story does not merely point vividly to the way in which excellence *can* lead to self-congratulation; it makes the hearer aware that excellence *does* do so. And it lifts this self-distortion of the good man, through recognition that he is a good man, to a level of clear visibility by contrasting it with the simple acknowledgment of weakness of the vicious man, and by favoring the latter. To hear this story is to see values reversed. If one's sense of values is not turned upside down, he has not heard the message. If the word achieves its effect, it has authority—the only authority it wants or needs. If it does not achieve its effect, no talk about the otherwise authoritative nature of the speaker makes much difference.

Jesus spoke this parable to those who were deeply immersed in the responsible, personal existence attained by Judaism. This provided the context in which his words came as disturbing and revolutionary threats. The continued presence of responsible, personal existence still provides that context today. The parable is shocking to just that degree to which the hearer is an agent of moral decision, and it is especially forceful if one is basically successful in governing one's actions righteously.

Some of those who heard Jesus could take the simple and radical step of joining themselves to the company that surrounded him. There they participated in a fellowship experienced as a reversal of the world and the beginning of the expected Kingdom. Some experienced this as a single, once-for-all repentance that was permanently decisive for their lives.

There may have been times and places in subsequent centuries where similar acts were possible. There may have been monastic or sectarian communities that so embodied the reversal of values that to enter them offered a permanent solution to the problem of coming to terms with Jesus' words. But if this had occurred at all, it has been exceptional. Jesus' words have had an enormous effect in history, but the effect has been far more equivocal and complex than this.

On a social and political scale Jesus' words have broken the self-evidence of established systems. They have thereby transformed resignation into revolutionary opposition. But the new systems that have replaced the old have also been vulnerable to the power of his word. Thus, where Jesus' words are heard, a permanent principle of restlessness is introduced into history.

The individuals who hear Jesus' words and are thereby uprooted from complacency about themselves cannot ordinarily find a place to go in which the new reality proclaimed in that word is actually manifest. Even those who have sought it in perfectionist sects and monastic communities have, for the most part, been forced to recognize the endless distortions of self-righteousness to which such movements are vulnerable.

Having recognized in oneself the Pharisee whose complacency bars the way to God, one becomes ashamed and finds in oneself also the publican who openly owns the need of help. Thus the parable that initially judges becomes, by its assurance of the justification of the publican, a word of grace. But the grace does not provide a place in which one can stand. Having repented, one returns to the world in which one lives and falls back into the habits of spirit and action of which one has repented. The process must be repeated. Or, if by some miracle one retains the spirit of humility and openness attained in the moment of repentance, one becomes gratified by this success and, in that moment, becomes again the Pharisee.

The moment of new recognition of perversion and the moment of new repentance are distinct. In the Christian life they gain separate dominance in special occasions. But they also tend to become coexistent elements in a single continuing existence. One knows oneself as continuously corrupting the gift of grace that comes with a continual mood of repentance. Always sinner, always justified, is Luther's formulation.

In this distinctively Christian structure of existence the self observes itself in its tension with grace and its unlimited capacity to distort God's gift. The self holds itself responsible for its way of dealing inwardly with this gift, as well as with the outward behavior that it knows itself to control. The self distinguishes itself from its body, its emotions, its mind, and even its will. It constitutes itself anew in each moment by its manner of relating itself to all of these. In its self-identity with itself and its distinctness from all other aspects of the psychophysical organism it identifies itself with the sequence of antecedent and anticipated selves. Thus the self establishes its self-identity through time and its "overagainstness" toward all other selves.

The self thus established has enormous capacities for discipline, controlled action, organization, experimentation, and creativity. It is untrammeled by the inhibitions and restraints that characterize people in many other traditions. It has immense power for analysis and for exercise of the will. It is thereby placed in conflict with other selves. Community becomes a goal difficult to attain. Each self is isolated from every other self, enclosed within impenetrable boundaries, and preoccupied with itself, its sin and virtue, its hopes and fears.

This structure of existence is far from what Jesus had in view. He called for a community of perfect openness. But his call has produced the strongest and most isolated individuals in history. These individuals by their aggressive vigor have brought the entire planet into the orbit of that history which measures time from the birth of Jesus.

In Part Three, especially in Chapter 13, we will turn to the question of whether Christian existence may yet become more nearly what Jesus had in view. But for the present it is sufficient to recognize how the authority of Jesus' words actually operates when they are heard. The example has been a typical one, stressing the reversal of expectation and the consequent crisis. But even here the same parable that afflicts the comfortable also comforts the afflicted. Jesus' words not only reverse or tear down the hearer's world; they can also build up a world and give the hearer a place to stand.[33]

In the language of Part One, both the reversal and the affirmation contribute to creative transformation in the hearer. The significant new possibilities for our lives are blocked by complacency and especially by self-righteousness. When this is shaken we are opened to creative novelty. But we can accept the destruction of our world and be open to the new only in the context of reassurance and affirmation. Jesus' words provide this as well; and for this reason we can say that they are the occasion for the realization of Christ within the hearer.

CHAPTER 6

Life in Christ

In the preceding chapter the impact of Jesus' message was illustrated chiefly in terms of its power to jar its hearers out of complacency and to open them to creative transformation. Even in this act of judgment Jesus' words also affirm and establish as well, and, from Paul to Ebeling, Jesus' total efficacy has been described chiefly in terms of the positive new reality into which, through the transformation of the old, we are introduced.

Jesus concluded the parable of the Pharisee and the publican by declaring the publican justified. We have seen how precarious is the experience of justification as a psychological state, and how readily it passes over into complacency. But there is in the mainstream of Christian thought, profoundly influenced by Paul, a sense of security in justification that operates at a deeper than the psychological level. This chapter shifts from the message of Jesus to the church's understanding of the saving efficacy of Jesus, and this is done in order to enlarge the understanding of the relation of Jesus to Christ as the incarnation of the Logos. The chapter proceeds (1) to analyze the existential problem of the need to feel justified, showing the need for an objective basis; (2) to set the problem of justification in the larger context of Paul's understanding of the saving relationship to Christ; (3) to provide a theory of how a past event can function as Paul believes the Christ event to function; (4) to interpret Paul's understanding of life in Christ in these terms together with the justification it effects; and (5) to describe that structure of existence which Paul normatively envisions as "in Christ" and which he himself in some measure seems to have attained.

1. In the sphere of influence of the Judeo-Christian tradition there is an urgent need to believe that one is in the right, acceptable, O.K., or justified. When we are criticized by others or even by ourselves, we try to defend or justify ourselves. We attempt to justify our existence by accomplishing something. The collective phenomenon of national self-justification reflects the need to believe that our collective as well as our individual actions are justified. To this end we expend our psychic energy and go to great lengths of self-deception. Even so our conviction that we are individually and collectively justified in what we are and do remains fragile and precarious. We are unconsciously fearful that our self-justifications do not succeed. At times we are forced to admit that indeed we are not justified. Self-contempt and self-condemnation become a new form of self-defense.

The problem is greatly eased if we can be persuaded that indeed we are acceptable just as we really are. We do not have to be different or to achieve something in order to justify ourselves. In this case we can be honest about ourselves without destructive anxiety and can be open to others without the predominance of defensiveness.

One approach we can take to feeling all right about ourselves is to reject any heavy demands. If we measure ourselves by the standards of what is average rather than by moral ideals, and especially if we adopt a rather cynical view of how others behave, it is much easier to feel justified in what we do. For example, if we measure our national policy in terms of enlightened long-term self-interest and concern for human welfare generally, we are hard pressed to justify ourselves as Americans. It is much easier if we derive our norms from the fact that strong nations generally use their strength for short-term self-interest and face-saving, with little interest in the pursuit of international peace and justice, while cloaking their actions under high-sounding rationalizations. When we measure our actions by these standards, we can accept American foreign policy without the need for self-deception.

This approach, though effective for some, reduces any remaining moral restraints upon mutually destructive behavior. Ethically sensitive people cannot adopt it. Yet those who reject it are led to the continuing self-deception and hypocrisy that characterize our collective and individual behavior.

The other possibility is that individuals feel that they are justified in spite of the fact that they are not just. This requires a distinction of the self from action and feeling that is particularly characteristic of Christian existence and hard to communicate apart from it. It also requires the belief that there is an authoritative source of justification other than the self.

The response to the need to be justified authoritatively by another is to point to God as forgiving us, saving what can be saved from what we make of ourselves even at the cost of suffering in his own life, and giving us anew in each moment an opportunity to begin afresh. Since God forgives us, accepts us, and gives to us what we can receive, it is appropriate for us to turn from concern with justifying what we have been, to be grateful and assured, and to open ourselves to the Logos as it comes to us.

This is an important and true way to view our relation to God. In itself, apart from the concrete actualities of our lives, it *should* suffice to overcome our self-justifying habits. We should be able to turn from preoccupation with the past and anxiety about the future to move forward in trust. But in fact we seem to be unable or unwilling to accept God's acceptance as decisive for our own self-understanding.

This inability or unwillingness is not simply a function of individual decision and perversity. It is also a product of the influence upon us of the world in which we live. Other people are engaged in trying to justify themselves, and in the process they put blame on us or belittle our efforts and achievements. We find ourselves called upon to defend our past actions and to justify our present existence before persons who often see our success as threatening theirs. The superego we have internalized also condemns us. The belief that God does not condemn us is quite abstract in comparison with the pressing fact that others do, or that we are in constant danger of putting ourselves in a position where they will criticize us. Furthermore, even though we feel that some of the criticism is unjust, we also know that we are in fact vulnerable to criticism. We sense that there is a tension between what we are and what we ought to be. God's forgiveness does not reduce that. Our uneasiness before the criticism of others stems in part from half-repressed self-condemnation.

To overcome this self-destroying and never-ending process of self-justification, something more is needed than the belief that God has forgiven us. That belief does not lead us actually to participate in his righteousness. We continue to resist his Logos. The belief serves as much to enhance our implicit guilt as to render us open to his Logos and thereby free from the need to justify ourselves.

Traditional Christian teaching is that we are justified in Christ. In some way, we are told, Jesus has objectively justified us, and recognition of this truth frees us from the need to justify ourselves. As given concreteness in its many theoretical formulations, this belief that we are justified by faith in Jesus Christ has exercised far greater power than theistic beliefs in themselves. But most of the formulations of the belief that carry this power have become incredible, and most of the intelligible proposals lack power.

The first such proposal is that Jesus justifies by revealing God to us. Not only are we indebted to him for the belief that God forgives, but also his conduct and teaching as reported to us in the New Testament vividly display that quality of divine forgiveness. Thus when stories of Jesus' forgiveness of sinners are told, and when they are as moving as those in the New Testament, my abstract belief in God's forgiveness is clothed with emotional force. If I imaginatively identify with the prostitutes and tax collectors and crucifiers, I can experience vicariously what it means to be forgiven.

This is quite true, but it does not go far enough. In this account it is the stories themselves that evoke my emotional response. Even if I believe that they are true and that they are somehow appropriate to representing the way God deals with me, they lose their power to the extent that I realize it is my emotional response that is decisive. Once I have understood the value gained from hearing the stories in a psychological way, their psychological efficacy is reduced.

The account of the effect upon us of the words of Jesus offered in Chapter 5 carries the discussion deeper. This can be combined with stories about Jesus that also shatter our preconceptions and our complacency. Precisely by destroying every possibility of self-justification the words of Jesus and the words about Jesus can open us toward God's grace. That is a part of the Christian experience that should be affirmed within any context. But in this chapter we are looking for something else. Christians have believed that in addition to the words of Jesus there is another form of power or grace that comes from him. Certainly the unsettling encounter with the words of Jesus has not been, in Christian tradition, the only way in which his redemptive action has been experienced.

2. How then has the tradition understood Jesus' saving efficacy, and in particular, how is this affirmed in Paul? The Pauline view h: been so overlaid by subsequent theories that its essential meaning is easily lost from sight. But it is the renewed encounter with the New Testament rather than intellectual assent to subsequent theories that has stimulated the deeper sense that Jesus' work was redemptive for his followers. New Testament study has made clear that the sense of Jesus' efficacy was great, but that it gave rise to a profusion of images in its explication rather than to any consistent theory. Most of this imagery suggests that the efficacy is attained by a powerful relation between the believer and Christ.

The Christ to whom we are related may be conceived either as the heavenly resurrected Lord or as the historical Jesus. A sharp distinction of this sort is rarely found in the New Testament. Christ is at once the Nazarene carpenter who died on a cross and the one who is at the right hand of God. It is this Christ to whom the Christian is related. Yet the weight falls on the side of the crucified one. In Paul we are related to him in his humility and passion so that in the end we will share with him in his resurrection; and Paul understands the eucharist as a reenactment of the table fellowship with Jesus on the night on which he was betrayed. Of course this past figure is viewed in the light of the conviction that he rose, and this conviction transfuses the meaning of the event.

The believer's relation to Jesus, known as Christ, is expressed by Paul in many ways. Christ is seen, served, preached, obeyed, and loved. Christ's grace is with his people, and they are crucified and dead with him. Christ, his suffering, and his life are in them. Christ is the head of his church, which is his body, of which Christians are members. Paul urges his readers to put on Christ, and states that Christ is formed in them. His life is made manifest in the bodies of believers. Through Christ the believer is related to God, receiving his grace, glory, and victory and entering into life unto God, peace with God, joy in God, and eternal life. But the dominant language in Paul's writings for this crucial relation is "in Christ." There is in Christ hope, faith, unity, the love of God, wisdom, one body, the new creation, the Spirit of life, and no condemnation. Christians are begotten in Christ, instructed in Christ, alive in Christ, and asleep in Christ. More often they are simply in Christ. To be a Christian is to be in Christ. To grasp what Paul means by being in Christ would be to gain an important clue to the Christian experience of redemption.

In *The Mysticism of Paul the Apostle*, Albert Schweitzer rendered an important service for Pauline scholarship as he had done earlier for the study of Jesus. To an unusual degree he detached himself from both the need to find truth in Paul and the desire to berate him, and he allowed Paul's own world of thought to come to expression. When he did so, it became clear that what Schweitzer called "Christ-mysticism" was the dominant characteristic of Paul's experience and thought.

Schweitzer points out that already in the nineteenth century Hermann Lüdemann showed that Paul's "being-in-Christ" was an ethicophysical relation and that Otto Pfleiderer described it as mysticoethical. Schweitzer believes it would have been more accurate to call it mysticonatural. But he notes that "under the influence of the distaste felt for the realism of Paul's mysticism, efforts have constantly been made to represent the being-in-Christ as an essentially ethical relation, only obscured a little at times by the shadow cast by a naturalistic conception." [1]

In Bultmann, too, the tension can be found. On the one hand, he recognizes that the idea of "in Christ" points to a relation of determination by Christ. It denotes the "fact that the individual actual life of the believer, living not out of himself but out of the divine deed of salvation, is determined by Christ." [2] But when Bultmann explains what this means, the causal relation between the past event and the present believer gives way to language about church membership and Christian living.

Walter Grundmann has recently introduced a more helpful image, that of a field of force. He writes: "Christ is for Paul the bringer of salvation whose crucifixion and resurrection are the salvation event. This establishes a time and a space of salvation after the manner of a spiritual field of force which has Christ, the bringer of salvation as its centre. . . . The *in* expresses the fact that salvation is operative in the field of force of Christ." [3] "Paul has in mind a field of force in which all events are spiritually caused and ordained by God through Christ." [4]

Viewed in terms of this image, Paul's language takes on rich meaning. He does not think of being in Christ as involving a mixture of ethical and physical, or ethical and mystical, or mystical and natural characteristics, because he does not think of reality as divided up in these ways. Even Grundmann's qualification of the field of force as "spiritual" betrays a modern duality of spiritual and natural that is foreign to Paul. The real past event of the crucifixion and resurrection of Jesus, involving his total being, has objectively established a sphere of effectiveness or a field of force into which people can enter. To enter the field is to have the efficacy of the salvation event become causally determinative of increasing aspects of one's total life. Faith, the ethical life, the church, and the sacraments are all to be understood in this context. Certainly it is the context within which the Christian experiences the deeper meaning of justification.

3. Schweitzer believes that Paul thought in a way "incomprehensible to us" [5] and that his "mysticism does violence to the facts of the natural world." [6] Certainly the notion of a historical event as generating a field of force runs counter to usual ways of understanding our relation with the past. But the approach adopted in this book is to seek a positive account of the kind of experience that is expressed in varied religious contexts rather than to reject them as incomprehensible or as doing violence to the facts. The basic question is whether we can conceive of past historical events as exercising an efficacy on successor events of the sort believed by Paul to be exercised by the salvation occurrences. If so, we must find our way between the dominant options of modern thought which treat the relation of the past to the present as either wholly objective or wholly subjective.

The objectivist believes that present events are exhaustively the effects of past ones. What now happens is, therefore, totally

caused by what has happened. In this view Jesus, as part of
what has happened, is one part of the complex pattern of causes
of what now happens.

The subjectivist believes that the past does not exist except in
the present. What exist are memories of the past. These and
these alone are efficacious. Memories of Jesus and beliefs about
him affect how we feel and act. But the historical Jesus himself
no longer exists or has efficacy.

Objectivists are right in saying that the past *is* objective to
the present. What happened happened, whether we know
about it or not. Our present beliefs about the past affect the
present and the future, but they do not affect the past.

But subjectivists also have their truth. There is decision now,
and that decision is guided by the content of present experience,
including present memories, images, emotions, sensations, anticipations, and beliefs. It cannot be guided by what is not
present. Beliefs about the past are part of the present matrix,
even beliefs about its objectivity and causality, but the past as
such in its pastness is not.

One solution to the problem of this double truth is dualism.
The objective world is seen as ruled by objective laws governing
the way the past determines the present. The subjective world
is seen as the wholly different sphere of thought and freedom.
Since Descartes, this division has played a major role in both
philosophy and theology. But if neither view separately gives
any clue as to how a personal relationship with a real past
person is possible, their addition in this dualistic way is equally
useless. At best it is more the statement of a problem than a
solution; for in fact the subjective and objective spheres are
intimately interconnected.

The alternative here adopted has been presented above in
Chapter 3. It is to affirm after Whitehead that events are not
simply located but instead pervade their causal future. This
means that every event sets up a field of force beyond itself. But
since each new event finds itself in the fields of force of many
past events, just what role each plays in the self-constitution of
the present event is decided in the present. The efficacy of the
past event is real and objective; each is truly given, but its exact
role is determined in the fresh decision of the present. Subjectivists are correct in thinking that only what is present affects

decision, but they miss the point that the past pervades its field and that its givenness is an important part of what is present.

Because the idea that the past is given in the present appears paradoxical, some further explanation should be offered. Consider a moment of present experience. It has a subjective and an objective aspect. One part of the objective aspect is the world presented by sense experience. The table or the tree that I see or touch is not me as subject in the same way that my pleasure or disappointment in them is. The table and the tree are in my experience, but they constitute the objective or given pole of that experience. I clothe this objectively given element with my private subjectivity. It is decided about. It is not part of the decision.

It can be shown by physical and physiological analysis that what is initially given are the causal influences of the table and tree upon my experience. I see them as contemporary with me, but in fact it is very recent past events in the table and the tree that affect me and cause me to see them. Those immediately past events are objective and given, but they affect my present experience by being objectively given in it.

The table and the tree are objectively given in my experience chiefly through the sense organs. But there can be other events in the brain that are not associated with sense organs, and these events can also be present as objective and given in experience. More important for our purposes, my own recent past experiences—of a fraction of a second ago—are present as objective and given in the constitution of new experience. This flow of experience in the psychic life of an individual person is the best instance to consider of how the past is given for the present and how its role in the newly self-constituting present is affected by the fresh decision; for it is possible to see that in each moment we are largely continuous with our past and yet not simply bound to repeat it. The subjective side of the present tends to conform to the past that is given as ingredient object. Therein lies the causal efficacy of the past. But the causal presence of other factors complicates this conformation. Furthermore, novel possibilities arise. Just what role the past as objective presence plays is settled only in the final decision that is the outcome. That decision affects especially the causal presence that its data will have in subsequent occasions. For example, if I repent of what I have done, the past actions will play a different role in my future experience than if I congratulate myself upon them.

Causal presence is not limited to my immediately past bodily states and personal experience. In some way, however trivial, what is given for me in each moment is affected by all that has ever happened. Between utter triviality and the massive importance of the immediate past lie all degrees of causal presence.

One major factor in determining the role that past events play in their present givenness is belief about them. What we usually call memory is a mixture of the efficacious givenness of what really occurred and our beliefs about the occurrence. The beliefs themselves represent the causal presence of other events in which the original one was interpreted. To sort out the present contributions of that past event from those of subsequent events is a matter of great difficulty. If the received interpretation conformed largely to fact, the original event will have a less diluted present efficacy than if it has been seriously misinterpreted. Past events once misinterpreted can sometimes renew their original efficacy when this is discriminated from the efficacy of the misinterpretations.

Our private past is bound up with the past of other persons so that what is causally present to a significant degree can include other persons as well. When we remember those persons we heighten the efficacy of their givenness as well as the efficacy of past interpretations. This makes for a personal relationship. The more accurate the history of interpretations that is intertwined with the causal efficacy of the other person, the more genuinely personal the relationship will be. If the interpretations are essentially distorting, the relation will be chiefly to these interpretations rather than to the person. The clarification of the truth about the past allows authentic memory to purify itself from this confusion.

4. The significance of this account should now be clear. For the subjectivist, memory is a subjective state. Hume, as a consistent subjectivist, said we could not distinguish it from other elements in present experience except by its relative indistinctness. An objectivist sees memory only as one of the phenomena necessitated by the complex pattern of events that constitute the causal past. The force of those events in the

present is determined entirely by them. The present, including memory, is the passive effect of this matrix of forces. But for the account here proposed, subjective and objective elements interact. Past entities are really, ontologically, effectively ingredient in the constitution of the present. They generate a field of force. The present entity determines just how effective that field of force will become in itself and in subsequent entities. The ontological fact of the present effectiveness of the past makes conscious memory possible in distinction from fantasy. The decision to attend makes the actual efficacy much greater. Jesus is one of those entities in the past that is really, ontologically, effectively ingredient in the constitution of the present. But of course he is only one of billions, and in an objectivist view his effect must be trivial. But when we recognize that the role of a past event now is affected by how it has been received and responded to by intervening events, we can consider that through myriads of channels Jesus' efficacy has been kept alive. When we remember Jesus we give the ever-present causal efficacy a much greater role in the constitution of our experience. We could not remember if the objective presence did not precede our remembering. The objective presence would long ago have become trivial if it were not frequently remembered.

Memory by itself does not suffice to describe the relation. There is also conformation. The force of the past is carried into the present by the conformation of the present to it. My emotions in one moment tend to conform to those in the preceding moments. But experience constitutes itself selectively, and it does not have to conform to what is quantitatively predominant. It tends to conform to what is proximate—to the attitudes and feelings of those in the immediate environment, and especially to one's own most recent past. But again, that is not necessary. Viktor Frankl tells how he maintained sanity and integrity in a death camp by thinking of his wife. Such attention raised to dominance her influence in constituting his experience moment by moment and so enabled him to avoid the destructive results of conforming to his more immediate environment.

There is some measure of conformation to all past events, and that again would include Jesus. But the possibility of conformation is greatly enhanced by attention and memory.

Thus the objective relation to Jesus is enhanced by a subjective one which then is passed on to its successors objectively. Conformation to Jesus is an ontological possibility that can be actualized to greatly varying degrees. It is possible because of the fact that Jesus existed. Its content or consequences is determined by who Jesus actually was. What role it plays in particular individuals depends on the many responses that others have made to this possibility and finally on their own free responses. The degree of response today affects the possibilities for further response tomorrow. One possibility is that the conformation will grow and become more and more determinative of all one's feelings, attitudes, and relations.

This discussion was begun to offer a post-modern conception of the effective givenness of the past that would enable us to make sense of the Pauline understanding of the relation of the believer to Christ. The proposal is that to put on Christ is to begin the process of conformation to him. To be in Christ is to have the conformation to Christ as the growing center of one's existence. Since Christ was distinctively related to God, to be in Christ is to be conformed in some measure to that relationship, hence through Christ one shares in grace, peace, and joy with God. Through the conformation, the righteousness of Christ becomes our righteousness.

The conformation is never finished. Paul looks forward to completion in the resurrection, but in this life we are influenced by many other things as well. Even though we are in Christ the power of many other elements and forces in our world opposes the forming of Christ in us. The stance that heightens our conformation is faith.

Now we are prepared to return to the question of justification. Paul says much less about it than we have been taught to think by Lutheran scholarship. But he does see that the attempt to justify ourselves is one of our central problems. He sees also that this is an endless and fruitless approach. He calls instead for our conformation to Christ. To conform to Christ is to allow ourselves to be shaped by his righteousness. That does not mean that we actually become righteous as he was righteous. But it does mean that his righteousness is formed in us. We belong to him and our identity is found in that belonging. We are part of a group of people who belong to him and constitute his body. Through Jesus Christ, or because we are in Christ, we share in his relation to God. Through him we receive sonship. Being conformed to him, we are conformed to his confidence in God and openness to God. Hence in our conformation we are freed from defensiveness. We no longer need to justify ourselves because we are justified in him. Finding ourselves justified as we are, we can respond positively to the new possibilities received from the Logos and be creatively transformed by them.

5. What has been described thus far does not yet do full justice to that element in Paul's teaching which led Schweitzer to speak of his realistic Christ-mysticism. For Paul, life in Christ finally entailed that the very center of his existence be constituted by Christ's presence. He can say that it is not he who lives but Christ who lives in him. In Bultmann's words, Paul "describes 'gaining Christ and being found in him' as the state of being completely determined by the salvation-occurrence." [7] This implies a structure of existence distinct from that both of Judaism and of most Christians.

Clarification of this structure requires a fresh criticism of the substantialist habits of thought that so easily come to the fore. If the self is understood to be a substance underlying experience, then it cannot be constituted by God without being God. The reason is that a substance cannot be constituted by anything except itself. It may be created by something else, but the creator remains external to the creature. The created substance can be the subject of relations with other substances, but it cannot include those relations within itself. The relations are external to the substance.

But today we can reject substantialist thinking about the self as well. Indeed, the intellectual and existential puzzles into which substantialist thinking leads give ample warrant to do so. It is better to recognize that there is no fixed entity or aspect of human experience that is uniformly designated by "I." Nevertheless, the word "I" is an important one and that to which it refers is of central interest. The one who says "I" refers to the ultimate subject of conscious experience and the ultimate agent of responsible action. That this subject and agent is not a self-identical substantial entity does not reduce its importance.

Every experience organizes itself around some center. This center is an aspect of the experience. It comes into being with the experience. But this aspect determines which other aspects are to be admitted to prominence and how they are to be related to each other. It does not have complete control, and in some instances it may even feel itself largely helpless. But it remains the subject from whose point of view other elements of the experience are appraised as threats or aids.

An example couched in the partly misleading terms of faculty psychology will help to make this clearer. A particular woman may identify herself with her rational will. Within her experience she also finds emotions, sometimes very strong ones. She sees these as something to be controlled and ordered in relation to her rational will. Sometimes she fails. She finds herself overcome by the power of feelings. The feelings are experienced as a force not identical with herself. A second woman may identify herself with her emotions. She is also capable of thinking, purposing, and willing, but, she sees these elements in her experience as tools useful for furthering her emotional desires. Her use of thought in the service of emotion may sometimes introduce tensions; for thought leads to conclusions she does not like, and it can be destructive in terms of her emotions. Hence the thinking is experienced as a force not identical with herself. Thus, by "I" one woman refers to her reason; another, to her emotional life.

Where the "I" in each momentary experience is located is largely determined by where it was located in earlier experiences in the same person's life. The immediately preceding experience is especially influential. That is, if a moment ago a woman's selfhood was found in her rational will, the present experience will also, in all probability, be structured in the same way. Change is possible, even abrupt change, but the overwhelming tendency is continuance.

Thus the "I" in each moment is ordinarily constituted by the inclusion in that experience of the previous experience and conformity to it. The "I" who finished a syllable is the continuation of the "I" who began it. The conformation is so close that for most practical purposes it can be regarded as an identity. People think of themselves as identical through time because the "I" in each moment is constituted by conformation to the presence in that momentary experience of the preceding experiences of that person. The new experience includes other elements as well. But from the perspective constituted by the presence of one's personal past these are felt as external ingredients with which to come to terms.

But there is no ontological necessity that the dominant conformation in each moment be to the predecessors in that personal life. Under hypnosis or in ecstasy other patterns of conformation are possible. In this case it is not the field of force of one's own past but that of some other event which constitutes the center or "I" from which all experience is organized. Or more probably some other field of force coconstitutes the "I" along with conformation to one's own past.

For Paul the coconstituting agent of his personal "I" was the salvation occurrence or Jesus Christ. Paul experienced himself as most fully what he willed to be as conformation to Christ constituted his personal selfhood. Thus all the conflicting fields of force emanating from his own past, his body, and his world were experienced as alien to what he truly was, namely, a bearer of Christ's life. As a bearer of Christ's life, he was open to being continuously creatively transformed by the Logos.

No other writer in the New Testament expresses a comparable self-identification with Christ. Conformation to Christ for most Christians even in the first generation did not penetrate to this level, but the power of the Pauline language and witness has made this structure of existence an attractive, if limiting, possibility for Christians for whom otherwise the self is constituted by conformation to the personal past and is always in tension with the conformation to Christ that is also occurring in some measure.

CHAPTER 7

From Jesus' Work to Jesus' Person

Jesus' words open their hearers to Christ by shattering established self-images in a context of ultimate reassurance. Entry into Jesus' field of force and progressive conformation to him likewise opens believers to the Christ. Clearly there is not an exclusive antithesis between these two ways of experiencing Jesus' efficacy, and most Christians in most periods of Christian history have understood their relation to Jesus both in terms of encountering his words and in terms of his objective efficacy. Yet a duality of focus has characterized Christianity from the early days; for example, some have understood Christianity primarily in ethical and legal terms, and others have understood it primarily in sacramental, ecclesiastical, and mystical terms. This duality has played a role not only in the interpretation of Jesus' work as savior but also in the understanding of his person.

One tradition in the early church saw Jesus primarily as the one teacher or preacher who through his words and deeds uniquely and perfectly revealed God and his will. Obedience to God's will is the way to eternal blessedness, whereas failure to follow this way must result in everlasting suffering. The other tradition in the early church saw Jesus as the one in whom the Logos entered history to overthrow the powers of evil that everywhere worked corruption. Through Jesus a new field of force began to work in which incorruptibility and immortality triumph. Few Christians in the early church rejected either of these traditions, and there was little explicit debate between them. But in the controversies about Jesus' person to be traced below in Chapter 9 the contesting parties were largely ruled by differing sensibilities as to the way Jesus saves, and similar differences to this day shape reflection on Jesus.

The former of these traditions comes to expression in the early church manual, the Didache, which presents Jesus as definitely distinguishing the religious and ethical way that leads to life from the other way that leads to death. It was continued by the second-century apologists, who presented Jesus primarily as so embodying the Logos as to reveal God and make known the way of righteousness. The apologist Justin Martyr tells the story of his conversion in terms of his recognition that God cannot be known through philosophy but only as he reveals himself by prophets and in Christ. Justin concludes with the wish "that all, making a resolution similar to my own, do not keep themselves away from the words of the savior. For they possess a terrible power in themselves, and are sufficient to inspire those who turn from the path of rectitude with awe." [1]

In this tradition God's exalted transcendence is centrally in view. Cyril of Jerusalem, for example, stresses that "what we say about God is not what should be said (for that is known only to him) but only what human nature takes in, and only what our infirmity can bear. For what we expound is not what God is, but (and we frankly acknowledge it) the fact that we have no sure knowledge about him; and that is to say that our chief theological knowledge is confessing that we have none." [2] Since "none could behold the face of Godhead and live, the Lord took him a human face that we can look upon and live." [3] Doctrinal purity and moral living are the essential elements in the appropriate response to this act of God.

For this tradition the clarification of what is required for belief and right action are found through the study of Scripture. Hence the exegetical school of Antioch largely eschewed the allegorical method, stressing the literal, historical meanings of the text. This bore rich fruit in the greatest preacher of the ancient church, John Chrysostom. His homilies were careful exegetical exhortations, emphasizing the ethical application of the text. His sermons show that theology was still able to fulfill its task in the church to a very large extent. Hans von Campenhausen comments that "the homilies of Chrysostom are probably the only ones from the whole of Greek antiquity which

at least in part are still readable today as Christian sermons.
They reflect something of the authentic life of the New Testament, just because they are so ethical, simple, and so clearheaded." [4] Many of these sermons give careful attention to the
words of Jesus, underscoring their point, and thus affecting the
existence of the hearers.[5]

Alongside and interpenetrating with this view of Jesus as the
revelation of God and his will was the second tradition,
continuing Paul's sense of a field of force initiated by the
salvation occurrences. The church as the body of Christ was
experienced as expressing that field of force and as incorporat-
ing believers into it through the community's sacramental life.
Christians could see themselves as a new race of people.
Irenaeus interpreted the inauguration of this field as the invasion of the world by the Logos. Mankind, which belonged
rightfully to God, was tyrannized by apostasy. Hence the
Logos, "mighty in all things, [reclaimed us], making us his own
disciples. Not failing in his quality of justice, he acted justly
against the apostasy itself, not redeeming his own from it by
force, although it at the beginning had merely tyrannized over
us, greedily seizing the things that were not its own, but by
persuasion." [6] Coming in the form of Jesus, the Logos perfectly
summed up or recapitulated human existence. The Logos
thereby "redeemed us by his own blood, and gave his soul for
our souls, and his flesh for our bodies, and poured out the Spirit
of the Father to bring about the union and communion of God
and man—bringing God down to men by [the working of] the
Spirit, and again raising man to God by his incarnation—and by
his coming firmly and truly giving us incorruption, by our
communion with God." [7]

Athanasius gave this sense of a redemptive field of force its
most influential expression. He too saw God as unwilling to
allow his creatures to be lost to corruption and death because of
their bondage to transgression. God responded through the
Logos, which had created the world and was the appropriate
means for re-creation. He who "has filled all things everywhere" [8] came in a new way as a man "to the end that, firstly,
all being held to have died in him, the law involving the ruin of
men might be undone . . . , and that, secondly, whereas men
had turned toward corruption, he might turn them again toward
incorruption, and quicken them from death by the appropriation

of his body." [9] "And thus he, the incorruptible Son of God, being conjoined with all by a like nature, naturally clothed all with incorruption." [10]

This same theme is the center of Cyril of Alexandria's passionate attack upon Nestorius, who seemed, by distinguishing Jesus from the Logos, to deprive the event of its power to transform the human condition. "The Only-begotten became like us, became, that is, a complete man, that he might free our earthly body from the alien corruptions which had been brought into it. . . . [Christ] is, so to speak, the root and the first fruits of those who are restored in the Spirit to newness of life, to immortality of the body, to certainty and security of divinity, so that he may transmit this condition to the whole of humanity by participation, and as an act of grace." [11]

The overwhelming concern in this tradition centering in Alexandria was for God's overcoming corruption and death in Jesus and establishing a new order of incorruptibility. To bring home the reality of the field of force deriving from the work of the Logos in Jesus, the literal meaning of Scriptural texts could be subordinated to allegorical meanings.

Both traditions led in the early church to reflections on the person of Jesus and to extensive arguments against those who denied or misrepresented the unique work of God in Jesus. For the adherents of the first tradition the need was to establish Jesus' absolute authority as teacher and revealer. To this end there were arguments from prophecy and miracles as well as appeals to the evident moral superiority of Jesus' teaching and the Christian life over all competitors. God's unknowability apart from his act of revelation was also stressed as well as the absolute importance of knowing him and his will in the light of the eternal consequences that hang on our response in this life. The understanding of Jesus that emerges from these arguments is of a man so empowered and indwelt by the Logos that his words and deeds give unqualified expression to God's purposes.

For the adherents of the second tradition the need was to establish that indeed the Logos has acted to overcome the power of corruption and death. To this end many of the same lines of argument were employed as in the first tradition. But, especially in the justification of particular beliefs about the person of Jesus, the weight shifts decisively to the experienced effect. What happened in Jesus must have been of such a nature as to explain what is occurring in the Christian community. Here believers find themselves freed from bondage to corruption and death and filled with confidence of immortality. Only the divine Logos can have accomplished this radical transformation of the human situation. Hence Jesus is the one in and through whom the Logos performed its soteriological and eschatological work.

The argument from what occurs in Jesus' field of force to the unique action of God in Jesus' person has been a dominant one down through the nineteenth century. In quite different ways, Kant, Hegel, and Schleiermacher all supported this kind of Christology. As long as this carried conviction, it tended to separate Jesus from other human beings. It cut, therefore, against another movement of the theological imagination that progressively saw the incarnation as affirming the full, concrete, particular creatureliness and humanity of Jesus. This expressed itself in the historical effort to free Jesus from his aura of supernatural mystery and sacral distance. More and more in the twentieth century Jesus had been understood to share our human fallibility and ignorance, our emotions of anger and resentment, our ambitions and fears, and our biological functions not only of eating, drinking, excreting, and sleeping but of sexuality as well. We not only assume that he was tempted, but that he yielded to temptation. In short, we have uncomfortably worked through our resistances to the recognition that in Jesus the divine became fully human. Jesus is altogether one of us. To have recognized this and what it means for Christian faith is a creative transformation in which we can discern Christ.

Those who have newly achieved freedom from the sacred Jesus and discovered the inner release that comes from recognizing in him a fully human participant in the ambiguous struggles of historical existence often view this as the last word in the understanding of incarnation and of Jesus' person. But this view is an illusion, for it is not possible to stop here. We can go only two ways. We can go on to say that because Jesus was just like us he no longer deserves any special attention from us but is to be viewed simply as one among many historically interesting and important figures. Or we can notice that because Jesus is, like us, fully human, there was a concrete particularity of the divine presence and action in him as there is in each of us. In view of the peculiar efficacy of both Jesus' message and his field of force to open others to Christ, the particular mode of the activity of the Logos in him is of more than casual interest.

The direction we now take is decisive for the future efficacy of Jesus, because the capacity of his words and his field of force to open us to the Logos as the power of creative transformation depends on our exposing ourselves to those words and to this field. This occurs chiefly through reading the Bible and secondary Christian literature and by participating in the life and liturgy of the church. These practices continue in some circles, partly through habit and partly because of intrinsic satisfaction received. But the habit and the satisfaction by no means ensure perseverance.

It is possible that some continuing attention to Jesus can be motivated, apart from belief in his distinctive authority, by the recognition that this attention sustains Christian existence. If one prizes this existence, one may cultivate whatever practices are needed for its strengthening. But this, too, is a precarious situation containing the seeds of its own decline; for it is the nature of Christian existence that every concrete embodiment of it must be judged and transcended. That means that Christian existence is a repeated process of giving itself up to what is unknown. This can happen only through the continual unmasking of our tendency to establish ourselves as we are and a repeated renewal of trust in the process of creative transformation. But our tendencies to self-satisfaction with our present participation in Christian existence resist the unmasking in the name of Christian existence itself. To undertake to overcome that resistance by developing our own discipline, which will include attending to Jesus, is a subtle form of self-salvation that conflicts with the essential nature of Christian existence. To select Jesus for attention because that benefits us is unlikely to lead to the kind of attention that exposes to judgment the benefits that are sought. It is to substitute the authority of our own opinions as to what is valuable for the authority of Jesus. Christian existence arose and developed where the authority of Jesus was recognized and evoked attention. That authority was grounded in the assumption that Jesus' relation to God was different from ours. Before we subordinate that authority to our own, it is worthwhile for us to consider whether our present knowledge of Jesus supports the recognition of distinctive authority in him.

In the past, Christians could argue from the saving power of Jesus' field of force to his divinity. Today that is not possible. The boundaries of this field of force have become too vague for us any longer to be sure of its power. On the one hand, it has reached out to embrace the whole planet. On the other hand, it is no longer clearly manifest with distinctive efficacy in avowedly Christian institutions. Precisely because the efficacy is one of opening people to creative transformation rather than of communicating a particular defined pattern of character or behavior, the field of force has generated numerous and highly diverse movements or traditions. In doing so, it has intermingled with many other fields of force so that everywhere, for good or ill, it has lost its earlier relative purity. When it has tried hardest to maintain that purity it has absolutized some one pattern produced by an earlier phase of creative transformation and thereby inhibited the continuing work of the Logos.

If concern for Jesus' continued efficacy leads us to ask about Jesus' distinctiveness, and if we cannot reason from the effects to the distinctive character of the cause, then we must turn to those who have directly investigated the cause—that is, the historical Jesus. We can turn again to historians whose interest is to determine as objectively as possible who Jesus was. We can ask whether they have learned anything that is relevant to our question about his distinctiveness and especially about the distinctiveness of his relation to the Logos.

Until the nineteenth century it was assumed that Jesus expressly affirmed his own deity. Even when Johannine and other sayings that did so most explicitly were recognized as those of the church, Jesus was still thought to have identified himself with the Son of Man, and that title was seen to have supernatural significance. The creative transformation that is the history of New Testament scholarship step by step removed from our understanding of the real Jesus all such claims about himself. It participated centrally thereby in the radical humanization of the Christian image of Christ that has dominated the recent history of the understanding of incarnation. But almost unnoticed, at the point when Jesus is most fully understood apart from any claim to deity or Messiahship, the scholar confronts the fact that at the heart of his message is an astonishing presumption of his own importance and authority.

It is characteristic of recent scholarship that none of the four writers treated in Chapter 5 deals thematically with the question of Jesus' authority but that all make important relevant statements. Machoveč stresses that Jesus' impact cannot be understood in abstraction from the attractive power of his personality.[12] The supposition that Jesus' ideas alone would have so great an effect on others is for Machoveč a modern illusion. Only when a man is one with his message, when the "proclaimer of the idea" is himself the "image of its actualization," [13] can he make it real to others as Jesus did.

Bultmann, Perrin, and Colwell treat Jesus' authority in terms of his teaching and actions rather than his person. They agree in excluding from the authentic sayings of Jesus those which refer various titles to himself. Bultmann, however, accepts the authenticity of sayings that speak of the future coming of an eschatological Son of Man and relate Jesus' ministry to him. This implies an exalted claim to authority on Jesus' part. Although Bultmann directs attention elsewhere, he notes that "there is indeed one estimate of him which is consistent with his own view, the estimate of him not as a personality, but as one sent by God, as bearer of the word." [14] And in a more recent essay, written in criticism of the new association of Jesus with Christian faith by some of his followers, Bultmann recognizes that Jesus "doubtless appeared in the consciousness of being commissioned by God to preach the eschatological message of the breaking-in of the kingdom of God and the demanding but also inviting will of God. We may thus ascribe to him a prophetic consciousness, a 'consciousness of authority.' " [15]

Perrin goes beyond Bultmann in his denial that the apocalyptic Son of Man sayings are authentic, and he says nothing either of Jesus' embodying his own word or "consciousness of authority." All the more remarkable are his numerous comments that witness to the extreme claims to authority implicit in Jesus' message and action. Perrin agrees with Ernst Fuchs that "*Jesus' conduct* was itself the real framework of his proclamation," [16] and he asserts that the parable of the prodigal son "clearly reflects the situation of the ministry of Jesus and is equally clearly designed to open men's eyes to the reality of that situation, *as Jesus himself saw it.*" [17] In his discussion of the

laborers of the vineyard, Perrin agrees with Eta Linnemann that
"there is a tremendous personal claim involved in the fact that
Jesus answered an attack upon his conduct with a parable
concerned with what *God* does!" [18] He notes that Jesus' words
beginning, "I tell you," contain a "direct challenge to dearly held
preconceptions of the period" and constitute "an indirect
personal claim of great magnitude." [19] And he sees that Jesus
calls for faith as "recognition that Jesus does, in fact, have the
authority to forgive sins, and recognition that the exorcisms are,
indeed, a manifestation of the Kingdom of God." [20]

Indeed it seems in Perrin's account that Jesus associated
himself and his ministry with the present reigning of God in a
way that implicitly claims an authority that goes far beyond
that of the prophets. "Jesus taught the same thing both by
proclamation and by simile: the decisive activity of God as king
is now to be experienced by men confronted by his ministry in
word and deed." [21] "The hotly debated question as to whether
this implies that the Kingdom is to be regarded as present,
inbreaking, dawning, casting its shadows before it, or whatever,
becomes academic when we realize that the claim of the saying
[Luke 11:20] is that certain events in the ministry of Jesus are
nothing less than an *experience* of the Kingdom of God." [22]

Colwell, too, turns attention away from titles. But he sees
evidence, in Jesus' "words and deeds of divine mission, of a
decisive mission for the Kingdom." [23] "Jesus taught with
authority; his words do not rest on external validation. His
authority is not scribally derived from Scripture, nor apocalypti-
cally from vision, nor prophetically from a reported call or word
from the Lord. He acted with authority: he called disciples,
cleansed the temple, exorcised demons, healed on the Sab-
bath." [24] "Forgiveness and salvation take place through his
word." [25] "Unless one admits that Jesus felt that he knew with
certainty the nature of God and God's will for man, the sayings
that are historically most probable are most inexplicable." [26]
Indeed, many of Jesus' sayings imply that "his relationship to
the Father was unique." [27]

All our writers share with the great body of New Testament
scholars the conviction that Jesus was truly, in every sense and
in every dimension of his being, a man. This is simply not in
question. In this respect the contemporary scene differs profoundly from earlier epochs of church history. It does not occur

to such historians as we are treating, for example, to wonder about a divine omniscience or omnipotence in Jesus. Yet all four are impressed by the distinctiveness of this particular man. They note his claim to a unique relation to the Logos, the Kingdom, or the Father, and they present this astonishing claim with respect. Jesus' claim might be ignored if his words did not carry the ring of truth. But in a world that has been deeply shaped by Jesus' influence, and among those who participate in the structure of existence that his words have brought into being, the claim cannot lightly be passed over.

Accordingly, the chapters that follow proceed to a consideration of the distinctiveness of Jesus' person in terms of his relation to the Logos. Chapter 8 proposes a way we can understand the structure of Jesus' existence that fits the picture that emerges from our four historians and the general consensus of New Testament scholars as to Jesus' implicit claim to authority. It then considers whether attributing this structure to Jesus grounds the kind of authority experienced in his words and accounts for the field of force attested by Paul and Christian tradition. Since the church has in the Chalcedonian creed an official statement of the structure of Jesus' existence, its conceptual meaning is explained as objectively as possible in Chapter 9, and the relation of the formulations in Chapters 8 and 9 is considered in Chapter 10. Chapters 9 and 10 are thus intended to make explicit the relation of the results of the approach to Christology in this book to creedal orthodoxy. They are not essential to the systematic development of this Christology itself.

CHAPTER 8

Jesus' Person
as Christ

When the question of the structure of Jesus' existence has been asked in the past, it has seemed that only two answers were possible. Either Jesus was simply a human being, in which case the structure of his existence was just like that of everyone else, or else he was the incarnation of God, in which case he was the one radical exception to an otherwise common condition. Limitation to these two possibilities follows when it is assumed that there is a universal structure of human existence or a common human nature.

The perspective of this book is quite different. Even in the very limited comments on structures of existence above, diversities appeared. In *The Structure of Christian Existence*, I set these modest diversities in the context of a wider, although still limited, variety. There is little common human nature other than the uniquely human capacity to be shaped in history into a wide variety of structures of existence. Each major culture and each major figure in history is to be freshly approached with the question whether the structure of existence embodied is familiar or different, common to others or unique. Here the pluralistic spirit is at work at the deepest level.

Rudolf Bultmann saw Jesus definitely as a Jew. That would suggest that Jesus embodied the typical Jewish structure of existence. It would not explain the distinctiveness of his message or the authority with which he spoke. Realizing this, Bultmann attributed to Jesus a prophetic consciousness.

The structure of the prophet's existence, at least in those

experiences which inspired the prophecies, differed from ordinary Jewish existence chiefly in the relation to God. Jews knew themselves as agents of decision and action, responsible before God to obey the divine law. Thus their existence centered in the will as the decider and determinant of action. The law was known by instruction and study. The prophet, however, was grasped by a direct awareness of divine purposes and requirements that constrained him to witness and overruled any resistance from his will.

The point at which the prophets were distinctive, i.e., their relation to God, is also the point at which Jesus appears distinctive, but the relation was not the same. The prophets spoke of a Word of God received by them, whereas Jesus presented his message on his own authority, sometimes explicitly so, while identifying God's purposes with his actions.

If Jesus' structure of existence is not identical with the ordinary or prophetic Jewish existence, perhaps it is the same as that of Christians. However, the picture of ordinary Christian existence presented in Chapter 5 discourages that identification. Christians know themselves as responsible for a purity they continuously destroy and hence experience a pervasive sinfulness as well as forgiveness. Jesus' words betray no sense of moral anguish or need to be forgiven.

Since the distinctiveness of Jesus' structure of existence, like that of the prophets, is associated with his relation to God, some suppose that he may be understood as a mystic. In a very broad sense of the term "mystic"—one that would include the prophets as well—this is correct. But if the mystic is understood to be the one who attains ecstatic union with God, there is no evidence that Jesus was a mystic. The mystic contemplates God in separation from the world to such a point that awareness of the world, the past, and the future drops away, and the content of the experience is God alone. Jesus' message deals in concrete particularity with ordinary men and women and their response to the coming Kingdom. Other mystics claim an actual identity with God clearly denied by Jesus.

There are, of course, other varieties of Jewish, Christian, and mystical existence with which Jesus' existence could be compared, but this brief survey should suffice to indicate the justification for considering Jesus in his distinctiveness. The datum for this reflection is the implicit identification of his

actions as directly expressive of God's purposes and the authority of his personal word. In the language of Ernst Fuchs, Jesus'
"conduct is neither that of a prophet nor of a teacher of wisdom,
but that of a man who dares to act in God's stead." [1] This
suggests that in some special way the divine Logos was present
with and in him.

The account of the Logos in Chapter 3 shows that it is
incarnate in all things. It shows also that the mode and function
of that incarnation vary. The Logos is now more, now less
determinative in the constitution of occasions. Although the
Logos is never entirely absent, resistance to creative transformation can be successful. What people believe, to what they
attend, and what they decide affect how the Logos is incarnate
within them. Structures of existence are correlated with different roles of the Logos.

To assert that the Logos was incarnate in Jesus in itself,
therefore, is true but insufficient. The Logos is incarnate in all
human beings and indeed in all creation, but it does not provide
all with certainty of God's will or the authority of direct insight.
If Jesus is a paradigm case of incarnation, and if the structure of
his existence as it incarnates the Logos is explanatory of his
assurance and authority, the possibility of a distinctive mode of
incarnation should be considered. In the fullest incarnation of
the Logos, its presence must constitute not only a necessary
aspect of existence but the self as such. Embodiment of this
structure of existence explains Jesus' certainty and authority.

This structure of existence is attributed to Jesus by Machoveč
as well. According to him, Jesus not only proclaimed the
Kingdom of God, he "incarnated this lived future in his entire
being." [2] He made the new age real only "because in him his
'word' was completely identical with himself, because in this
sense he was the 'word,' because he was its human 'incarnation.' " [3]

These phrases might be interpreted in a purely psychological
sense to mean that Jesus was completely possessed by his hope
for the Kingdom. But this would underestimate the depth of
Machoveč's insights. The lived future for him is no mere idea
but the controlling reality of fully human life. Although there
may be ontological differences in the interpretation of its status,
the lived future is fundamentally identical with the Logos as
that has been explained in Chapter 3, and Machoveč also makes

the identification with the Logos in these quotations. In Jesus there is a distinctive incarnation because his very selfhood was constituted by the Logos. The remainder of this chapter is devoted to clarifying what that means and how it can be.

In the last section of Chapter 6 it was pointed out that "I," or the organizing center of human existence, is usually constituted by conformal continuity with the "I" of preceding moments of the same personal life. We saw that Paul seems at times to have experienced his "I" as coconstituted by the presence of Christ in him, but that in ordinary Christian existence the call to conformation to Christ or to live from the field of force generated by the salvation-occurrence is experienced as coming to the self from without.

Similarly in ordinary Christian existence the "I," constituted by conformation to its own past, experiences the new possibility provided by the Logos as challenging it from without. It is to be taken account of. It may be felt to some extent as help, to some extent as demand and threat. A person may conform to a considerable degree to the possibility offered by the Logos. But the Logos is felt as a force other than the self and as acting in relation to the self within the total synthesis that is the actual experience.

Although this is the most familiar structure of existence, it is not the only possible one. There is no necessity that the chain of experiences reaching far back into the personal past be so completely constitutive of present selfhood. This is not the case with very young children. In primitive tribal existence identity may be based more on the tribal experience than on the private, personal one. Buddhism has devised techniques for breaking the common way of identifying oneself and for becoming more impartially open to the many ingredients in experience. Various forms of mysticism suggest the possibility of still other structures of existence.

In another possible structure of existence the presence of the Logos would share in constituting selfhood; that is, it would be identical with the center or principle in terms of which other elements in experience are ordered. In that structure the appropriation of one's personal past would be just that ideal appropriation made possible by the lure of creative novelty that is the immanent Logos. If this occurred, the usual tension between the human aim and the ideal possibility of self-actualization that is the Logos would not occur. The relation of the person to God would not be the confrontation of an "I" by a "Thou." That confrontation assumes that the "I" derives its existence elsewhere than from the "Thou" and is then modified in that relation. This is the case when the "I" is constituted by its reenactment of elements in preceding experiences of the person and its anticipation of its own projections into the future. Then the Logos may be gratefully received and its claim may be recognized as a just and righteous one, but it is felt as coming from outside the "I" and as challenging the natural tendencies of the "I" to seek its own narrower interests. But in the structure now under consideration, the "I" in each moment is constituted as much in the subjective reception of the lure to self-actualization that is the call and presence of the Logos as it is in continuity with the personal past. This structure of existence would be the incarnation of the Logos in the fullest meaningful sense.

This full incarnation of the Logos does not abolish the continuity and identity of the human self. The ideal possibility for one moment is based upon what the self had been in preceding moments. That self constituted itself in anticipation of a novel future. The call to novel realization in which the Logos makes itself present fulfills that anticipation. Thus the "I" in each moment is at once the inclusion of the "I" of the preceding moment and the aim at novelty that is the presence of the Logos. Self-identity is not lost by identifying with the Logos but perfected thereby.

A human "I" fulfilled through its identity with the immanent Logos, which is at the same time the Logos become fully incarnate, is the center of an existence which, like all other human existence, includes much whose source is neither the past "I" nor the Logos. Events in the body contribute to the psychic life, experienced as emotions of pain and pleasure, hope and fear, longing and compassion. The gaining of information, the formation of concepts, and the shaping of images occur through the same processes as in other structures of existence. This "I" too lives in tension with other ingredients in its conscious and unconscious life. It has no more defense against them than do others. There is nothing to prevent these from drawing the human "I" apart from its identity with the Logos. But when the structure persists or is renewed, one tension does not exist; that is the tension between the "I" and the ever-new form that the Logos takes in each moment. The turmoil of life continues and makes its mark. Suffering is not reduced but increased by the greater openness to the suffering of others. But the center from which it is experienced is at one with the divine aim.

This structure of existence has been described as a theoretical possibility, but the interest in this structure has been that it fits with what we know of Jesus. It is appropriate to the confidence with which he acted in ways condemned by the tradition and law of his time. If Jesus existed in full unity with God's present purposes for him, then even the rules that he acknowledged as embodying God's past purposes could be freely set aside. It is appropriate to his style of teaching in which he directly presented the situation as he knew it without citing textual or empirical support. If he viewed reality from a perspective coconstituted by the immanence of the Logos in him, then what he saw could be unabashedly announced as there in the fullest and most objective sense possible for a creature. It is appropriate to his remarkable identification of his own ministry with the work of God. If the "I" who acted was coconstituted by the presence of the Logos in him, then God was indeed immediately active in the action.[4]

Those who think in substantialist terms suppose that the structure of existence, the constitution of the "I," must be settled and identical throughout life. This view blocks recognition of the complex history of structures of existence. In the study of this history, interest focuses on the emergence of distinctive structures and their influence. Those in whom the distinctive structures appear usually live much of their lives within the structure out of which the new one emerges. Prophets through most of their lives are related to the word of God in the same way as their contemporaries, but what chiefly concerns us is the relation that emerges when the Word comes to them. Mystics through most of their lives share the structure of existence of their culture, but what happens to them in ecstasy defines their existence as mystics. The enlightened Buddhist is not born enlightened, but we attend especially to that structure of the Buddhist's existence which is experienced as enlightenment. Christians do not continuously exist as radically self-transcending selves, but it is the fullest form of

such existence that interests us. Paul's self-identity with Christ
was for him an ever-to-be-renewed relation. The structure of
existence that obtains in sleep and daydreams is important too,
but it has probably changed little since prehistoric times, and it
is likely to be much the same in prophets, mystics, Buddhists,
and Christians.

Just as a prophet is not continuously receiving the Word of
the Lord, a mystic is not continuously in ecstasy, and a Buddhist
is not born enlightened, so also we may assume that the
distinctive structure of Jesus' existence did not characterize his
infancy or remain constant through sleeping and waking states.
When it emerged and how steady it became are subjects on
which we have little information. The stories of his temptation
in the wilderness, his struggle in Gethsemane, and his forsaken-
ness on the cross are not historically reliable, but they witness
to the belief on the part of his disciples that he was not
continuously free from the tension between his "I" and the
Logos. To affirm today that he was fully human entails this
same assumption. But our attention is directed also and
primarily to the new thing that occurred in him. That new thing
was the full incarnation of the Logos.

There is no *a priori* basis for determining whether others
have participated in this structure of existence. That remains
an open question. Perhaps there are fleeting approximations in
the lives of some Christian saints, but of this we have no
adequate evidence. There might be someone of whom history
has left no record who was constituted much as Jesus was, but
that is an idle speculation. So far as we know, Jesus is unique.

The distinctiveness of Jesus can be spoken of in terms of
Christ. Christ is the incarnate Logos. As such Christ is present
in all things. The degree and the kind of Christ's presence
varies. The fullest form of that presence is that in which he
coconstitutes with the personal past the very selfhood of a
person. That would be the paradigm of incarnation. In that
case Christ would not simply be present in a person but would
be that person. The distinctive structure of Jesus' existence was
characterized by personal identity with the immanent Logos.
Hence it is a matter of literal truth to affirm the identity of Jesus
with Christ. In all things Christ is present. Jesus *was* Christ.

Since there are many today who see no reason for interesting
ourselves in any distinctiveness of Jesus' structure of existence,

attention was paid in the preceding chapter to the importance of this question. The continuing efficacy of Jesus' words and of his field of force is bound up with continuing decisions to attend to him. Such decisions are affected in turn by beliefs about his distinctive authority and efficacy. To speak of such authority and efficacy is to assume something distinctive about his person, about the structure of his existence. A theory has now been offered as to Jesus' structure of existence. In concluding this chapter, we will ask: (1) Does this account explain and justify the inherent authority of Jesus' words discussed in Chapter 5? (2) Does it explain how his field of force can have the effects attributed to it in Chapter 6?

1. Unless our belief about Jesus encourages us to open ourselves to being reshaped by his words, those words will have diminishing efficacy. Jesus spoke with an implicit claim to authority and the structure of existence attributed to him above was ordered to that implicit claim. The question is whether belief that Jesus was the Christ in the sense there explained appropriately directs our attention to his words.

This question can best be answered by returning to the parable of the Pharisee and the publican and its effects as presented in Chapter 5. If Jesus had the same structure of existence as ours and hence the same basis for understanding and insight, then the idea that the publican is justified when he confesses his need of help, whereas the Pharisee is not justified when he thanks God for his virtue should be set impartially alongside other theories. Its initial power to challenge and open the hearer should not be unduly decisive. Many ideas that strike us as illuminating on first encounter turn out, on fuller consideration, to have limited validity. It is easy to bring reasonable objections against this one. Viewed in this way, it can be little more than one hypothesis alongside others. Or it can be understood to be an account of the specific events taking place in Jesus' day without any wider applicability.

But if Jesus experienced reality in a distinctive way, and if his way of experiencing reality had special validity, then a stronger conclusion is to be drawn. The point that strikes initially as insightful and illuminating will be attended to as well grounded; the appropriate response will be to examine its potential relevance over wider and wider areas.

The present theory of Jesus' structure of existence justifies
the expectation that his perception of the human situation had
distinctive validity. Especially in the light of his teaching we
can recognize that each of us is bound to a particular perspective in interpreting what happens. We see others in terms of
their potential to threaten or support us. Even if we cultivate
openness to others, we do so in terms of calculation of how that
will affect us. This is true even of our relation to God.

I can to some extent transcend this situation. I can recognize
that in fact I am only one among many. I can see that the others
have perspectives in terms of which their existence has to them
the importance mine has to me. I can attain to rational
principles of impartiality and disinterestedness of behavior. The
recognition of those principles can have some influence upon
my actual behavior. It can even modify my attitudes. But all of
this is constantly checked by the very powerful pull of my
continuing egocentricity of perspective. I still do not *feel* others
in terms of their objective rights to equal consideration with
myself. Hence in fact even my attempts at disinterested reflection include a large defensive element. Much of my thinking,
even my most moral thinking, is defensive.

In this way I can recognize that there are truths about the
human situation which my own perceptions attain in only
fragmentary and subordinate ways. I can recognize that these
truths are likely to threaten my ordinary ways of judging others
and understanding myself. I can recognize that a man who did
not need to justify his past and protect his future would be able
to see reality in a more objective and profound way.

The theory here proposed is that Jesus operated from a quite
different perspective. His "I" was coconstituted by the incarnate Logos. Thus God's purpose for him was his purpose rather
than being a threat to his purpose, as we often experience it.
His personal existence did not require justification and protec-
tion in the way ours does. Therefore, he did not need to
interpret the human situation with the distortions we introduce.
He could distinguish both the validity of moral ideas and the
ways they are distorted for self-justification with a disinterested
freedom we cannot attain. In offering his insights to others he
did not need, as we do, to glance to the side to see that they
supported his self-image. Thus he could speak with a unique
purity, simplicity, and directness.

2. We are drawn into Jesus' field of force by the belief that in that field of force we will be justified, or more broadly, rightly related to God. The belief entails both that the field of force is one of peculiar strength and that its nature is such as to alter favorably our relation to God. The question is now whether what has been said of Jesus' structure of existence supports this belief.

The field of force of any event is a function in part of its intrinsic character. In most of our experiences conflicting elements are reconciled in such a way as to impoverish the whole and to dull its intensity. But there are times when we feel peculiarly alive, when the rich potentialities for experience that pour in upon us are synthesized into new forms that allow each to make their full contribution. These moments exercise an influence upon their future that is greatly disproportionate to their temporal endurance or frequency. We can dimly imagine what it might be for us to be continuously alive in this full sense, in each moment growing beyond our past through its inclusion in a richer whole that includes others as well.

The central tension that makes such aliveness rare in our experience is that between our selves and the Logos. As long as the Logos is felt to be alien to our selfhood, the possibilities it offers us are felt in part as a threat to selfhood. This is particularly true because the call of the Logos is to accept pain and suffering as a continual part of existence. This call is felt as demand and judgment against which the dynamisms of self-defense and self-justification are called into play. These syphon off the energy that might be fulfilled instead in embodying what the Logos offers. The moments of full aliveness are those in which these processes are broken through and the fresh possibilities of the moment are wholeheartedly welcomed and realized.

Jesus' structure of existence as described above was one in which the tension of self and Logos was overcome in coalescence. It was, therefore, one that made possible a unique cumulative richness and aliveness of experience in which intense suffering and joy were united. It is understandable that such experience, culminating on the cross, should produce a field of force of truly unusual magnitude sustained and extended through repeated acts of remembrance.

That this field of force tends to justify those who are drawn into it or more generally to open them to the Logos has been shown in Chapter 6. The account of Jesus' structure of existence in this chapter fits with what was said there. Jesus was fully open to the Logos, thus undercutting all need for self-justification. To whatever extent there is conformation to that structure, the believer too is opened and freed from defensiveness.

CHAPTER 9

The Christ
of the Creeds

In the preceding chapter the incarnation of the Logos in Jesus
was described in terms of a contemporary understanding of the
Logos, a modern ontology of events, and the results of recent
historical scholarship. No reference was made to official doctrines of the structure of Jesus' existence in the tradition. Yet
no new formulation is possible except within the tradition that
made incarnation the central Christian dogma. This tradition is
that of the early church, culminating in the creeds of Nicaea and
Chalcedon.

The summary in Chapter 7 of the Christological concerns of
the early church showed that they were homologous to those
that motivated the account of Jesus' structure of existence in
Chapter 8. Hence the structure of existence attributed to Jesus
in the preceding chapter is an appropriate contemporary expression of the religious concerns that expressed themselves in
the ancient creeds. But for many Christians this is not suf-
ficent. For them the creeds have an authority that is not
exhausted in this way. A contemporary formulation must be
seen not only as expressing the same types of soteriological
concern but also as asserting in detail the same conclusions as
those formulated in the creeds. Even when their authority is
taken more loosely, the creeds are recognized as touchstones
for later statements about the person of Jesus. In recognition of
the importance of the historic creeds, this chapter sketches the
history of the formulations of Nicaea and Chalcedon to clarify

the meanings of the conceptual decisions involved in the final formulation.

The conceptual decisions were governed not only by considerations of intelligibility and plausibility but much more by soteriological, liturgical, exegetical, and political factors. An adequate description of the Christological controversies in the early church would need to display the issues in terms of these soteriological concerns as well as in terms of liturgical customs and methods of Biblical scholarship, while recognizing the effect of political intrigue and imperial purposes on the outcome of debates. The aim of this chapter is the different and much more modest one of clarifying the conceptual meaning of the final outcome. Chapter 10 compares this conceptual meaning with the structure proposed in Chapter 8.

The process of conceptualization began immediately with the earliest Christian community, and its first stages can be traced in the New Testament itself. In the first chapter of *The Foundations of New Testament Christology,* Reginald Fuller has provided a helpful schematization of three of these stages: the earliest Palestinian stage, the Hellenistic Jewish stage, and the stage of the Gentile mission. Although it is increasingly clear that such neat divisions are artificial,[1] that, for example, Palestinian Judaism already contained Hellenistic influences, Fuller's diagrams offer a convenient way to picture the development.

The earliest Palestinian Christians looked back to the earthly ministry of Jesus, whom they viewed as Lord and Son of Man, and they looked forward to his return as Messiah, while "Jesus' present status was not yet a matter of reflection."[2] Hence Fuller diagrams this Christology as follows:

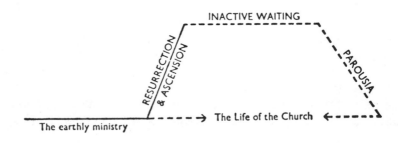

"A major shift of emphasis took place in the second, Hellenistic Jewish stratum. Hitherto the continuing work of Jesus had been thought of as an extension of the earthly work or as an anticipation of the parousia. Now it is evaluated for its own sake." [3] The exalted Jesus is viewed as presently reigning in the Christian community as Christ and Lord. Also there emerges the idea that Jesus was sent into the world to fulfill his mission. This is diagramed by Fuller as follows:

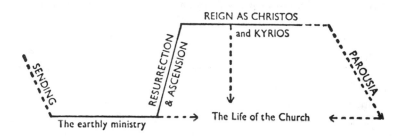

Fuller continues: "The search for redemption in the gentile world was centered not upon a hope of national restoration like that of Israel, but on deliverance from the powers which held man in thrall—fate and death. If the gospel was to be relevant it must offer redemption from this plight. Hence, the missionaries to the gentiles took another major step in affirming the Redeemer's pre-existence and incarnation. They developed a Christological pattern in which the pre-existent One descended into the realm of our human plight at the incarnation, defeated the powers on their own ground, and reascended. In so doing he became the head of a new order of humanity and reversed the fall of Adam." [4] Fuller represents the pattern thus:

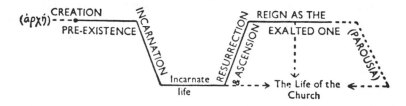

These diagrams visually clarify the distinction between the two great Christological debates of the following centuries. One debate was about the nature of the top line in the third diagram, that is, the preexistent and exalted Christ. Who was he, and how was he related to God? The second debate was about how this exalted divine being was related to the human Jesus. The Nicene creed was the church's official word on the first of these questions. The Chalcedonian creed was its most important response to the second.

Both creeds were formulated reluctantly. They did not arise out of any desire in the church to have comprehensive and authoritative statements of faith. They were in no sense summaries of the church's teaching. Most emphatically they were not intended to promulgate new ideas. They were, instead, attempts to resolve disputes that rent the church, and to resolve them in a way that was as continuous as possible with the settled faith of the church. All participants in the debates assumed what our historical consciousness now makes suspect —that there was a common essence of Christian faith that remained unchanged through the centuries. Theologians understood themselves as only explaining this common faith. The bishops in council understood themselves to be testing the alternative verbal formulations against their collective understanding of this common faith. When they recognized authentic elements within two conflicting schemes of conceptualization, they had to affirm both, whether or not they could achieve conceptual consistency and clarity.

The upper line in these diagrams was often designated as the Logos. The term "Son" could be used interchangeably with Logos,[5] and it was preferred in the creeds; but because it could also be used to refer to the human Jesus, theological issues are often more clearly stated in Logos language. Hence the first major Christological issue faced in the early church can be formulated thus: How is the Logos related to God? Christian interest in this question presupposed that the Logos was incarnate in Jesus, but similar discussions were conducted by philosophers or Jews without reference to Jesus.

Insofar as reflection was shaped by the dominant imagery of the Old Testament, the basic alternative was between Creator and creature. On the side of Creator was God alone. On the side of creation were not only the world we know but also the angels and other supernatural powers. In Jewish speculation about the preexistent state of the Son of Man or the Messiah, there was little question that, however exalted he might be, he was a creature. Most references to the preexistent Christ in the New Testament are naturally understood as expressing this same assumption, even if the preexistent one is distinguished from all other heavenly creatures by the closeness of his relation to God and his decisive role in creation. This is sometimes called the "angel Christology." That name misrepresents it somewhat by the implication that the Logos was one angel among many, whereas it was viewed as superior to all the angels and as the agent of their creation.

In the context of the two-story world view the angel Christology was conceptually quite clear. First, the existence of heavenly created beings among whom one was superior to the others was perfectly acceptable. Second, it was understandable that these beings could take human form and appear on earth and then subsequently return to their heavenly place. The language used, of God's sending his Son into the world and then exalting him, expresses this understanding.

However, this view by no means had universal support. There were many Christians who held that only if in Jesus God himself entered the world could the new Christian field of force be understood. They were unwilling to distinguish and subordinate the preexistent Christ or Logos in relation to the Creator. Indeed, for many, Christ was the only God who mattered.

The view of the Logos as God received a relatively clear conceptual formulation in modalism. The simplest form of modalism viewed Father, Son, and Spirit as three successive forms in which the Godhead has been actualized. As Father, he created and ruled the world. Then he became Son in order to save the world. Now as Spirit he inspires believers. This form of modalism is called Sabellianism[6] and was widely opposed. However, Father, Son, and Spirit could also be viewed as three modes of the one Godhead without this chronological distinction. The single divine being was seen as eternally constituting itself in a threefold way, one way being as Son or Logos. This view early gained wide acceptance in the West. It received careful formulation in the writings of Tertullian.

Both of these positions accept and assume the sharp distinction of a unitary Creator on the one hand and the creatures on the other, with no intermediate possibility. But the dominant philosophical mind of the time offered another model. This model has been partly spoiled by modern science. Today it is known that when the heavenly bodies emit light, this costs them something of their store of energy. But until the Renaissance the heavenly bodies, unlike earthly bodies, were supposed to possess an unchanging permanence. Light radiated or was generated from them without any change in them. The light grew dimmer as it moved farther from its source. It was supposed that God could (and did) in a similar way generate other orders of beings without in any way being affected thereby. These participated in his nature, as a creature did not, but they derived from him and were subordinate to him.

The greatest and most influential Christian thinker between Paul and Augustine was Origen. Origen was a great Biblical scholar and a devout Christian. He was also affected by the philosophical climate of his day, which he adapted to Christian use. It was natural for him to think of God the Father as the One from whom the Logos was generated. From the Logos in turn there derived the Spirit. In this conceptuality the Logos is not identical with God, but it is nevertheless a divine being and not a creature.[7] Its worship is appropriate even though it is subordinate to the ineffable Father.

There are, then, three fairly clear conceptualizations of the relation of the Logos, understood as the divine in Jesus, to God: (1) the supreme supernatural creature, (2) one of the eternal modes of the Godhead, and (3) the eternal and primary emergence from God the Father. Most Christians were satisfied with the use of Biblical language about Christ and were not concerned with the problems raised by such conceptualizations. They were content to share in the life of the church under the Lordship of Christ without raising these issues to clear consciousness. Even those who were reflective often fused and confused the alternatives.

But there were some clearheaded Christians who were impatient with this confusion and thought that it led to errors. Among these was Arius, a presbyter in Alexandria. He was an adherent of the angel Christology, which he correctly thought was highly congruent with the dominant imagery of the New Testament. He certainly did not suppose that this Christology demeaned Christ. The Logos was the first of all creatures, and all other creatures were made through him. This Logos became man for our salvation in Jesus and was exalted by God to heavenly rule. It seemed to Arius that such a creature was quite capable of fulfilling the soteriological work of revelation and teaching. As Arius saw it, to identify this creature with God would be to destroy the most fundamental religious and conceptual distinction. It involves attributing to the radically transcendent Creator the characteristics of change and suffering. To Arius that was sacrilege.

By his vigor and articulateness Arius forced a decision on one of the issues that had thus far been avoided. Hence a council assembled at Nicaea in 325 to delineate the relation of the *ousia* (substance or essence) of the Logos to that of the Father. Arius insisted that they were different. The *ousia* of the Logos was creaturely, that is, it was created out of nothing as were all other things. Arius' formulation was widely offensive, because most Christians wanted to stress the close connection between the Logos and the Father, not the contrast. Hence Arius' teaching was rejected. But it was not easy for the bishops to agree on a positive formulation. How could they affirm the close connection of the Logos to the Father without losing the distinction between them and, especially, the primacy of the latter on which the Origenists insisted?

The Nicene creed solved this problem by distinguishing sharply between begetting and making. The Son was begotten from the Father, not made by him. Hence he was not a creature. Also, this relationship does not imply that the Father was once alone with himself, and then begot. The council explicitly condemned the Arian doctrine that "There was when He was not, and, before being born He was not." It affirmed that the Son was begotten eternally.

Up to this point the modalists and the Origenists were in agreement against the Arians, but the modalists were not quite satisfied. They did not want to leave open the possibility that the Logos or Son could be viewed as belonging to an intermediate order of being, somewhere between God the Father and the creatures. Arius had explicitly denied that the Son was of the same *ousia* as God the Father. The modalists wanted the creed to avow just what the Arians denied, that is, that the Son is *homoousios* (of the same substance or essence) with the Father; and they succeeded.

The word *homoousios* could be understood in two senses. In one, all human beings are of the same *ousia*, that is, the

substance or essence of humanity. In this sense, the Origenists
at the council accepted the term, even though it was foreign to
them. They agreed that the Logos belonged with God and not
with creation. But the assertion that the Son was *homoousios*
with the Father could also mean that there is no real distinction
between them, that Son and Father are simply different names
for, or aspects of, one entity. This the Origenists certainly did
not believe; for in their eyes the Logos was both distinct from
and subordinate to the Father.

In the intense quarrels that followed Nicaea, the Origenist
party alternated between supporting and opposing the Nicene
creed. When supporters of the creed gave it a modalist
interpretation, moderate Arians were able to secure the support
of the Origenists and the rejection of the hated word *homoousios*. When the Arians grew confident of their position and
again spoke of the creatureliness of the Logos, the modalists
were able to reestablish their alliance with the Origenists. There
was a period in which the emperor was ardently Arian, and it
was during this period that missionaries went out to the
Germanic tribes in northern Europe. These tribes later con-
quered Rome as Arian Christians. Even so, the Nicene formula
gradually won acceptance, even by the Arian barbarians. It was
reaffirmed at the Council of Constantinople in 381, and there-
after it has been little disputed.

It is sometimes thought that the Council of Nicaea established the doctrine of the Trinity. This is not strictly accurate.
No account was given of the Holy Spirit, and no category was
offered in which the Father and the Son can be understood in
their distinction. The term *hypostasis* (which was later considered synonymous with *prosōpon*, or "person") was there synonymous with *ousia*. Hence, by implication, the Nicene creed
affirmed that Father and Son are of the same *hypostasis* as well
as *ousia*.

During the course of the ensuing debates the doctrine of the
Trinity did come into being. The modalists gained support for
their understanding that the substance of Father and Son was
strictly one by allowing that they could be distinguished as two
hypostaseis or *prosōpa* embodying this identical substance.
Meanwhile, with relatively little advance disputation, the Council of Constantinople (381) affirmed that the Spirit, too, was of
one substance with the Father and the Son. To distinguish the

generation of the Spirit from both that of creatures and that of the Son, the Holy Spirit was affirmed to "proceed" from the Father. The traditional formula, one *ousia* in three *hypostaseis* was finally established in the East and understood as identical with the long-accepted Western doctrine of one substance in three persons.

What the formula means is still subject to widely varying interpretations. Official theology has generally followed the modalist view, placing the emphasis upon the unity of the persons. It thereby preserves a strict monotheism. The three are modes in which the one Godhead relates to the world. Strictly speaking, God as such acts in all the actions attributed to any one of the persons. That is, all the persons are involved in the actions of each. When pressed to its logical conclusion, this view makes the distinction of the three no more than a confusing concession to Biblical and liturgical language.

At the opposite extreme there are those who think of the *ousia* quite abstractly. As three men or women share the common essence of humanity, so three divine persons share the common essence of deity. This view can hardly be distinguished from tritheism except for the insistence on perfect unity of purpose and character among the three persons.

Views of the Trinity as worked out by theologians often fall between these two extremes. They usually begin with the unity and undertake to explain the multiplicity within that unity. They have thereby countered the philosophical tendency to view God as an undifferentiated simplicity, but they have done little to explain who Jesus was.

The doctrine of the Trinity arose out of the attempt to understand the relation to God of that which was incarnate in Jesus. It established that what was incarnate in Jesus, that is, the Logos, was God. It continued to assert that what was incarnate was God as Logos rather than as Father or Spirit, but in the end the official formulations undercut any significance that distinction had possessed. The doctrine of the Trinity tended to become a mystification rather than a clarification of Christian belief. Even so, its fundamental conclusion was a fortunate one. The idea that either a supernatural creature or a divine emanation is that with which Christians have to do in Jesus is conceptually and religiously unsatisfactory. The Logos Christology in this book assumes with the Nicene creed that the

Logos is fully God. By denying any ultimate difference between the Logos and God, the official doctrine of the Trinity restores the question of Christology to one that is more intelligible today. In Jesus—the official doctrine maintains—we have to do with deity itself. But now the question is, How? What is the relation of Jesus to the Logos, which is now identified as God?

This issue, ultimately responded to in the Chalcedonian creed, was approached in two ways in the early church.[8] One could begin with Jesus as a man and ask whether and how he was related to God. One could begin with God and ask in what way he became a man. The extreme form of the first approach was called Ebionism. The Ebionites opposed all tendencies to deify Jesus. He was the Messiah and would return to bring in the Kingdom. He had thus a distinctive mission, but he was in himself a man like other men. The extreme form of the second approach was docetism, according to which the seemingly human features of Jesus were mere appearance. God did not take on real flesh.

Although the vast majority of Christians thought there was something special about Jesus' relation to God, on the one hand, and insisted that his human features were real, on the other, the attempts to understand him developed as modifications of these two extremes. The major centers in which reflection was carried out were Antioch and Alexandria, and it is convenient to identify these two schools with the two approaches. At Antioch one began with the man Jesus, who reveals God and shows Christians the way to salvation, and one asked in what way God was present to and in him. At Alexandria one began with the divine Logos, which entered the world in a new way in Jesus, and one asked what was involved in its assumption of human form.

The simplest and most readily understandable form of the Antiochene Christology was adoptionism. According to this view, Jesus was a man of such supreme virtue that at his baptism God announced his adoption as his Son and poured out his Spirit upon him. Thus Jesus was set aside as the Son of God by God's act and inspired by God in response to his own peculiar merit.

Adoptionism was condemned, but the fundamental thrust of this approach was not thereby stopped. One who began with the humanity of Jesus could agree that even before the baptism God was present to him and inspiring him. Indeed, one could accept the view that from Jesus' very conception God was actively present to him, protecting him from sin and guiding him into truth. Thus Jesus' will from birth was united with the will of God in perfect harmony and obedience. This idea of a moral union of Jesus with God was characteristic of the Antiochene Christology. It provided an adequate grounding for the divine authority of Jesus' words and person.

The Antiochenes pushed the exaltation of Jesus as Christ as far as their starting point and their conceptuality would allow. They tried to find ways to express the presence of God in Jesus more forcefully than through the perfection of obedience and the harmony of will. They would speak of the Logos as fully indwelling Jesus. But they had no adequate conceptuality to explain what this could mean. Their radical distinction between the transcendent divine and Jesus as human seemed to deny any real union and unity.

The Alexandrian problem was just the reverse. The Alexandrians strongly rejected docetism, for they were governed by a concern to show how the Logos in its incarnation effected the transformation of the human condition, overcoming corruption and death. Hence, they asserted the reality of Jesus' flesh, but they initially thought of the flesh as simply the body and as devoid of a human soul. In place of the human soul of Jesus was the Logos. The position was stated clearly, if extremely, by Apollinarius, and it was his formulation that was condemned.

Despite the condemnation of Apollinarianism, the Alexandrian tradition continued to think in terms of the Logos assuming humanity. This always meant that some aspect of what is human in other persons was transformed in Jesus into the Logos.[9] The Alexandrian leaders were now careful to assert that the humanity assumed included a human soul and reason. They were quite willing to recognize extensive participation in humanness on the part of Jesus, for it was crucial for them that the Logos redeemed humanity by assuming it. But they were convinced that the divine and the human were indissolubly united in one Christ, and that in his ultimate being and unity he was divine. Thus their problem was to find the right name for that in Jesus which was the Logos as the one finally active agent

in Jesus' humanity as well as in his deity, and to avoid
attributing to God such human characteristics as birth, suffering, and death.

The issue between these two approaches to Christology came
to a head over the way Mary, the mother of Jesus, was treated.
From the Antiochene point of view, Mary bore a human being in
whom the Logos dwelt. From the Alexandrian point of view the
fetus in Mary's womb was the Logos itself in process of forming
about itself the human Jesus.

In Constantinople the question arose as to whether it was
appropriate to speak of Mary as *theotokos,* that is, the one who
bore God. The patriarch Nestorius was Antiochene in his
Christology and did not favor this expression. His opposition
aroused the anger of Cyril of Alexandria, who insisted in
typically Alexandrian fashion that the true nature of Jesus was
that of the Logos and, therefore, of God himself. Cyril succeeded in having Nestorius deposed and exiled. Cyril, however,
finally compromised with the Antiochenes in allowing that in
Jesus were to be found two distinct natures, divine and human,
the former consubstantial with God, the latter consubstantial
with us. The Antiochenes, in their turn, agreed that in Jesus
these two natures were in full union, a union they interpreted in
terms of the Logos indwelling the man. This compromise was
expressed in a formula drawn up by the Antiochenes in 431 and
subsequently accepted by Cyril. The Antiochenes also allowed
the word *theotokos* to be used, and they sacrificed Nestorius on
political grounds.

After Cyril's death this compromise broke apart. His earlier
insistence that there was only one nature in Jesus, that is, the
Logos nature, was vigorously renewed.[10] The Cyrillian party
asserted that Jesus was composed *from* two natures, but in his
concrete existence these two natures became one, the Logos-
nature. It was to deal with this doctrine that a council was
called at Chalcedon.

The Council of Chalcedon (451) was a vindication of the
earlier compromise. The two natures of Jesus, one consubstantial with God, the other consubstantial with us, were reaffirmed,
and to avoid any possible misunderstanding these words were
added: ". . . the difference of the natures being by no means
removed because of the union." Similarly, the union of the two

natures was reaffirmed, and this union was now defined as a coalescence in one *prosōpon* or *hypostasis.*

The creed was a masterful compromise. It embodied the ideas most precious to both parties by asserting on the one hand the full deity of Jesus and on the other his full humanity. By stressing that there were two natures in Jesus, it satisfied the Antiochene insistence that Jesus was truly a human being and that human characteristics were not to be attributed to God. By insisting on the unity of Jesus as a single *prosōpon* or *hypostasis,* it satisfied the Alexandrians that the deity was not being viewed as something external to or separable from the actual man Jesus.

But like many compromises, it remained ambiguous and could be read through either Antiochene or Alexandrian eyes. The distinction centers around the one *hypostasis* or *prosōpon.* From the Antiochene perspective this one "person" is Jesus, the one about whom it has been said in the creed that he has a fully human nature. This fully human nature is indwelt by God himself. Between the human nature and the indwelling God there is neither opposition nor tension, but perfect union. The human will of Jesus is perfectly in accord with the indwelling Logos. The one person, Jesus, embodies the nature of God just as fully as he embodies the nature of humanity.

From the Alexandrian point of view the one "person" is the Logos or the eternal Son. This one person retains in his incarnation his full deity. But in the incarnation he also assumes the nature of humanity. This assumption in no way qualifies the fullness of the deity, but what is assumed also has all the properties or characteristics of human nature.

The depth of the difference between these two Christologies is manifest in the aftermath of the council. The thoroughgoing Alexandrians were profoundly offended by the creed. Its affirmation of a fully human nature in Jesus compromised their sense that in Jesus it was the Logos who established their salvation. The object of their worship could not have a human nature that was not itself fully deified in such a way as to cease to be merely human. Large segments of the church remained steadfastly monophysite, that is, they affirmed that Jesus had a single nature and that this nature was divine. These segments developed into the Coptic churches. The Antiochenes, however, were more satisfied that their basic concerns were met. Even Nestorius would have been willing to subscribe to the creed, but his condemnation remained, reinforced by the adoption, by the council, of certain of Cyril's writings against him. A Nestorian church rose and prospered in the East, reaching as far as China.

Monophysite and Nestorian churches were, at times, comparable in strength to the Chalcedonian church. It was the military conquest by Islam and the Mongols of those eastern areas in which the other churches flourished, rather than a theological superiority on its part, that gave the ecclesiastical victory so decisively to Chalcedon.

The monophysite schism was by far the more pressing within the Empire. Hence every effort was made by the supporters of Chalcedon in the East to achieve reconciliation with the monophysites. This led to the dominance of the Alexandrian interpretation of Chalcedon, which came to official expression a century later at the Second Council of Constantinople (553). Its formulation stressed the unity of Christ, denying that God the Logos, who performed miracles, was another than Christ, who suffered, and strongly implying that the one *hypostasis* of Christ was the Logos.

Nevertheless, the distinctness and reality of the humanity in Jesus was not denied, and in the last of the ecumenical councils, the Third Council of Constantinople (680), it was reaffirmed. The issue there was about Jesus' will. To appease the monophysites and to make clear the authority of the Alexandrian interpretation of Chalcedon, it was proposed that Jesus be declared to have had a single will, that of the Logos. This position is called monothelitism, and it would have made clear that the Logos was the one agent of all Jesus' acts. By the same token it would have truncated Jesus' humanity. Rather surprisingly, in view of the trends of the period, monothelitism was rejected. Jesus' consubstantiality with us in our humanity was held to entail a human will as part of the human nature.

Christological controversy was a predominantly Eastern matter. It was in the East that the great theological schools concerned themselves with conceptual clarity and rigor, and large numbers of people were caught up in doctrinal debate. The West had more practical issues in view and was deeply divided only over these. Yet the West played a decisive role in the Eastern debates.

With respect to Christology, the West was early satisfied by some phrases that were adopted without intensive analysis or debate. Their paradoxical character and the difficulty of gaining a clear understanding of what they meant did not greatly disturb the Westerners. Indeed Tertullian, who did more than any other man to shape Western Christology, rather relished the paradoxes. It was Tertullian who first spoke of a Trinity composed of three *personae*. For the unity he used, among other terms, the word *substantia*. In his account of Jesus, Tertullian spoke of one *persona* composed of two *substantiae*. Although the word used later was *natura* instead of *substantia*, here at the beginning of the third century the West already had Latin formulations that gained permanent acceptance.

That both Nicaea and Chalcedon adopted formulas fully congenial to the West was no accident. The word *homoousios* was included in the Nicene creed at the insistence of the Emperor Constantine, whose chief adviser was a Western churchman. The prestige of the bishop of Rome was such that he often had the deciding voice in theological disputes in the East, and the letter, or "Tome," of Pope Leo tilted the scales at Chalcedon in favor of the formulation "one person with two natures." Of course the Western influence could not have imposed Greek translations of the Latin phrases upon the East had not the debate in the East brought the Eastern bishops to see the need for the kind of compromise these phrases afforded. But the choice of language was influenced in large measure by the less reflective decisions made earlier in the West.

After Chalcedon, the West continued to play an important role, chiefly as defender of that council. Fear of schism with the West restrained the leaders of the Chalcedonian East from going farther than they did in their accommodation with the monophysites. This was especially important in the monothelite controversy; for, apart from the intervention of Rome, the East would have accepted the idea that Jesus had a single, divine will.

Even so, a fundamentally Alexandrian interpretation of Chalcedon triumphed in both East and West. The crux of the issue was not one will or two but the character of the one *hypostasis* or person of the one Christ. The creed was open to the Antiochene interpretation that this one person was the union of the two natures, but within a century after Chalcedon, Antio-

chene theology lost its vigor. Western influence continued to
protect the doctrine of the human nature of Jesus, but the West
had never concerned itself with the question of the relation
between the one *hypostasis* of Christ and that of the Logos.
Even Leo's Tome had been ambiguous, inclining more to the
Alexandrian view than did the Chalcedonian formula itself.

Hence, although there was opposition in the West to the
attack on the Antiochene interpretation of Chalcedon at the
Second Council of Constantinople, the Pope concurred with that
attack, and the resistance finally ebbed. The authority of the
Council of Constantinople was accepted. Only gradually was
the consequence clearly affirmed that the only person of Jesus
was God himself and that his humanity was impersonal or made
personal only by the Logos. John of Damascus, writing in the
eighth century, still hesitated to draw the conclusion with full
consistency,[11] but in the end the doctrine of the impersonal
humanity of Jesus became traditional.

CHAPTER 10

Christ and the Creeds

The deepest commitment of the Alexandrians was to affirm that in Jesus the Logos had truly established a new order of reality or field of force. The special interest of the Antiochenes was that Jesus was and remained in this process truly a man who revealed God and taught his way. The intention of the Chalcedonian creed was to satisfy these concerns, both of which are faithful to the New Testament and liberating in their effects on the believer. It is ironic that the dominant results of the Chalcedonian creed in much of Christendom have been otherwise.

The major reason for the failure of the creeds to liberate believers has been that their formulations have been abstracted from the living context of both Antiochene and Alexandrian faith. They have been read, instead, as describing a radically supernatural being, the God-man. That a full human nature is asserted in the Chalcedonian creed has not prevented the dominance of the view that the God-man is remote from the actual humanity known and experienced by believers. Belief that Jesus was this mysterious God-man became itself the criterion of Christianity.

Jesus thus became, for post-Chalcedonian believers, not the man in whom the Logos was incarnate but a supernatural being. He was the transcendent, omnipotent, omniscient ruler of the world, lawgiver and judge, walking about on earth in human form. Jesus himself did not function as mediator between the transcendent God and humanity; rather, mediators were required to relate ordinary people to Jesus. The truth of this picture could not be established by Jesus' message, life, and death, but only by miracles, especially a miraculous conception and a miraculous resurrection. Since even this evidence could not make Jesus' deity intelligible, the creed was to be believed on authority, by the sacrifice of the intellect. The willingness to make this sacrifice became the test of whether one was regarded as a Christian. One was supposed to be saved by the worst kind of work, that is, a dehumanizing one.

In addition, the focus of Christian attention was redirected from the future to the past. The supernatural fact of Jesus as God was located at a particular point in the past. Relation to that past fact was the crux of Christianity. The present was to be lived in the light of the past. That meant, primarily, that the present was to be lived in obedience to the past and to the institutions that affirmed the past and developed and guarded its consequences. Jesus functioned as law.

Finally, under the influence of the creed become dogma, Jesus became a sacred object. In relation to him no ordinary critical questions or inquiries were allowed. He could not be viewed as a historical figure or compared with others. He was to be worshiped rather than studied or even encountered. He was absolute, and the religion that worshiped him was therefore the absolute religion. All other religions were supposed to be essentially misdirected or false.

This statement is harshly formulated. It is not intended as a comprehensive characterization of the Christianity of any period. It intends only to describe the tendency at work in Christianity insofar as it became a religion of dogma, whose key dogma was the Chalcedonian creed. It is intended to place in bold relief the contrast of the actual effects of this creed with the concerns that led to its formulation.

Rejection of dogmatic Christianity and specifically of this creed is not new. The *sola scriptura* principle of the Reformers weakened the power of the creeds, although the Reformers did not reject them. Explicit rejection of their authority was present in some of the sects of the Reformation period, but even these, in most instances, freed themselves only in part from the supernatural Jesus largely assimilated to the absolute God. The full rejection of Chalcedon awaited the Enlightenment and was carried forward by liberal Protestant theology.

In reaction against the supernatural Jesus, the Enlightenment affirmed a purely human Jesus, identical in nature or structure with all other men. This opened the way to two types of interpretation of Jesus. One type of interpretation has been common in liberal Protestantism: Jesus was a man like other men—only better. He was wiser, more pious, more free, more obedient to God, and more loving. If one's general conceptuality allowed, one could speak of a fuller immanence of God in Jesus. If one wished to exalt Jesus still further, one could describe the degree of Jesus' superiority in glowing terms. One might even assert perfection in him, in contrast to the imperfection of all others. The one caveat was that the difference must be one of degree and not one of kind.

The problem with the liberal Jesus is that he is hardly more historical than the post-Chalcedonian one. The great concern has been to insure that what is said of him *could* be true of a human being. But there is little historical evidence to support the view that what is said of him was true of that *particular* human being, Jesus. There is, of course, some evidence of his wisdom, piety, freedom, obedience, and love. But careful investigation indicates that the bridge from historical knowledge to strong statements about any of these matters is a fragile one. Many of the affirmations of liberal Protestants must be recognized as sentimental projections of favored attributes onto Jesus.

A second type of interpretation has been a ruthless iconoclasm. Reimarus, who initiated the quest of the historical Jesus, followed this route, presenting Jesus as a thwarted revolutionary. This iconoclasm reappears in a very different form in the recent writings of Morton Smith, who presents Jesus as a magician.[1]

This interpretation is more fully historical in the sense that it presents an intelligible and possible figure who is interpreted in the same categories historians use to interpret others. Its difficulty is that since the picture it offers must necessarily be a reversal of the dominant New Testament picture, it must build in a tendentious fashion upon exceptional elements in that account and construct a theory as to why and how the early church engaged in such extensive and successful deception. The net result of the dominant quest of the historical Jesus has been to abandon efforts to know so much about his personality and purposes as either liberals or iconoclasts have claimed. As summarized in Chapter 5, it has provided us with reliable knowledge of his authentic sayings.

The sentimentality of liberalism, the destructive character of iconoclasm, and the dilution of Christian beliefs about Jesus in the scholarly quest led to a reaction in favor of a supernatural-ist, and Chalcedonian, view. Søren Kierkegaard had taught that the either/or of Christianity was the belief or disbelief that a particular man was God. In twentieth-century neo-orthodoxy this doctrine was reaffirmed. Chaldecon was reasserted in full Alexandrian garb complete with the doctrine of the impersonal humanity of Jesus. The person of Jesus was now understood to be his self or "I," and Jesus was viewed as lacking human selfhood. In the words of Emil Brunner, "When Jesus Christ . . . speaks to us as 'I' . . . God Himself is really speaking to us." [2]

Protestant scholarship has done little toward a transforma-tion of the positive meaning of Chalcedon. When Chalcedon is accepted, the acceptance is in terms of a supernatural and sacral Jesus and an exclusivist faith. When Chalcedon is rejected, the interpretation of its meaning is the same. The radical historical scholarship that has freed the meaning of the New Testament from its alien world view, from its supernatu-ralism and exclusivism, and has thus made it accessible and relevant to the contemporary consciousness, has largely passed Chalcedon by.

Catholic theologians have not been so free to reject or ignore the ancient creeds. This has commonly retarded their efforts to speak in an effective modern idiom. But the acceptance by Catholics of critical historical scholarship in conjunction with an understanding of the development of dogma has recently given rise to creative appropriation of Chalcedon that seeks to do justice to its real intentions and frees it from Alexandrian interpretation. Most impressive is the work of Piet Schoonen-berg, who expressly adopts the Antiochene interpretation of Chalcedon: "In Chalcedon itself . . . the one person of Christ is not described on or from the basis of his preexistence, but is much more the result of the concurrence of the natures." [3] He goes beyond the Antiochenes in arguing that it is the divine that becomes hypostatic in the human person rather than the human nature that becomes hypostatic through assumption by a divine person.[4] If Chalcedon had always been interpreted in this fashion, many of the worst distortions of Christianity could have been avoided. A view of a genuine incarnation is here found in Chalcedon without transforming Jesus into a supernatural being. Yet, Schoonenberg is not able to make clear how the incarnation in Jesus is distinctive, and he one-sidedly subordinates the divine to the human in Jesus.

There is a second, closely related direction in which the intentions of Chalcedon can be affirmed and rescued from the misrepresentation that followed when the creed became dogma. Both Alexandrians and Antiochenes wanted to affirm the immanence of God in Jesus. But the categories available to the church fathers were substantialist ones, and they had to attempt to explain the relation of the Logos to Jesus in those terms. Whitehead declares that, in struggling to express this immanence, "these Christian theologians have the distinction of being the only thinkers who in a fundamental metaphysical doctrine have improved upon Plato." [5] "In the place of Plato's solution of secondary images and imitations they demanded a direct doctrine of immanence." [6]

Nevertheless, the substantialist categories prevented the adequate articulation of the immanence which the fathers tried to express. The Antiochenes succeeded in maintaining the full humanity of Jesus and affirmed the indwelling of the Logos within him. But they could offer no adequate conceptualization of this immanence. They spoke of a moral union, that is, of a perfect harmony of Jesus' will with that of God, but this did not fully overcome the externality of the relation of Jesus and God, despite the intention.

The Alexandrians insisted unequivocally upon the immanence of God in Jesus, and they stressed the interchange of characteristics between the divine and the human in him. But, because of the substantialist conceptuality, their formulations were in constant danger of suggesting that some element of what would otherwise have been human in Jesus was displaced by the Logos. In the major interpretation of Chalcedon, it was the human person of Jesus that was thus displaced.

Incarnation for the Antiochenes could be understood only as the closest imaginable proximity and harmony of the divine and the human substances, which still retained their mutual externality. Incarnation for the Alexandrians could be understood

only as the substance of God clothing itself in aspects of
humanity without being affected by that act. The efforts of both
Alexandrians and Antiochenes to go farther were hampered by
the available images and language. But both struggled to show
that God was present in Jesus in the fullest sense without
destroying the distinction between God and Jesus or denying
Jesus' full humanity. At Chalcedon the bishops tried to say this
by declaring that the two natures of Jesus were "without
confusion, without change, without division, without separation." But no concept of substance really renders this intention
intelligible. New conceptualities are now available that abandon the idea of substance and make possible a fuller and less
paradoxical expression of the creative and valid intentions
behind the Chalcedonian creed. The real enhypostatic immanence of God in the person of Jesus can be understood and
believed without any sacrifice of the intellect, and apart from
authoritarian grounds.

A third shift is also needed and made possible by the other
two. If we understand Jesus as having a fully personal humanity and God as genuinely immanent in him, it becomes possible
to assimilate the thought of God in important respects to what
we know of Jesus. If it is in Jesus that we perceive what God's
immanence is and does, then it is from Jesus that we should
learn what God is like. We can and must reverse the long
history of retaining ideas of God uncongenial to what is
apparent in Jesus.

This should not mean an identification of God as Jesus.
Immanence is not identity. There are ontological questions
about God that cannot be decided by studying Jesus. But the
way that God relates to the world should be visible in Jesus. If
so, then God is not one who forces and compels but one who
lures and persuades. He is not one who gives a fixed, eternal
law to which external obedience is demanded on threat of
punishment, but one who calls people beyond every established
structure and principle for the sake of creative new possibilities.

Fourth, when we take our clues as to the nature of God from
Jesus, we will modify some aspects of the patristic understanding of the Logos. The fathers intended to mean by Logos what
was meant in the New Testament, where the Logos is bound to
Jesus and understood from him. But inevitably their under-

standing was affected by the wider use in the Hellenistic world with which they rightly established contact.

The Antiochenes thought of the Logos chiefly as the unchanging wisdom and will of God. Thus God's revelatory presence as Logos in Jesus is understood to make manifest a truth and a purpose that in their own nature are eternal. In this view the New Testament reluctance to spell out a Christian ethic is unrecognized, and Christian existence is too readily understood as a particular pattern of living valid for all times rather than as openness to ever-new possibilities.

The Alexandrians thought of the Logos chiefly in terms of its incorruptibility and immortality. In this they were correct, but they derived from this premise the conclusion that the field of force generated by the incarnation of the Logos in Jesus was largely exhausted by its work of rendering human beings incorruptible and immortal. They failed to recognize that the one Logos calls persons in different times and places to quite varied modes of realization, each of which is to be transcended in its turn.

Fifth, although recognition that the historical effects of the Logos are dynamic and ever-changing helps to adapt Logos Christology to our pluralistic age, before we can safely return to affirmations about the distinctive incarnation of the Logos in Jesus, we must reflect still further on the pluralistic context in which such affirmations are to be made. In the early church these affirmations intended to destroy all other religious claims or at least to subordinate them to Christianity. Unless great care is taken, Christians and others alike will hear the same imperialist claims in our assertions today. This can be checked only by a full recognition of the variety of structures of existence among which that of Jesus is one and that of Gautama, for example, is another. Only then can an account of Jesus as distinctively incarnating God leave open the question of the relative importance of that event in comparison with Gautama's enlightenment.

Some of these shifts implement the intention of the Chalcedonian creed, and some relativize it. Together they open the creed to serious consideration in our pluralistic age. They make possible its realistic comparison with the structure of Jesus' existence proposed in Chapter 8. That comparison will be undertaken in terms of three creedal phrases and one implicit theme: (1) Jesus as "consubstantial with the Father in Godhead"; (2) Jesus as "consubstantial with us in manhood, like us in all things except sin"; (3) the deity and humanity "coalescing in one *prosōpon* and one *hypostasis*"; and (4) the primacy of the divine initiative.

1. Clearly, in the present view Jesus is not "consubstantial" with the Father, for the notion of any two entities being of the "same substance" is rejected. However, the doctrine chiefly intended at this point, where Nicaea is echoed, is fully affirmed. The Logos incarnate in Jesus is God himself. Furthermore, the presence of the Logos in Jesus is in a genuine way structurally coconstitutive of his selfhood. For the Logos to be constitutive of his fundamental being, in substantialist perspective, required simple identity. However, where experiential events are taken as fundamental, no two entities can ever be simply identical. Only abstractions can be present in two events in an identical way, and the intention of the creed is violated if the divine in Jesus is conceived abstractly. It is the Logos itself that is present. In such presence the distinction of what is present and that in which it is present remains. Hence, Jesus was not the Logos as such but the Logos as incarnate, that is to say, Christ.

2. Jesus meets us in his authentic sayings as one who shares our common humanity, yet does so without the anxiety and guilt that characterize human beings generally. The creed sums this up by the phrase "consubstantial with us in manhood, like us in all things except sin." It was an excellent formulation, given the inevitability of substantialist concepts, but, because of its substance language, it creates problems. According to it, there is a human substance that can take two forms, sinful and sinless, without being affected in any other way. In that case, man's fall does not affect his "substance." But then the fact of the universality of sin becomes mysterious. If human substance is equally capable of a nonsinful form, one would expect this to appear regularly as an option alongside the sinful one. But it does not.

The intent of the creed can be better expressed if substance categories are abandoned. Jesus was in every respect, without qualification, a human being. Human beings embody many structures of existence. In all but one of those structures they constitute themselves around a center that is distinct from God's presence in them. This distinction gives rise to an existential anxiety that in turn breeds guilt and a pervasive sense of a difference between what one is and what one ideally might be. In addition, the distinction of the self from the immanent Logos is the occasion, although not the cause, of sin. Jesus, without in any way ceasing to be human, participated in that one structure of existence in which the self is coconstituted by the presence of God. In that structure alone there is freedom from existential anxiety, and one is without guilt and sin.

3. When substance categories are used, no clear conception can be gained of the meaning of the creed when it speaks of "the difference of the natures being by no means removed because of union, but the property of each nature being preserved and coalescing in one *prosōpon* and *hypostasis*." There is no ordinary meaning of substance that allows for two substances to coalesce. The creedal affirmation is made in the face of this absence of any applicable model. It expresses the firm insistence on maintaining the continuing real humanity of Jesus while he incarnates the Logos, even if that cannot be conceptually understood. The great concern was to avoid the diminution of the human that follows from the Alexandrian theology, in which some element of the human is in constant danger of being displaced by the Logos.

If substance categories are abandoned, the real integration in Jesus of the human and the divine can be stated intelligibly. In Jesus, who is a single person, the presence of the Logos and of his own past coalesce in each new act of self-constitution. There is no question of the incarnation diminishing the humanity. All humanity includes in some measure the immanent Logos, which is the lure to the fullest possible human realization in each moment. The more fully the lure is responded to, the more fully the human potential is actualized. The optimum realization would occur when human existence constituted itself in unity with the lure, as in the case of Jesus. This perfect incarnation of the Logos is at the same time the highest embodiment of humanity. Thus the coalescence of the Logos and humanity, in which each becomes hypostatic in the one person who is Jesus, far from diminishing or depersonalizing

Jesus' humanity or transmuting it into something else, enriches and completes his humanity.

4. Although no phrase in the Chalcedonian creed explicitly asserts the primacy of the divine initiative in the incarnation, this primacy is implied. It is more explicit in the Nicene creed and in the whole course of the discussion leading up to Chalcedon. The church condemned views such as adoptionism that suggested that Jesus as a man achieved a measure of virtue that led God, as a response, to adopt him as his Son. One main reason for the persistence and ultimate victory of the Alexandrian interpretation of Chalcedon is that it seemed to make clearer that God rather than a human being is the primary actor in bringing incarnation into being. And, indeed, as long as substance conceptuality controls the discussion, this is the case. To ensure the divine initiative, the church succumbed to the pressure to reduce the human in Jesus to a purely passive role in spite of the creedal statements of Chalcedon and the Third Council of Constantinople.

When substance categories are abandoned and the model of experience sketched in Chapter 3 is substituted, the divine initiative can be affirmed without an Alexandrian interpretation and without the denial of free agency to the human Jesus. In this interpretation the aim at a certain optimum attainment grounds the becoming of every moment of experience. The event that is the experience must itself make the decision that constitutes its own actuality in relation to the proffered possibility. If the possibility is hardly more than the repetition of the past, there is little room for significant decision. The decision is largely made for the occasion by its situation. But if the aim is at realization of a creative and novel goal, then the decision as to whether, and to what degree, to embody that possibility has considerable latitude and importance.

The initial aim is the immanence of the Logos. It is God's gift and presence to the occasion, God's grace. The decision is the locus of freedom. The greater the grace or the higher the possibility that lures the occasion into existence, the greater the scope of the freedom that is elicited. In other words, the greater the effective presence of the Logos, the greater the human freedom in the determination of what will in fact be attained. If God's initiating efficacy and the freedom of response are complementary in human experience, then there need be no basic problem in recognizing both the divine initiative and the human freedom in Jesus. God gave to Jesus distinctive possibilities of actualizing himself around the immanent Logos. At least at important times in his life Jesus freely chose to constitute his own selfhood as one with this presence of God within him.

PART THREE
Christ as Hope

CHAPTER 11

Christ as
the Image of Hope

Part One presented Christ as the everlasting Logos in its effective presence in the world. Part Two grounded the understanding of Christ in the historical Jesus. This attention to present and past now requires supplementation and fulfillment by a focus on the future in Part Three. This chapter justifies the affirmation of Christ as Logos and interrelates it with the conclusions of Parts One and Two.

If one asked Christians of either the Alexandrian or the Antiochene school what Christianity was all about, they would most likely have answered that it was the means by which human beings could enter into a blessed immortality beyond the grave. They differed, not on this goal, but only on the way in which the work of Jesus as the Christ was related to it. They jointly won out over competing philosophies and religions of their time because they offered a greater hope with more confidence, and they won out for this as much as for any other advantage offered. In the West, Augustine pointed out the contrast with Stoicism in just these terms.[1]

This eschatological focus of early Christianity did not cease with the Middle Ages or with the Reformation. On the contrary, it was the self-evident context in which theological issues were discussed. It is true that, especially among sectarian groups during the Reformation period, visions arose of a society radically different from any that had been known, and in the name of these visions there were vigorous protests against the established order. But these revolutionary movements no more rejected belief in salvation beyond death than did the more conservative efforts of Roman Catholics or Calvinists to establish societies that were conformable to Christian principles. Even in the seventeenth and eighteenth centuries, when leading intellectuals sought to establish a rational religion based on evident truths against the particularities of competing and warring Christian bodies, life after death was not questioned as being of supreme moment for religion.

The moralistic faith in rewards and punishments after death according to one's virtue or vice in this life finally elicited a reaction at the outset of the nineteenth century. This is most clear in Friedrich Schleiermacher. Schleiermacher saw Christianity as a fulfillment of human potentialities in this life rather than as a preparation for another. This fulfillment he saw as possible here and now rather than only in a historical future. And he developed this new, deeschatologized understanding of Christianity in the most influential dogmatics of the nineteenth century, *The Christian Faith.* Thereby Schleiermacher set the stage for a fundamental refocusing of what is Christian.

There were many factors other than Schleiermacher's romanticism that contributed to the new era of noneschatological Christianity. The scientific world view increasingly crowded ideas of another world to the edges of credibility, so that Christians who did not want to struggle against the dominant modern world view found it easier and wiser to give up talk of another world altogether. Progress seemed to many a historical reality given deeper sanction on the one side by Hegel's dialectical view of history and on the other side, later in the century, by the rise of evolutionary thought in biology. This allowed for an assurance of meaningful life here and now benefiting from the progress already attained and contributing to the process without any necessity of another world or a vision of an End of this one. Where there are opportunities for contributing to the betterment of the lot of human beings here and now, concern for what happens to them beyond the grave appeared irrelevant or obstructionistic. Indeed, otherworldliness increasingly seemed the enemy of social progress and human responsibility.

The fact of progress supported belief in the fundamental goodness of things, and confidence in that goodness—the goodness of nature, humanity, or historical process—ensured that progress would continue. Largely unnoticed, the sense of progress that made the modern, secular consciousness possible took on the characteristics of the sacred. It was in this context that Schweitzer found so shocking the fact that Jesus himself was caught up in the eschatological vision of the End of the world we know.

But faith in progress had already disappointed the more sensitive spirits. They examined the condition of the interior life and found it desiccated by what was called progress. Nietzsche saw progress leading to the wretchedness of the last man, who did not even know he was wretched. By the middle of the twentieth century the lonely voices of nineteenth-century protest had become the orthodoxy of the humanistic intelligentsia. Within the humanities the images of progress became objects of ridicule. New images of hope were hard to find. They had power only to the extent that they embodied and then reversed the hopelessness of the dominant vision. Dialectical theology shared in this mood and now finds its fullest expression in Thomas Altizer's vision of hope as coincident with despair.

The paradoxical character of the images of hope in the mid-twentieth century separated hope from public affairs. Reinhold Niebuhr almost alone among dialectical theologians brilliantly integrated his paradoxical hope with political activism. But he could not pass on even to his admirers the subtle motive of committed action without an image of a significantly better future. Existentialist theologians interpreted Christian faith in terms of a mode of individual existence that required no hopeful expectations of a better future.

Teilhard de Chardin perceived that the crisis of hope goes deeper still. He saw that lack of hope would ultimately destroy that zest for life apart from which the human enterprise cannot continue.

> Although we too often forget this, what we call evolution develops only in virtue of a certain internal preference for survival (or, if you prefer to put it so, self-survival) which in man takes on a markedly psychic appearance, in the form of a *zest for life*. Ultimately, it is that and that alone which underlies and supports the whole complex of bio-physical energies whose operation, acting experimentally, conditions anthropogenesis.
>
> In view of that fact, what would happen if one day we should see that the universe is so hermetically closed in upon itself that there is

no possible way of our emerging from it—either because we are
forced indefinitely to go round and round inside it, or (which comes
to the same thing) because we are doomed to a total death?
Immediately and without further ado, I believe—just like the miners
who find the gallery is blocked ahead of them—we would lose heart
to act, and man's impetus would be radically checked and "defeated" forever, by this fundamental discouragement and *loss of
zest*.[2]

The 1960's witnessed a violent burst of protest against the
loss of images of hope. The existentialist tendency to find
satisfaction in the analysis of alienation from neighbor gave
way to passionate visions of community. Analysis of inner
emptiness was displaced by images of religious wholeness
borrowed chiefly from the East. Cynical acceptance of the
ambiguities of social order gave way to a new, revolutionary
utopianism.

Christian thinkers participated fully in the protest movements of the 1960's. Many of them expended their energies
chiefly in freeing themselves from what they found irrelevant
and restrictive in their inherited Christianity, while others
devoted their attention to the interpretation of the changing
cultural milieu. Both of these groups tended to distance themselves from the church and in many instances from the name
Christian. But a third group, largely inspired by the creative
imagination of the Marxist revisionist Ernst Bloch, reacted
against the deeschatologization of Christianity and recovered
within the Christian tradition the centrality of the theme of
hope. Jürgen Moltmann gave name and content to this movement with his book *The Theology of Hope*.[3]

We are too close to these events to appraise them reliably.
The swift decline from public prominence of many of the visions
of hope of the 1960's can lead to cavalier judgments of their
faddishness and to the assumption that we are returning to the
empty hopelessness of the 1950's. A few even judge that the
wild experimentation of the 1960's has paved the way for a
renewal of particularistic and exclusivistic Christianity. But
there is more continuity into the 1970's than these judgments
recognize.

Much that was formerly self-evident about our world has
become questionable. The heretofore unspeakable has now
been spoken. There is no going back. Our consciousness has

been raised with respect to race, religion, sex, consumption, the natural environment, and their profound conjoint interconnection with all our values and attitudes. The vicissitudes of thought and imagination in the recent past are beginning to rearrange the order of credulity that was established by the secular consciousness. Our scholarly books and our established institutions, both church and university, are still dominated by a sense of probability and reasonableness that is continuous with the outlook of the early decades of this century, and for these institutions the objects of sense experience still govern the sense of reality. But this mentality no longer carries conviction or inspires creative work or imagination. Indeed, the world produced by the older notion of the credible is in shambles intellectually, politically, socially, and biologically. It is sad that Christian theology seems so fully bound to this dying conceptuality, when in the study of other religions the Western mind finds freedom to think new thoughts. In this respect as in others, Christianity may be saved through its interior acceptance of pluralism and its creative transformation through openness to other traditions.

Out of the chaotic religious explorations of the 1960's, in the 1970's we may be witnessing the rise of more ordered esoteric traditions. Interest in these traditions is often private and escapist and as such is not relevant to our present concern for hope. But through such spokesmen as William Irwin Thompson the esoteric elements in the counterculture are finding voices that cannot so easily be written off by open-minded persons. They represent and advance a revolution of sensibility and belief that may indeed embody hope for the future. Furthermore, in Thompson's case it appears to be possible to render in partly credible ways the conviction, widely held in esoteric communities, that as our culture decays a new one is already being born that can save humanity from or through catastrophe in ways that are unintelligible to the still dominant modern mind.[4]

In a culture in which such esoteric grounds of hope can gain a hearing, the credibility of Christianity suffers not so much from the boldness of its claims as from their reduction to common sense. Our problem is not that we believe too much but that we do not believe enough. We must cease to be afraid to be thought fools for Christ's sake. In the face of threatening catastrophe we need great images of eschatological hope, but most of us are still engaged either in defending powerless propositions or in reducing our images to triviality. We need free imagination that breaks courageously into transcendence, but most of our efforts are still directed to explaining that what we have to say does no violence to the dominant but dying modern consciousness. Of course, the imagination we need is a disciplined one, but the discipline should not consist in the dogmatic inculcation of the crudely inadequate world view that has governed our minds in the recent past.

Before launching into a consideration of Christian images of hope, we need to consider the structure of hope itself. Ernst Bloch has given major attention to this question. He points out that, down to the nineteenth century, philosophical efforts were devoted to the situating of human beings in a fundamentally realized cosmos. Such a vision had no place for hope as a basic category, since what exists is stable and permanent. Hegel transformed philosophy by temporalizing it, but even he saw the temporal process as unfolding what was already implicit from the beginning. It was Marx who called for thought to cease describing an existent world and to begin to transform it into something that never heretofore existed. But even Marxism keeps falling into deterministic visions of inevitable dialectical developments.

To understand the structure of hope we must recognize that "what is usually called reality is surrounded by a gigantic ocean of objectively real possibility." [5] This possibility is "partial conditionality," [6] that is, what already exists does not fully determine what will be. Bloch holds that within this ocean of possibility there are some possibilities, the entertainment of which "is merely wishful thinking, or hocus-pocus." [7] But there are others that have that kind of relation to the world which makes them effective in the transformation of the world. The entertainment of these possibilities is the structure of hope.

Now it should be clear that the structure of hope is nothing other than the structure of creative transformation described in Chapter 3. It is the entertainment of just those possibilities that have the power to reorder the actual so as to go beyond it. I have argued, as Bloch does not, that the order among the possibilities that makes them effectively relevant is the divine Logos. The structure of hope is the incarnation of this Logos whereby it is effective in the structuring of actual experience. Hence, the structure of hope is Christ.

That there is creative transformation (and, therefore, also hope) is the fundamental reason for hope. As Bloch says, "In the prison of mere already-existing-things we could neither move nor breathe." [8] That is, if there were no yet unrealized possibilities effectively relevant to our world, there could be only inertia, entropy, and decay. The future could only be the inevitable outgrowth of these negative forces. There is reason to hope that the future can go beyond the past and the present because there is a principle of creative transformation everywhere at work, whose nature it is to bring into being just that which cannot be predicted until it occurs. Our hope for the future is based on the unpredictability of that future, that is, its partial undeterminedness.

That the future is undetermined is our hope, for we know that the principle of this indeterminacy is the creative transformation we trust as Christ. This means that we cannot project particular future possibilities and cling to them, governing all action according to its tendency to achieve these goals. Every goal we entertain must itself be subject to creative transformation in the process of seeking it. This is the profound truth that Henry Nelson Wieman has repeatedly shown.[9] But we need a unifying image to guide us in our hopeful openness to being transformed. We need an image of that kind of existence that is optimally open to this transformation and hence appropriate as an eschatological image of what human beings should be and may become. Christ provides such an image as well. And, indeed, a major reason for concern with the particular structure of Jesus' existence is that he may provide us as Christians with the needed image of hope.

This is because we cannot rest content with our present Christian structure of existence. Though we may prize it, we cannot but experience its ambiguity as well. Our alienation, insecurity, guilt, and the hiddenness of God from us are not particular problems of individuals who have failed to be sufficiently Christian. They are inherent in the structure of our Christian existence. In principle they are overcome in Christ, and in fact they are so alleviated that we can live creatively with them, but there is no going beyond tension and incompleteness in the Christian existence that we know. The overcoming in principle of these ambiguities in Christ is in part through hope. Christ grounds the hope that what we now experience is not the final possibility for humanity. Jesus provides the decisive image for such hope.

It is true and important that Jesus, who is the image of hope, is entirely one with us in our humanity. The New Testament supports this emphasis on his likeness to us. Our hope is for human fulfillment and only a fully human being could image that hope. But it is equally true that if the particularity of Jesus' existence differed in no respect from ours, or if he only participated more fully in the distinctive structure that we know in ourselves as Christians, he would not constitute an image of hope. The New Testament proclaims not only that he was like us but also that we shall be like him.

The structure of Jesus' existence presented in Chapter 8 provides the requisite image of hope. It differs from that structure of existence we now find dominant within ourselves and indicates a possibility for our human future. As we yield ourselves to the Logos to be creatively transformed by it, we have an image of one in whom the self was coconstituted by the presence of the Logos so that the tension between the self and the call to the new was overcome. That structure, as our eschatological hope, is Christ.

The emergence in Jesus of that structure of existence in which the human self coalesces with the immanent Logos is the recovery at a new level of the structure that predominates in all things apart from human beings. In simple entities the Logos does constitute the center from which their self-constitution occurs. The entity may not completely fulfill its potentiality, but there is no competing center within it. The painful tension between the "is" and the "ought" does not occur. That tension can arise only when personal individuality appears. This is constituted by the dominant inheritance of character, novel experience, and purpose from a single route of antecedent events, namely, those that are one's personal past. The inheritance from that route claims determination over all other experience. In the move from animal existence to primitive existence to civilized existence to axial existence, and especially in the particular form of axial existence brought into being through the prophets, this self-identity strengthens itself over against the immanent Logos.[10] Alienation from the Logos grows with the heightening of individual personality. One strong religious impulse is to return to the primordial condition of unity with the Logos by the abandonment of personal selfhood.

The structure of Jesus' existence recovered unity with the Logos at the level of conscious human existence. Personal existence was not negated but fulfilled. What had been achieved through the long history of estrangement was not rejected, but the unity with the Logos that had been lost was regained. His existence was like "pre-fallen" existence except that it took up into itself a history that is not only fall but also enrichment.

Jesus may have thought that what was happening in him could happen in his hearers as well. His call for perfection seems to imply this, as well as the sense of the Kingdom's beginnings. But if so, he was mistaken; the historical process was not ready for universal incarnation. The actual effect of his ministry was rather to drive the process of personal individualization, and therefore also of estrangement, further still. The Kingdom being realized in his own ministry became the resurrection at the End of history. Only there could the final unity occur. But for just this reason Jesus, as Christ, becomes the image of Christian hope.

Part One showed that faith in Christ, who is the Logos at work in our world and in ourselves, expresses itself in artistic and theological creativity, in love, and in critical and constructive reason. Part Two dealt with Christ as he was incarnate in Jesus, and it displayed faith as attending to Jesus' words and as conformation to him in his field of force. In Part Three we see that faith in Christ as we face the unknown future is hope.

These stances toward present, past, and future are not separable from one another. The openness to creative transformation that is faith in relation to the present can be sustained only in a context of hope, but the hope and the images of hope are themselves expressions of creative transformation. Both the openness and the hope require that we be renewed in our openness by the support of a community that expresses the field of force generated by Jesus and that is renewed by encounter with his words. Jesus opens us to the present working of the Logos by assuring us of our future. Hope enables us to hear the words of Jesus and to conform to him.

This means that apart from Christ there is no hope for a better future. This is not merely pious rhetoric. It follows from the identification of Christ as the Logos as it confronts every settled world with some novel possibility for its creative becoming. Apart from the Logos there could be only the running down of the world governed by slow inertial decay. In the strictest sense there would be neither anything to hope for nor any possibility of the attitude of hope. This is an unreal picture of the world, but it has a powerful grip on human imagination, and when human beings are grasped by such a hopeless vision they become closed to creative transformation. The loss of hope shuts Christ out from effectiveness in human affairs.[11]

Whenever hope is present in history, Christ is present, whether recognized or not. But apart from the history of Jesus, hope is distorted, and Christ's effective presence is blocked. Affirmation of Christ can itself also become a basis for distortion when Christ is idolatrously identified with particular results or embodiments of his past presence; but where the Christ image is powerful, it helps to correct these distortions and to remove the obstacles to faith as openness to creative transformation.

Christ transforms the world by persuading it toward relevant novelty. Thus Christ is himself the hope of the world. Christ calls us to envision a hopeful future. The basic image by which we can do so is Christ. The credibility of Christ as the image of hope depends both on the recognition of Jesus as Christ and the experienced power of Christ as creative transformation. Openness to creative transformation depends on hope. The circularity of all theology, and indeed of all thought, is peculiarly manifest in this logic of hope.

This book as a whole intends to offer Christ as an image of hope. The more immediate hope is that Christ can be named again in our time without either obscurantism or embarrassment, and that when he is named, the urgently needed process of creative transformation can become more effective. The cultural loss of the capacity to name Christ has weakened basic hopefulness and threatened the continuing effectiveness both of the Logos itself and of the human response and appropriation through critical and constructive reason. The recovery of the ability to discern the Logos, to recognize its creative-salvific power, and, hence, to name it again as Christ would give to a post-Western culture, now global, the courage to struggle against the patterns of self-destruction that now control it.

If this is to happen, the Christian consciousness must be freed from its fear that to move forward in the acceptance of the secular and pluralistic world threatens its faithfulness to Christ. The secular consciousness must be freed from its fear that to acknowledge its own positive principle as Christ will be betrayal of its critical and open spirit. The pluralistic consciousness must be freed from its fear that to name Christ as universal is to close itself to the independent power and truth of other traditions. The thesis of this book is that faithfulness to Christ requires immersion in the secular and pluralistic consciousness and that it is precisely there that Christ now works, impeded by our failure to recognize him and by our continuing association of faith with past, particularized expressions of Christ.

That Christ might return explicitly to the imagination of the secular and pluralistic consciousness is evidenced by what has occurred in the recent history of art. Jane Dillenberger notes that "from the death of Rembrandt in 1669 until the twentieth century a hiatus occurs in the creation of religious art." [12] She then goes on to show that in our century some of the greatest artists have turned again to Christian themes. Significantly, when she devoted a complete book to this recent Christian art, she entitled it *Secular Art with Sacred Themes*.[13] The return to Christian art is not a return to investing the particular images with sacred power. That power remains in the art that is served and not in its products or what is represented. But if it is realized that what is depicted is also the power that is served, the Christ image may again represent the unity of creative transformation and of hope.

Although Christ is the central image of Christian hope, he cannot stand alone. Openness to Christ requires that there be images of a hopeful future toward which he leads and through which we may be led to him. I have called for boldness and discipline in the fashioning of such images. Since our received images have died and there is no return to either the supernaturalist or the trivialized forms of Christian hope, the task is a large one that will demand the best efforts of many Christians. What I can offer in Part Three are select expressions of the Christian imagination of the recent past, combined with suggestions of my own. They are offered with the intention of encouraging the hope that Christian images of hope are possible and thereby energizing the now dormant efforts to share in the creation of more effective images.

To call an image of hope Christian is not an idle matter. Not every image that a Christian happens to like can be so named. I have applied in this connection four criteria. First, the image must itself be the recent product of creative transformation; it will not do to resuscitate old images, however orthodox. An image is Christian only if it has been forged or reforged in the heat of the crosscurrents of contemporary thinking. Second, an image is Christian only if it is reformable through a continuing process of creative transformation and depicts a future in which such creative transformation can continue. A fixed image, or an image of a fixed condition of perfection, may have its value, but it is faithless to Christ as Christ is understood in this book. Third, the image must be such that to accept and live by it is to be open to the process of creative transformation in the present. No image is Christian that leads to closure or to indifference to the events that transpire in our world here and now. Fourth and finally, an image is Christian if it can be seen to have arisen through encounter with Jesus' words or as a result of immersion in his field of force. The requirement is, not that the author of the image consciously affirm indebtedness to Christ, but that the Christian see such indebtedness, where it exists, in a historical as well as an ontological form.

The focus on Christian images is not intended to disparage other images of hope. On the contrary, the intention is to clarify the Christian images of hope in such a way as to maximize openness to others without imperialistically claiming them as Christian. An image is not Christian if it is not open to this appreciation and to being inwardly transformed through it. But this process of Christian growth toward universality cannot occur except by the expansion and transformation of Christian images. It is these Christian images that are sought.

There can be no question here of demonstration of the truth of any of these images. Hope is a matter of the unseen and unknown. Further, there is today no widely convincing image of hope, even among Christians for whom hope is recognized as essential. We await the emergence of a new and powerful image. At present it may help to see how a number of images that superficially appear quite different and even conflicting are capable of merging toward a unified image.

Accordingly Chapter 12 describes the most hopeful image I know of a radically different organization of human relations in a new kind of city. In this "City of God," human life could become more human while at the same time the natural environment would be freed from the repressive and destructive aspects of our present way of life.

Chapter 13 supplements this account of a possible transformation of our outward relations by a proposal for the inner reconstitution of human relations. Since Buddhism is an especially persuasive challenge to Christians, the proposal is of a way Christians could inwardly be transformed through appropriation of elements of the Buddhist ideal.

But openness to radical transformation in a time when all human life is threatened requires grounding in another dimension as well. Chapter 14 presses the question of hope to its transcendent basis. It offers Whitehead's vision of the Kingdom of Heaven as answering the question posed by the loss of temporal passage and the ambiguities of even the greatest historical achievement.

Chapter 15 examines the central traditional Christian conviction of the resurrection of Jesus. It shows that in the thought of Wolfhart Pannenberg the resurrection image is correlated with our modern understanding of reality and presented as the answer to the problem of death.

In the final chapter, Chapter 16, through critical development of the several images, their potential for mutual support and supplementation is displayed. Finally, they are jointly viewed as pointers to the basic image of hope as Christ, already offered in this chapter.

The most glaring omission from this selection of images of Christian hope is the Omega of Teilhard de Chardin. This does not mean that he is ignored; for I have borrowed from him already in this chapter, and the image of the City of God presented in the next chapter is inspired by him. In the final chapter I rely upon him in working through the diversities toward a unity of hope. Indeed, Part Three is dedicated to Teilhard as the visionary Christian thinker who has done more than any other to restore the possibility of hope to the contemporary Christian imagination.

CHAPTER 12

The City of God

We are surrounded by multiplying signals that our civilization cannot continue in the directions of its recent past. It has been based upon economic growth, and growth has now become self-destructive. Even where this destructiveness is not recognized and efforts at growth continue unchecked, growth seems to be impossible. Shortages of resources combined with public expectations that growth itself has created now stymie and frustrate every effort to continue the path of ever-increasing production of goods. Even so, the frantic efforts to sustain familiar institutions in which no one any longer really believes continue to accelerate the pollution of the environment and the destruction of our fellow creatures. There are indications that pollution may be changing planetary weather—in ways that can only accelerate crises in agriculture and economics. Crime increases, the family system decays, schools and churches cease to command general respect, communities are fragmented, and political life is polarized. Our cities become year by year less livable.

There is no lack of futurists, both revolutionary and conservative, who assure us that science and political management will solve all our problems and that we can look forward even yet to an economic and technological golden age. There is no lack of critics who show us on point after point how continuation of present practices threatens to lead us all into destruction. There is no lack of suggestions of how to solve one problem or another in isolation from the total situation. But what is rare is to find persons who, having heard and taken seriously the prophetic warnings of imminent danger, propose comprehensive solutions commensurate with the problems. That is to say, there are few images of a truly hopeful future for mankind.

Even the hope that Christ can be named again, of which the preceding chapter spoke, is profoundly shaken by the realization of how near our civilization may be to collapse. Other civilizations have risen and fallen in the past, and Christ has continued his incarnation in the world. But our civilization has become global, and in its collapse it threatens to take with it not only the human species but all higher forms of life as well (for example, if the ozone layer is seriously depleted). This is a new realization, and where it dawns it alters the whole context of theology. Christ himself, as the incarnation of the Logos in the life of our planet, is threatened.

In the imagination of the 1950's, the adventure and suffering of human existence were located in an essentially static historical context. One could afford the luxury of subtle hopes and even of despair. Despite the atomic bomb, that there would be a human future did not seem to be in question. In the 1960's we finally learned that historical existence of any sort depends on its physical base and that this base is being rapidly eroded. The self-contained world of human imagination was rudely jolted by the threat that forces wholly outside of it might soon entirely destroy it.

In this context, images of Christ as hope seem, from one side, pointless. They have meaning only if there will be the time for them to gain force in the imagination and existence of mankind. But there is another side to the problem. Just as in recent years it was realized that the self-contained world of the humanistic imagination has an unnoticed natural environment apart from which it cannot exist at all, so also we have learned that what happens in and to that natural environment is profoundly shaped by the images by which we live. The images of progress banished from the humanist's world continued to dominate the world of economic and political life. There they have been crudely identified with technological advances and a rising gross national product. These controlling images have so shaped our actual treatment of the environment as to threaten life itself.

The images of progress that dominate our public affairs

cannot be displaced by the sophisticated humanist's cynicism or subtle paradoxical hope. Also the destruction of these images by despair will only serve to leave short-term greed the unquestioned master of the public world, reducing the likelihood that total catastrophe can be avoided. There is no hope for appropriate response to our final crisis as a species unless there are hopeful images to guide such a response. Hence, the hope for a new ability to name Christ is not irrelevant. The effective presence of the hope would make its own realization, in transformed ways, more nearly possible.

Still, this image, geared to an assumed ongoing history, is far from sufficient. Realistic images of a hopeful future for mankind must now be fashioned in the teeth of the threat to the existence of a world in which any images at all can arise. To be governed by the hope of a new ability to name Christ today, one must be convinced that to act in the light of that possibility will be appropriate to sustaining the context of all action and that this image of hope can be fleshed out in a realistic image of a viable human society.

But these cannot be images of an improved economic, political, moral, and educational order within the basic structures of our present world, whether capitalist or communist. The power of such images has been broken by the more radical ideas of the 1960's. The apparent failure of these in their turn does not return us to where we were but leaves a vacuum that has not yet been filled. Furthermore, we now see that the basic order of society in our worldwide civilization is itself responsible for our headlong course toward racial suicide. Action geared to sustaining that order by its moderate adjustment does not help. Only action guided by images that have taken account of the depths of our need for change can serve us.

A realistic reinterpretation of hope renews the prophetic-apocalyptic Marxist vision that only after catastrophe can there be positive rebuilding. Individual habits and patterns of social and economic power are too entrenched in our world to be changed by mere recognition of future danger. They will not be voluntarily surrendered. Hence, only as they collapse of their own weight can a situation be created in which a new order that is humanly and ecologically viable emerge.

This is probably true. The recognition of its truth alters all the lesser hopes that guide responsible action. The question is only how horrendous the catastrophe must be. What magnitude of famine or plague, economic and political collapse, social chaos, or environmental degradation will be required to shake humanity out of its self-destructive drive? The ultimate danger is that nothing will suffice except the culmination of that drive itself in the end of the species. The hope is that far lesser calamities will lead us to shift our direction. But we will not shift unless we sustain the zest for life of which Teilhard speaks. And we will not know how to shift unless we have images that direct our energies in new ways. We cannot wait for catastrophe to begin critically to shape our images.

The need for such images is urgent. Without them even well-intentioned governments and enlightened Christians are blind and their noblest actions are likely to be counterproductive. Many of our efforts to relieve poverty worsen the condition of the poor. Feeding the hungry and healing the sick increases the global problem of starvation. Our efforts to save our cities hasten their collapse. Attempts at racial integration often heighten racial animosities. Programs to save or improve local environments run counter to the environmental needs of the larger society. The increase of individual freedom produces an anarchy that is likely to give rise to totalitarianism.

Also, without an image of hope, people are unwilling to give up what security the existing system affords. Even catastrophe could serve to heighten resistance to change. Paradoxically many of our society's victims, for example the elderly, oppose most bitterly attempts to alter it. As we lose the prospects of all segments of our society increasing their wealth because of the ever-expanding economic pie, each will fight tenaciously to hold and increase its relative position—unless a new image of hope becomes effective.

One attractive realistic image of hope that has taken into account many dimensions of the problems we face is *The California Tomorrow Plan.*[1] This is a plan for a livable society in viable relation to its nonhuman environment and a program for its attainment by the year 2000. Built into the plan is the process for its own reshaping through experience and imagination as steps are taken to realize it. In relation to established habits and entrenched interests, it is so radical that the chances of its implementation appear to be slight. Yet, in relation to the magnitude of the problems, it is so moderate that even its success would probably be too little, too late.

If we are faithful to Christ, we will encourage the development and implementation of more images of hope of this order and scope—however fragmentary and insufficient they may be. But we will also seek elsewhere for more radical and fundamental images. Today most images of hope are of a return to earlier styles of human existence.

One such image is that of the renewal of the hunting and gathering society. It can be beautifully embodied, as by Gary Snyder, who participates in a tribal life of this kind. It is realistic in the sense that people can live that way and can, in terms of many of the deepest human needs, live well. Its advocates believe, indeed, that such a life, and only such a life, is truly in tune with the deepest rhythms of bodily and psychic functioning. But apart from experimental groups, it is realistic only for a world that will have passed through catastrophe of scarcely imaginable magnitude.[2]

Another vision of hope is that of a return to a simple agricultural society. On the basis of labor-intensive farming and basic handicrafts, largely self-sufficient communities could develop. To discourage free enterprise, mobility, and growing gaps between rich and poor, property would be held in trust as in a feudal system and therefore would not be subject to sale and purchase. Such communities would not be destroyed by the breakdown of global economic systems or by regional collapse of transportation or energy transmission. Moreover, the environmental damage caused by a given population living close to the land would be very small compared with that caused by the same number of people living in our industrial, technological, growth-oriented society. Warren Johnson has proposed practical means for starting such communities.[3] In a context where most of what is called realism offers solutions that only accelerate our drive to destruction, Johnson's radical ideas deserve more attention than they have received.

Basically the visions of both Snyder and Johnson, as well as the more moderate proposals by Barry Commoner, are of a return to earlier social orders. Since continuation of our present order is suicidal, these visions must be taken seriously. Perhaps our species has overreached itself. Perhaps it has been precisely hope for something more that has led us toward annihilation. Perhaps all our vaunted achievements express only a self-destructive hybris. There is much evidence today that we as a species have transgressed the boundaries, that we will pay an enormous price, and that the survivors should learn the lesson forevermore to abjure history and civilization.

If this is indeed the truth about the human condition, we who hold the prophetic-Christian faith must confess to great responsibility for our collective transgression. Christians have always looked to the future to vindicate the present and, in doing so, have made humanity restless in the face of the injustice, ignorance, and poverty that have characterized history. Either we have been fundamentally wrong or there lies ahead a way that is not primarily a return to the past but a forward movement—a movement that will so redirect science, technology, urban culture, and interpersonal relations that a large human population within a limited biosphere will be assured of a decent life.

The possibility of any plausible vision of hope along these lines is widely discounted. But there is one person who is proving the possibility by offering the vision. Paolo Soleri, artist-architect-visionary-prophet, a voice crying in the wilderness, sees the profound connection between cities and civilization, and he affirms both. Our problem, he says, is not that we have become urbanized but that we have built our cities in such a way as to sacrifice our relation to nature for the sake of urban values; and the ironic result is that for most of their inhabitants our cities no longer provide even urban values. Cities have become agents of dehumanization as well as of denaturalization. They require ever-increasing per capita consumption for a rapidly declining quality of life.

Soleri believes that the fundamental problem of the city is that it is two-dimensional—a thin web of human construction and life stretched over a large area. As it spreads, it destroys both the natural surface and the possibility of rich interrelationships among its people. Thus it alienates the affection and loyalty of its inhabitants and at the same time becomes more and more inefficient in its use of energy and raw materials.

Soleri recognizes that our present cities are strangling themselves and sucking their environment into the vortex of their ruin. But he does not for that reason turn his back upon the city as such. He prizes the humanizing power latent in urban life. And, to make that power manifest, he proposes a radically new kind of city, an architectural ecology, or an "arcology."

The image that Soleri holds up is an image of hope. For one thing, an arcology would greatly reduce the threat to the environment because it would use only a fraction of the space, energy, and resources required for building or maintaining our present cities. Problems of waste and pollution could be solved with relative ease. For instance, the waste heat from underground factories would provide the energy for the business and homes above, and the air would be kept unpolluted by making the automobile a rare plaything rather than a necessity. For within the arcology everyone would have convenient access to all its inner facilities, as well as to the world of agriculture, wilderness, and recreation outside. Diversities of opportunity for human interaction would be offered as well as easy participation in the decision-making processes. Residential segregation by race, age, and social or economic class would no longer be a major problem, for the whole city would be a single unit.

These claims are not merely the fantasy of wishfully combining mutually exclusive values. They point to real possibilities vividly displayed in Soleri's breathtaking models. In nature, Soleri observes, effective organization is always three-dimensional. A thin layer of living cells spread out in two dimensions over the globe could accomplish little; but concentrated in three-dimensional forms, cells constitute the vast and varied world of plant and animal life.

Until now, cities have been two-dimensional, hence they have overreached themselves and become cancerous. The effort to solve the problem by concentrating huge skyscrapers in their centers expresses a real necessity, but in itself it does not help. Indeed, most of the efforts to improve cities have for some time now been self-defeating.

To visualize the problem, imagine a million small cubes each representing a two-story building. The cubes can be spread out in a square a thousand cubes on each side. Of course, this arrangement disregards the need for transportation. To provide for this, groups of buildings will have to be organized into city blocks with space left between them for streets, sidewalks, driveways, parking lots, filling stations, etc. The distances, already great, will be extended. Thus, providing space for motor vehicles increases dependence upon them. As the square grows larger, distances to the open areas outside of it also increase. But life in a vast, solid mass of buildings and streets is intolerable; large areas must be opened up for recreation and greenery. Playing fields, gardens, and parks must be scattered through the city, and these will require additional streets and parking lots. The city is now so big that access from one part of it to another is extremely difficult. A freeway system must be built, and to make room for it large sections of the city must be torn down. These sections are moved to the outside of the city, thus once again extending the whole, increasing dependence on motor vehicles, and heightening the need for open space scattered throughout. Each step in the solution of the problem adds to the problem, requiring that further steps be taken. Just to slow the pace of decline within the city demands enormous efforts.

The million small cubes could also be formed into a single large one, with three dimensions of one hundred cubes each. This single cube, too, will have to be enlarged to allow for movement within it. But distances in the three-dimensional city are but a fraction of those in the square. Motor transportation will not be needed; elevators, escalators, moving sidewalks, bike trails, and walking paths will suffice. The need for open space within the cube will also be much less, since the inhabitants can quickly walk outside to enjoy forests, fields, and recreational facilities. Still, space should be allowed for gardens, playgrounds, swimming pools, tennis courts, and public squares scattered throughout the cube. Extra space for these purposes equal to a third of the volume of the original cube can be gained by increasing it just 10 percent on each side. Distances within it will remain small—less than a tenth of those within the two-dimensional city.

Obviously, this picture is highly artificial. No city is laid out in a perfect square, and Soleri does not envision building huge solid cubes. He is an artist and a humanist. Vast areas are left open for light and air to penetrate throughout the arcology. But even if most of the space is left open, the three-dimensional city will occupy barely one percent of the land surface of the present two-dimensional city. Nor does this scheme involve crowding. Each family, business, industry, shop, school, and church would be left with just as much space indoors and out as it now has.

Savings could be effected here, too, but that would depend on decisions over and above the choice of the arcology as such. What each family would give up would be its isolation, not its privacy.

These staggering claims for what arcologies can mean for the human race are only a part of what Soleri believes they will accomplish. Soleri states the importance of a commitment to an architectural ecology ("the Arcological Commitment"):

> The Arcological Commitment is not indispensable
> (1) Because it is the solution to the ecological crisis, although it is that.
> (2) Because it is a better alternative to the degradation of waste-affluence-opulence, although it is that.
> (3) Because it is the true resolution of the pollution dilemma, although it is that.
> (4) Because it is the only true answer to the global crisis of energy-production-consumption, although it is that.
> (5) Because it is the only road to land, air, water conservation, although it is that.
> (6) Because it is a necessary answer to the sheltering of an exploding population, although it is that.
> (7) Because it is structurally desegregating peoples, things, and performances, although it is that.
> (8) Because it is a forceful instrument against fear and disillusionment, although it is that.
> Most generally, the Arcological Commitment is not indispensable because it is the best instrument for survival, although it is just that. . . .
> All these are remedial reasons important for man but only instrumental to the specific humaneness sought by him. They are manutentive and restorative. They are not specifically creative. By their implementation, the refound health of man could never be a substitute for grace but only a threshold to it.
> The Arcological Commitment is indispensable because it advocates a physical system that consents to the high compression of things, energies, logistics, information and performances, thus fostering the thinking, doing, living, learning phenomenon of life at its most lively and compassionate, the state of grace (esthetogenesis) possible for a socially and individually healthy man on ecologically healthy earth.[4]

Soleri does not know when arcologies will be built on a large scale, but he is convinced that they must and will come. Imbued

as he is with the vision of Teilhard de Chardin, he sees the
human odyssey in the context of the total development of life on
the planet. Like Teilhard, he has deep faith that the evolutionary energies of the universe which have brought life on earth to
its present high pitch are working through the present crises to
a new level. The next step, after the explosion of population
around the world that we have witnessed in recent centuries,
will be "implosion"—and that means arcology.

But Soleri is not waiting passively for this next step in human
evolution to occur. He has drawn up general plans for dozens of
highly varied and beautiful arcologies. Of some of these he has
built huge models that have been exhibited in leading art
museums and featured in architectural and art journals. And
now, since the realists of our time still view all of this as
dreaming, he has himself begun to build.

But is Soleri's direction one that Christian realists should
take seriously? Must we not recognize that, given the control of
our behavior by habits, and given the slow changes that occur in
building practices and city planning, arcologies are an issue for
some subsequent generation rather than our own? Should we
not concentrate our energies on alleviating the plight of those
caught in the decay of our present cities rather than on
dreaming of new cities in which these problems would not
occur?

This "realism" in our time is analogous to that of the
individualists and pietists of earlier generations who insisted
that Christians should minister to personal needs but not
meddle with the social structure that creates the needs. We
should have learned by now that the attempts to end the
suffering of people in the cities by tinkering with political and
economic changes is futile. We win an occasional battle, but the
war goes overwhelmingly against us. True realism would be to
consider why we always lose and to begin to work on the deeper
causes of urban decay. Realists of that stripe will not want to
postpone arcologies for another generation or two.

The most common hostile reaction to Soleri's vision is that
his cities would be human beehives. What is expressed in this
protest is that in the arcology rugged individualism would have
to be subordinated to the collective well-being. Property could
not be so absolutely private as some suppose our present
system still allows. Individuals would be part of a larger whole.

Those who sense that the arcology would carry us in the direction of new dimensions of interpersonal connections are correct. This is indeed Soleri's intention. He sees the ideal city as being an organism within which particular communities and individuals perform their differentiated roles and make their diverse contributions. He believes that there is no loss of individual fulfillment or freedom in participating in such intensified mutual relationships. He writes:

> If we have a superorganism made up of men, men retaining their own uniqueness, then such an organism will be made of thousands or millions or more of brains. Furthermore, each of these brains will contain a mind, that is to say, will overgovern that power of choice among the endless propositions of the possible, the one-at-a-time performances making the present.
>
> This will be the fundamental distinction between the city and the anthill, the beehive, the termite colony, and so on: not just brains by the score but also minds by the score. The romantic and rugged individualists will speak out immediately about the mindlessness of the human beehive. They might want to glance at the nightmarish suburbia with its six billion individuals, but it is their privilege not to reason about mankind and the staggering logistics it is faced with.[5]

But even if we are prepared to recognize that we can now preserve our personal freedom and dignity only as we move forward to more intense and intimate interconnections with others, must we not also admit that the unlimited capacity of the human being to pervert what is potential for good into the material for evil introduces into the arcologies all the problems that we face in our present world? Is it not an illusion to look for real progress? Again, the "realists" raise their objections, and, of course, they are correct. Soleri speaks of building the plumbing for the City of God. The plumbing does not determine how the city will be used. But the plumbing will make possible a viable life in the context of a healthy biosphere. That possibility cannot be discerned today apart from some such radical change. Christians cannot withdraw from action because they know that no social, political, economic, or urban structure guarantees virtue. We need an image of hope to sustain our action, and Soleri offers that image.

Soleri knows that the City of God must be much more than plumbing. He asks the help of the psychologists, biologists, chemists, physicists, engineers, agriculturalists, industrialists, lawyers, political scientists, economists, sociologists, and a host of others. Such help is hard to find, for the environmental crisis has vividly exposed the disjointedness of the many specialties. Each moves in ruts established by its limited questions and its limited conceptualities. But Soleri's vision could serve, as few others could, to precipitate creative transformation within these specialties. For those who can endure it, the encounter with a radically different organization of space can provide the occasion for fresh thinking capable of fleshing out the image of hope. At least the image inspires the hope that this is possible. In the process, Soleri's own images will also be transformed.

Is Soleri's vision of the City of God a form of Christian hope? He does not so designate it, but the Christian can discern Christ in it. It is not the call to return to an earlier condition by giving up what our tradition has accomplished. Instead, it carries forward our tradition by a great leap of the imagination. It is a creative transformation at once of thought, planning, and art. Furthermore, life within the arcology would be one in which the process of creative transformation would be enhanced.

Soleri is but another example of the mystery that frequently where the Christian discerns Christ most clearly the agent of Christ refuses to identify herself or himself as a Christian. Yet Soleri is far from indifferent to the issues of faith. Indeed, he has become increasingly interested in theology in recent years, although in his continuing quest for universality he eschews traditional Christian language or associates it with past meanings that he opposes. He affirms "a God which does not exist as yet," and he distinguishes the religion in which he believes from pantheism "since the pressure which characterizes it is the need to transcend whatever it is that makes it up to that point." [6]

In an unpublished paper, "Relative Poverty and Frugality" (June 1974), Soleri recognizes implicitly that the Omega-God is somehow already operative. "The laws of mass energy would have ended their reality (usefulness), since the whole of mass energy would have transcended itself into Logos. But then this transcendence is not a hypothesis or a future possibility. It is a daily occurrence. We, the humankind, are matter transcended into spirit; a raw, dark, violent, excess-prone spirit as yet."

Despite the obvious congeniality of Soleri's theology to the Christology of this book and despite the fact that he is an enthusiastic disciple of Teilhard de Chardin, Soleri does not name Christ. He distances himself from everything in Christianity that is restricting, particularizing, authoritarian, antiquarian, and supernatural. Teilhard experienced more than most what is restrictive and authoritarian in Christian tradition and institutional life, but he saw more clearly than Soleri that this is not Christ. Teilhard found Christ in Christogenesis, the process of creative transformation that takes on through Jesus and the Christian community the particular character of uniting humanity into a new community of love. Christogenesis is the bearer of the energies of evolution. Soleri understands himself as servant of those energies that Teilhard named Christ. If with Teilhard we strip from Christ all that does not belong to him, we will not falsify Soleri's faith by naming what he serves in our Christian way.

CHAPTER 13

The Perfection of Love

The vision of a new kind of city provides hope that the human race could live with its environment in a way that would allow for the flourishing of both human beings and our fellow creatures. In that context we could nourish other hopes. One such hope is that through the interiorization of pluralism our understanding and existence will be transformed and we can move toward a new spiritual unity. Since openness to others is love, it can only be through the perfection of love that such unity is achieved. If so, the spiritual unity we envision is at the same time the fuller incarnation of Christ. This chapter fashions an image relevant to one phase of the creative transformation that is required.

Naming the Logos (the principle of creative transformation) as "Christ" makes possible and necessary the inner acceptance of pluralism, and thereby moves the process of creative transformation into a new phase. Since the Christian finds the Logos incarnate in Jesus, faith in Jesus cannot be in tension with the interiorization of the radically different achievements of other traditions or in opposition to their claims. But even the identification of Christ with the Logos does not make the inner encounter with other traditions easy. In this identification what is meant by the Logos is transformed by its identity with Christ, and, equally, what is meant by "Christ" is transformed by identification with the Logos. Furthermore, although Christians can discern the working of the Logos in all traditions, we see that other traditions do not intend primarily to order themselves by and to the Logos. Hence, some of the meanings that we are called by Christ to enter and to appropriate are alien to him.

As the depth of the differences among the religious traditions is grasped, the spirit of pluralism is in danger of relapsing into mere tolerance of diversity. It seems that one can find identity only in one tradition or another. It would seem safest to study other traditions only to attain objective understanding, or if one enters them subjectively, it would seem safest to do so in a provisional, temporary way that will not alter one's own basic attitudes, vision, and structure of existence. For example, if one's own position is tolerant openness, one cannot inwardly appropriate the intolerant closedness of another. It would seem that the intolerant character of another tradition can be recognized and tolerated, but not internalized.

Yet this is not sufficient. The affirmation of pluralism is not mere tolerance. Those who enter the pluralistic consciousness want others to join in it. They are not indifferent observers of the mutual hostility of traditions, but, rather, they seek the conversion of all to the pluralistic spirit. The call of Christ does not allow us to relapse from the effort at inner appropriation of other traditions to mere objective toleration.

The situation is bewildering. Traditions are in profound disagreement; they offer radically different ends; there is no common essence in terms of which diversity can be minimized; one cannot simply accept them all. There must be choosing, and these choices will inevitably be shaped by one tradition or another. There is no position of neutrality from which their respective values can be perceived and integrated into a new syncretism. What then can the call for interior appropriation mean?

This question can be answered in general terms only by saying that to become open to real otherness while remaining rooted in one's own tradition provides an opportunity for the creative transformation of that tradition. After initial resistance, Christian theology was open to Greek philosophy, and, without ceasing to be Christian, it was inwardly transformed by its interiorization of the Greek mind. Similarly, after an initial struggle, Christian theology was open to modern science, and, without ceasing to be Christian, it was inwardly transformed by its interiorization of the scientific method and results. Today, after an initial struggle, Christian theology has opened itself to the traditions of Asia, and, without ceasing to be Christian, it will be transformed by the radically different consciousness they embody.

This generalization can be given concreteness only in particular instances. We cannot inwardly appropriate everything at once. There is vast diversity and conflict among the traditions of the Orient as well as between them and the traditions of the West. The pluralistic consciousness calls for painstaking labor with no successful outcome antecedently envisioned. Even so, we do need images to guide our efforts and to give some sense of what it would mean for our own tradition to be transformed through uniting others with itself. The remainder of this chapter undertakes to offer an image of a hopeful outcome of the Christian appropriation of Buddhism in two senses. First, it proposes that Christianity can be creatively transformed through interiorization of this alien tradition. Second, the result of this creative transformation is a new mode of existence toward which Christian hope may aspire.

Buddhism has striking parallels with Christianity. Its relation to the religious matrix of India is analogous to that of Christianity (and Islam) to Judaism. It has shown a remarkable ability to spread to other cultures, and it has flourished chiefly on foreign soil. Like Christianity, Buddhism points to a particular historical figure and celebrates his work and his authority in canonized scriptures. Gautama, like Jesus, is often worshiped by his followers. The universalistic claims made for the truth and importance of Gautama's teachings by Buddhists are much like those made by Christians in respect to Jesus. The relation of Buddha to Gautama is analogous to the relation of Christ to Jesus.

However, the role of Gautama in Buddhism is not identical with that of Jesus in Christianity. Although Buddhists recognize that Buddhism as a movement was initiated by Gautama, they stress that Gautama is but one of many who have attained Buddhahood. He is one among numerous manifestations of the Buddha principle or the Buddha-nature. The once-for-all uniqueness of Jesus is not asserted of Gautama.

Can, then, the universal claims made by Christians and Buddhists be reconciled? The universalist claims of Buddhism are that the Buddha-nature is present in all things and that the enlightenment attained by Gautama is the goal of all things.

This leaves open the possibility that Jesus might also have attained enlightenment. Hence, Buddhists can in principle embrace a figure like Jesus as another Buddha.

The universalist claims of Christianity are that the divine Logos is present in all things and that it is fully incarnate and redemptively effective in Jesus. This leaves open the possibility that Gautama might also have incarnated the Logos in a redemptive manner. Thus the Buddhist and the Christian each can approach the normative figure in the other tradition in an attitude of openness.

Nevertheless, this approach has limited value. What Buddhists have found in Gautama is not the same as what Christians have found in Jesus. Furthermore, the historical evidence confirms the actual differences between the two figures. If Gautama was the normative manifestation of the Buddha principle, Jesus was a poor representative of it. If Jesus is the incarnation of the Logos, Gautama's embodiment was inadequate. There appears to be a conflict between the Buddhist assertion that the ultimate reality in all things is the Buddha-nature and the Christian assertion that the ultimate reality is the Logos; for Buddha-nature and Logos differ.

Before this is accepted as a contradiction, more careful scrutiny is needed. The two terms, Buddha-nature and Logos, are fluid in their meanings and connotations, and neither can be defined exactly. Each has both an objective use to describe the reality man encounters and knows and a subjective use to describe man's inner being. The objective use of Buddha-nature suggests a flux, a substancelessness, an emptiness, a void, an absence of conceptual meaning. The subjective use suggests detachment, openness, release, quiescence, serenity, and silence. The objective use of Logos suggests order, agency, relevant novelty, creative transformation, and intelligibility. The subjective use suggests critical and creative reason, love, purpose, disciplined imagination, and authentic speaking. In spite of these differences, it is possible that both Buddha-nature and Logos characterize ultimate reality. For example, ultimate reality may be both flux and order, and this is recognized in East and West. In Buddhism the ideas of *dharma* and *karma* carry strong connotations of order characterizing the substanceless flux. In the West, already in Heraclitus, what is ordered by Logos is flux. Between some forms of Buddhism and some forms of Christianity, therefore, the respective affirmations of the ultimacy of Buddha-nature and of Logos need not be contradictory.

If this is so, the issues between Buddhism and Christianity are shifted to another plane, the specifically religious one. They have divergent understandings of salvation and, therefore, of the means of attaining it. For the Buddhist, salvation is the realization of the universal Buddha principle normatively embodied in Gautama. For the Christian, salvation is new life through faith in Christ. Here there is explicit conflict and apparent contradiction. Realization of the Buddha principle and new life through Christ differ.

Since the meaning of salvation diverges, the conflict is not a contradiction. By salvation the Buddhist means enlightenment, and enlightenment is associated with the detachment, openness, release, quiescence, serenity, and silence listed above as subjective expressions of the Buddha-nature. By salvation the Christian means Christian existence, a life in which freedom expresses itself in community in active love.

The contradiction disappears if we interpolate accordingly. Enlightenment is attained only through the realization of the universal Buddha principle normatively embodied in Gautama. Christian existence is attained only through faith in Christ. There is still room for discussion of the truth of these claims, but there is no contradiction between them. Buddhists may be correct about the enlightenment they prize, and Christians may be correct that Jesus is the source of the mode of existence they find normative. Indeed, it would be historically surprising if these claims were far from the mark!

Nevertheless, the real conflict between Buddhism and Christianity is not so easily overcome. The Buddhist believes that enlightenment is the fundamental answer to our deepest human need. The Christian believes that Christian existence is the fundamental answer to our deepest human need. They could reconcile their claims by agreeing that some people need one and some the other, but this would be a profound break with the universalistic character of both traditions. Alternately, they could regard enlightenment and Christian existence respectively as among the desirable attainments for all people, but this demotion of their respective goals to secondary status would be a still more drastic break with their traditions.

In *The Structure of Christian Existence*,[1] I concluded that Buddhism and Christianity had produced two structures of existence, each final in its own direction. Buddhism has broken the dominance of the self, or "I," in its continuity from the past and into the future. In doing so, it has freed people from defensiveness, anxiety, and self-concern. It has achieved a unique serenity and openness. Christianity, however, has heightened self-transcendence to the utmost. Christians objectify themselves and assume responsibility both for what they do and for what they are. Thus selfhood is intensified to the highest degree. This makes both possible and necessary the peculiar form of Christian love, *agapē*, as concern for the other in her or his otherness.

I was not able to see how these two radically different solutions of the ultimate human problem could be reconciled. Christianity and Buddhism each might respect the other from a distance and see that it was indeed successful and unsurpassable in its own terms, but this recognition would not lead to the appropriation by either of the attainments of the other, since these attainments were radically opposed. One could not simultaneously annihilate and intensify selfhood. Pluralism seemed to entail ultimate and irreconcilable differences and the irresolvable bifurcation of humanity. Hope's longing for unity seemed frustrated.

This conclusion is difficult for either a Christian or a Buddhist to accept. Both are concerned for the unity of humanity. Each views its basic image (i.e., Christ or Buddha) as universal in relevance. The fact that, despite the differences, each can be moved by the other's image offers hope for ultimate reconciliation.

In the mutually appreciative encounter of Christianity and Buddhism, each recognizes a lack within itself. The Buddhist recognizes as a limitation the lack of attention its adherents direct to the particularities of the world. Buddhism has failed to nourish scientific inquiry and social ethics. A Buddhist may be a scientist, and being a Buddhist may make one more disciplined and open to truth, but there is no inner connection between Buddhism and science. If science disappeared, there would be little impulse within Buddhism to renew it. Similarly, Buddhists who are in positions of social responsibility are given by their Buddhism the strength, poise, openness, and disinterestedness to carry out the responsibilities. But there is little impulsion within Buddhism to assume such responsibilities, and there has been little Buddhist reflection on the complex questions of power and justice.

Christians, however, are aware of the problems generated by the strong personal selfhood of their tradition. Anxiety, alienation, brittleness, pride, and self-seeking are too intense to be overcome by the love and community we affirm. The fading of the vivid sense of God's personal reality has left the self isolated and lonely. In contrast the serenity of the Buddhist appears as a needed release.

The fact that Buddhists and Christians can each recognize attractive features in the other's positions does not guarantee that their achievements are compatible. But it does suggest that each, in interaction with the other, may go through a further transformation. In now unforeseeable ways, this process may lead to a new whole in which the essential convictions and achievements of both are preserved. The Buddhist experiences the Buddha principle as manifest in Gautama as the essential spur to this further development. The Christian experiences the universal claim implicit in Christ as the impetus.

Although the manifold changes that might make for a Christianized Buddhism and a Buddhized Christianity cannot be predicted, an indication of what might be involved in some of them will give reality to the suggestion that such developments are possible. One change from within Buddhism will be suggested briefly first, and then a possible transformation of Christianity will be developed more fully.

Buddhist philosophy is multifaceted. In some of its forms it tends toward an extreme pluralism; in others, toward monism; in still others, toward nihilism.[2] But all these philosophies are united in their commitment to display the absence of substantial reality and value in the objects that ordinary experience invests with such reality and value. Buddhist pluralists analyze the objects of desire: possible possessions, other persons, the self. They show that all of these are composites of elements that are in a continuous flux of becoming. Fully recognizing this leads to nonattachment toward them, that is, to the readiness to let them go.

When reality is denied to the elements as well, then the result is either to view only the whole of things as having reality or to stress the emptiness or voidness of all things. Buddhists do not thereby deny, in every sense, the existence of things; but they insist that everything is empty of substance and, hence, of anything to which one might be legitimately attached. Here again the philosophical analysis serves the cause of nonattachment to particular entities.

In Mahayana Buddhism, when nonattachment is fully attained, those who are enlightened are concurrently filled with compassion. Being attached to nothing, they are compassionate toward all. They are aware of the distinctions within the flux, but they no longer discriminate among the forms or between themselves and others.

This is a beautiful ideal also from the Christian perspective. However, this universal compassion does not lead to the kinds of social engagement that the Christian takes for granted and that have become matters of pressing concern in the homelands of Buddhism as well. The reason is that the initial analysis through which nonattachment is fostered so denies the intrinsic value of particulars that discrimination among particulars as better and worse is undercut. The compassion that results is diffuse since concentration on relative evaluation of alternative courses of action requires an attention to particulars that has been negated.

These statements could be challenged. Indeed, it is difficult to make this point in language that is not misleading. A Buddhist landscape, for example, is profoundly attentive to the particular. However, the particular is valued as re-presenting all particulars, or the totality of things, rather than being valued in terms of its distinctiveness and unique value. Critical discussion of the relative values of different economic and political structures in particular times and places is not encouraged by this view of the particular.

However, not all Buddhist philosophy equally disparages interest in the particular. It is possible to deny substantiality to particulars while recognizing that, however ephemeral they may be, their particularity has its own value. It may be possible to do this in such a way that nonattachment is cultivated in the Buddhist sense. If so, then the compassion that follows from nonattachment can be directed toward particulars in their particularity in a way that allows for and even fosters reflection about the matters of social ethics that have heretofore been too much neglected in Buddhism.[3]

From within Christianity a quite different development will be required. It will involve a change both in the understanding of the self and in its actual formation.

Most Christian anthropology has been substantialist. Even when the word "substance" is not used, it is implied. The soul, person, or self is thought of as an entity that has its existence in itself. It is the subject of feelings and actions, but it is thought of not as constituted by those feelings and actions but as underlying them. In some modern formulations it is regarded as transcendental, that is, as standing outside the empirical and phenomenal spheres in such a way as to be fundamentally independent of them. In Kant's sense it is noumenal.

This view of the self has been challenged in the West, especially in recent times. Hume was unable to find such a substance underlying the flux of experience. The German idealist tradition reaffirmed an ultimate nonempirical agent, and this view was retained by Edmund Husserl, the founder of modern phenomenology. However, it was rejected by his pupils Martin Heidegger and Jean-Paul Sartre. Sartre wrote a book on *The Transcendence of the Ego*[4] to argue that the ego is an intentional object in experience rather than the underlying or transcendental agent-subject in experience. Thus existentialism has desubstantialized the self in a way that overcomes one of the features of Christianity that is most objectionable to Buddhism.

However, the existentialists have not gone far enough. Some of the objectionable characteristics of substance still linger in their characterization of selves. Heidegger depicts a single *Dasein* as remaining self-identical from birth to death. It lives in a world with other *Daseins,* but fundamentally it does not interact with them. Each *Dasein* is open to Being, and each includes its world. But the *Daseins* can only be pictured as having parallel routes.[5] Even the obvious tendency to be influenced by others is depicted as the enemy of authenticity, which is attained instead by fully recognizing that one must live out of one's own resources in terms of one's own project on the lonely road toward death. Living toward death takes on special significance because the fact that death must be endured absolutely alone frees one from the illusion that one can depend on others or that what others do or think has any real importance. This picture of the *Dasein* is the one that arises inevitably when persons are conceived as substances. Persons must be seen as mutually external, alongside each other, each remaining self-identical from creation to destruction.

Sartre shares this basic vision. He goes farther than Heidegger in his discussion of interpersonal relations, but his discussion does not alleviate the picture of mutual "overagainstness" that Heidegger offers. On the contrary, mutual relations are pictured as mutual threat and destruction. We objectify each other by the look. In *No Exit,* the protagonist sums up the climactic insight that arises from this analysis: "Hell is just—other people!" [6]

Heidegger and Sartre do not represent the Christian understanding of the self on this side of their thought. Christianity has always regarded persons as existing in community and community as constituted through mutual love. Even so, these existentialists have brought into clarity of focus certain tendencies implicit in the substantialist view of self, with which Christians have too often identified. Selves conceived as substances can act upon each other only externally, and there is an inherently negative element in being acted upon in this way.

The step beyond the existentialists that Christians must take is a fuller rejection of substantialist thought. Substances remain identical with themselves while their accidents or attributes change. Buddhists have stressed that there is no such self-identical substance enduring through time and especially that the self has no such status. Christians should agree. They should more fully appropriate the recent stress on a social self, that is, on a self that emerges out of the social matrix. The powerful experience of self-identity through time requires explanation, but it can be understood in terms of the special intimacy of relations that one moment of human experience has with its predecessors and successors and the tendency for the members of this series to embody similar patterns. It need not be explained by a numerical identity that strictly unites past, present, and future experiences.

Once the strict numerical identity of self from birth to death is given up, interpersonal relations can be understood in a different way. Real influence of one upon another becomes intelligible. This influence need not have the objectionable character involved when it is thought of as the action of one substance upon another. Instead, the influence can be understood as a contribution to the constitution of experience.

This allows also for the recognition that the amount and kind of unity that exists in one person or another can vary. Self-identity through time is a matter of degree and can be constituted in diverse ways. The structuring of existence has been encouraged by the Buddhist tradition in one way, and by the Christian tradition in another. A common conceptuality can show the real possibility of both structures of existence.

The Christian structure of existence has developed a strong self, capable of self-objectification and of acceptance of responsibility for itself. It has also encouraged a heightened awareness of self-identity through time. Perhaps, under the influence of Buddhism, this stress on self-identity through time, with its concomitant separation of personal selves from one another, can be modified in such a way that Christians can appropriate what they find most attractive in Buddhism.

Any modification of the self-other relation of Christian existence must take account of the existential grounds for the stress on self-identity through time. This stress has been intricately involved in the ethical dimension characteristic of the Jewish heritage of Christianity. Christian ethics requires that the person in the present moment accept full responsibility for past actions and commitments on the one side and be able to make trustworthy promises of future actions. The ideal of faithfulness assumes and encourages a heightened identity of self through time. Any tampering with the idea of self-identity appears to threaten this important Christian concern. Furthermore, the Christian teaching of love briefly adumbrated in Chapter 4 does not directly challenge the separateness and mutual externality of selves. It can be understood even when the selves are viewed as separate substances acting on one another from without.

Nevertheless, the thrust of the New Testament is to subordinate ethics to love rather than to view love as one ethical requirement among others. That we have not carried through this shift in our actual Christian existence is painfully apparent from Christian history. As we encounter the Buddhist critique of self, we now sense that our failure to subordinate ethics to

love may be the result of our continued cultivation of the
self-identity through time peculiarly appropriate to a primarily
ethical emphasis.

The change that would be involved in a primary emphasis on
love can be envisioned only if we follow Buddhism in the denial
of a substantial self. In a nonsubstance view the identity of the
self through time is a matter of degree determined by the
strength of the inheritance of feelings, pattern, and purpose
from moment to moment in one linear succession and the
relative weakness of inheritance from others. My sense of a
particular future as *my* future governs my identity with that
future now. I dread suffering in that future in a way that is
qualitatively different from my concern about the suffering that
someone else is likely to endure. Hence, my present action is
motivated much more strongly by the effort to ward off
suffering for myself than by the desire to prevent the suffering
of others. But the teaching that I should be just as concerned
about the neighbor as about myself challenges this discriminat-
ing attachment to a particular future. Insofar as I really become
concerned about the neighbor's future in the way I am concerned about my own, the neighbor's future would become my
future. The neighbor's future would no longer be so sharply
distinguished from the anticipated experiences associated with
my body.

When selves are thought of as substances with given self-
identity through time, the way in which one feels one's own past
is supposed to be entirely different from empathy. Empathy has
then to do with the relation of one person to another; it is an
external relation. But reflection on empathy tends to break
down this substantialist view. If one really has empathy for
another, then the feelings of the other penetrate one's being and
effectively share in constituting that being. The self that is
affected by the other internally, even in small measure, cannot
intelligibly be regarded as a substance.

When the substantialist view of self is rejected, it appears
that much of the identity of the self through time can be
understood by the peculiarly intense empathy that one has for a
particular set of past experiences, namely, those associated
with one's own body. The sense of identity with these past
experiences is so strong that it leads to notions of absolute
identity, which in turn lead to viewing all relations with others

as purely external. Real empathy with others, however, to whatever extent it occurs, belies the absoluteness of this distinction.

The ordinary situation is one in which a moment of human experience has intense empathy with (or inheritance from and conformation to) past experiences of the same person and very limited empathy with the past experiences of others. Empathy with the personal past remains stable. Empathy with others is fleeting. The degree of inheritance from the one set of past experiences is so much greater than that from the others that it is easy to conceptualize the two modes of relation as entirely different. Such conceptualization heightens the actual difference and inhibits empathy for others. The breakdown of such conceptualization can help to open experience to a greater degree of empathy toward others. Christian conceptualization has typically weakened empathy, but a call for empathy is present in the tradition. If the conceptualization is changed and the call is heightened, the result could be a lowering of the barriers that separate one self from another.

To transform an association of individualized persons into a more intricately interconnected community would not destroy the ideal of faithfulness, but it would alter it. The reason I can now commit my future self to act in certain ways is that I have considerable control over that self. I have much less control over others. This situation would not disappear in a community structured by love, but the emphasis would shift from "I" to "we." Where one experienced oneself as deriving much of one's being from others and contributing oneself to them, one would be less inclined to function as an individualized person in relation to both past and future commitments. Each person would be supported by others in the fulfillment of commitments made, and each would be inclined to make commitments only as others shared in them. The ideal of faithfulness would shift its primary focus from the lonely individual to the corporate community.

The Christian will sense another danger in this talk of subordinating ethics to love. Love as empathy and *agapē* is too easily imagined as binding together a community of like-minded persons in a warm and supportive intimacy that shuts others out. Primitive Christianity too often stressed love of the brethren at some expense to outsiders. Sensitivity training and human potential groups in our own time can too easily create ingrown and self-satisfied communities of mutual support.

But both Buddhist and Christian images warn against this persistent misconception of love. The Buddhist transcends all discrimination through enlightenment. Jesus exemplifies a love that shares the pain of the suffering and extends concern to those least able and least willing to reciprocate. The ultimate ideal must be a community of mutual love, and to whatever limited extent that is even now realizable, it is not to be disparaged. But, for the Christian, the way forward lies through love of the oppressed as well as of those who oppress us. This love can express itself adequately only as it plans, organizes, and acts. But even in this process it can be guided by an image of perfection of love, and it can attempt in fragmentary ways to realize that communion in the midst of pain and alienation. Clarification of the ideal of transcending individualism can help both to undergird sustained efforts for justice and to direct them. The diagrams on the facing page represent some features of the possibility that is envisioned.

Diagram 1 represents the general metaphysical situation as a flux of events or experiences. The symbol) at the center represents my experience as it is now coming into being. The diagram presents the total situation from my present perspective. I am affected by all the events that have taken place in my past, represented by capital O's to the left. In its turn, my present experience will affect all the events that lie to the right, that is, in the future, represented by small o's.

Diagram 2 indicates that, within the flux of events, forms of personal order obtain. My experience is a part of a sequence in which each inherits from a particular strand of past experiences in a dominant way, thus constituting me as a person and projecting my personal identity as the succession of b's. Other successions (A-a and C-c) constitute other persons. We are mutually external to one another. The successions O-o represent sequences of bodily and nonhuman events.

Diagram 3 indicates how perfect *agapē* would ideally modify the situation represented in Diagram 2. My present experience would be concerned for the futures of A and C in the same way as it is concerned for the future of B. This is indicated by representing all these future events as b. The diagram is misleading if it suggests that my present decision influences the

1

```
O O O O O O     o  o  o  o  o  o
O O O O O O     o  o  o  o  o  o
O O O O O O )   o  o  o  o  o  o
O O O O O O     o  o  o  o  o  o
O O O O O O     o  o  o  o  o  o
```

2

```
A A A A A A     a  a  a  a  a  a
O O O O O O     o  o  o  o  o  o
B B B B B B )   b  b  b  b  b  b
O O O O O O     o  o  o  o  o  o
C C C C C C     c  c  c  c  c  c
```

3

```
A A A A A A     b_a b_a b_a b_a b_a b_a
O O O O O O     o   o   o   o   o   o
B B B B B B )   b   b   b   b   b   b
O O O O O O     o   o   o   o   o   o
C C C C C C     b_c b_c b_c b_c b_c b_c
```

4

```
B_a B_a B_a B_a B_a B_a   b_a b_a b_a b_a b_a b_a
O  O  O  O  O  O          o   o   o   o   o   o
B  B  B  B  B  B )        b   b   b   b   b   b
O  O  O  O  O  O          o   o   o   o   o   o
B_c B_c B_c B_c B_c B_c   b_c b_c b_c b_c b_c b_c
```

character of the serial successors of A and C as much as those of B, or that the diversity of future events is reduced. Subscripts are used to indicate this continuing variety. The extension of the b's expresses only the kind of importance these events would have for my self-constitution. It represents with respect to the future what it would mean for me to love my neighbor as myself. Perfect love transforms the neighbor's future into a part of my future in anticipation of which I now constitute myself.

Diagram 4 illustrates the ideal consequences when perfect

empathy is added to perfect *agapē*. Instead of inheriting from one serially ordered set of past experiences as my own, feeling other aspects of the past as alien, I inherit from and partly conform to the feelings of others in a way that resembles my inheritance from and conformation to the succession of B's. This does not mean that the differences between the A's and B's and C's are reduced. The use of B's throughout represents only the similarity of the way in which I am related to all the events in this wider past.

Such diagrams have many limitations. They represent only my perspective. In Diagram 4, if the perspective of A-a were adopted, all the letters would be shown as A's and a's. This would not imply a change of character of the events; it would imply only that, from the perspective adopted, perfect empathy would open that experience to the entire past and perfect *agapē* would open it to the entire future. If all human experience attained this character, diversity would continue, but the separating sense of mine and yours based on the externality of personal selves represented in Diagram 2 would be transcended in a sense of ours. Whitehead described this condition as "Peace," which "is self-control at its widest—at the width where 'self' has been lost, and interest has been transferred to coordinations wider than personality." [7]

Another limitation of the diagram is that the O's used to buffer the persons from one another are represented as having no other function. In fact, they stand for events in the body and the environment of the body which also are causally efficacious and can be empathetically appropriated. Indeed, a heightened *agapē* for, and empathy with, the events in the body and the natural environment is particularly important in our time, but these diagrams are designed to highlight relations among human persons. Therefore, the O's are needed as buffers to indicate that, as long as we live in a bodily form, relations with others do not have the same immediacy as relations with our own past experiences. However much we live from and for others and thus reduce our isolation, estrangement, and "over-againstness" toward one another, we cannot expect our mutual separation to disappear. Diagram 4 is an ideal to be approached, but it cannot be fully attained.

The Buddhist ideal is sometimes formulated as the full realization of the situation represented in Diagram 1. The distinction between human experience and other events is minimized. The flux is to be recognized as flux. The events within it are all seen as instances of dependent co-origination, which pass on their contribution for good or ill to the whole of what comes afterward. In Mahayana Buddhism this reinforces the view that the fullest realization is the one that is for all rather than for the individual alone.

The Christian ideal represented in Diagram 4 differs from this, although not necessarily from actual Buddhist intentions. The difference can be made clear only if the self is distinguished from the person or psyche. The series of capital and lowercase B's in Diagram 2 represents the continuing person or individual psychic life. The momentary self is not represented in these diagrams. It is the "center" within each experience from which, or in terms of which, the past is selectively appropriated and the future anticipated. The symbol) in Diagram 2 is the center constituted by the reenactment of elements from the antecedent B's and by anticipation of subsequent b's in such a way that the distinction between self and person is of little importance. To develop in the direction of Diagrams 3 and 4, however, the self must become increasingly transcendent of this personal past and future in order to constitute itself in relation to the inclusive past and future. The limitations of personal individuality are overcome by strengthening selfhood, by differentiating the self from every other function in experience and action, and by the self accepting full responsibility for itself. Unless and until the self is strong and assured, it cannot expand from private self-identity to corporate inclusivism. The losing of the personal self through the widening of interests, of which Whitehead speaks, is possible only through the heightening of the momentary self.

Whereas this heightening and strengthening of selfhood appears to conflict with Buddhist teaching, the ideal represented in Diagram 4 closely approximates the Buddhist one in that the self grows out of the whole process through dependent co-origination. It does not perpetuate itself. The self in one moment of experience does not arise out of a single preceding self, as is characteristic of the Christian existence we know, but it arises out of the whole past, especially including other persons.

The difference between Buddhism and what is here proposed

as a Christian goal may be stated in another way. Buddhism
has negated the self and thus inhibited the development of
strong, isolated selfhood. The Christian goal is to go beyond
fully developed personal individualization. It is an expansion of
the self to include others. Yet the expansion does in fact
achieve a result highly analogous to that attained in Buddhist
enlightenment. Perhaps it might someday be recognized by
Buddhists as a fulfillment of their goal, a fulfillment which
nevertheless is free from limitations that have characterized
Buddhism in the past.[8]

That Christianity and Buddhism could each be so transformed by their internalization of each other as to move toward
a future unity is an image of hope in a time of fragmentation.
But many Christians perceive the postpersonal existence here
adumbrated as more disturbing than enticing. Our Western
ideals are bound up with personality and personal fulfillment,
and postpersonal existence is too easily heard as a return to
prepersonal existence. Soleri's vision of the city as organism
inspires this fear despite his expressed conviction that people
will find fulfillment rather than loss in the new levels of
interconnectedness. To allay this kind of fear, Teilhard spoke of
the preservation of the personal in the organic unity of the
Omega.

The encounter with Buddhism may prove an essential step
for the West to free itself from its attachment to individualized
personal existence as a final good. The West is prepared for this
encounter by its increasing recognition of the appalling price in
human misery and risk to human survival that has been paid for
our achievements in personal existence. We have become
disillusioned with the view that these problems can be solved by
appeals for justice and personal righteousness. We recognize
that radical changes are required. But we are frightened by the
prospects of change. Perhaps the encounter with the transpersonal existence of the Buddhist, the recognition of the serenity
and strength it embodies, the experience of Buddhist medita-
tion, and the study of Buddhist philosophy will give us the
courage to venture into that kind of radical love which can carry
us into a postpersonal form of Christian existence.

CHAPTER 14

The Kingdom of Heaven

In the two preceding chapters images of hope have been proposed that are realizable in this world without reference to any transcendence except that of the Logos itself. If there are in principle no obstacles to purely worldly hopes of this kind (except perhaps the difficulty of finding them attractive or believing they can be realized), the Christian task would be to criticize and refine the images that are offered and, as they are appropriated, to endeavor to realize them. But in fact there are obstacles to hope which arise at other levels and which must be addressed on their own terms. This chapter offers an analysis of what is required for hope and, following Whitehead, shows how his understanding of the world and its relation to the Kingdom of Heaven meets these requirements.

For historical hope to be sustained, three things are needed. First, there must be some conviction that the future is open, that human action can shape it to a significant extent. Second, there must be concern for the future of persons other than oneself, for a purely private hope is not historical. Third, a sense is needed of the possibility of being in or with a wider process tending to produce the desired results, for pure rebellion against the nature of things is not hope.

Jesus' teaching of the Kingdom of Heaven gave vividness and conviction to these three elements. The coming of the Kingdom called people to urgent decision and to the expression of that decision in action. The content of the Kingdom depended on this response to its coming. Far from being a private fulfillment, the Kingdom was a new community, a new world, and a new age. By positive response to the coming of the Kingdom, one entered the community that was being borne into the Kingdom by the Kingdom's own power.

William Beardslee shows that this pattern was present not only in Jesus' proclamation of the Kingdom but throughout early Christianity, for example in Paul, Mark, and Q (the sayings source used by Matthew and Luke to supplement Mark). In Mark, for example, the believer is called upon to participate vigorously in effecting the new reality that is expected. One is to be open to "the other's future through the route of loss of concern for one's own." [1] There is "an immense sense of the new presence of divine reality, which carries with it a likewise powerful sense that this divine reality is moving forward to its fulfillment." [2]

To keep these requirements for hope alive demands constant vigilance. The openness of the future must be defended against every form of determinism and fatalism. Concern for others must be defended against those who criticize this ideal as either impossible or harmful. And the existence of some process that favors positive historical developments must be shown against those who discern only the processes of decay and entropy, or only chaos and conflict, or only untrammeled power.

The discernment of the Logos as Christ and the account of human response thereto as critical and constructive reason satisfies these conditions. The Logos brings novel possibility that reopens the future at every moment. It calls for the expansion of horizons of concern and interest. By continually incarnating itself, the Logos constitutes a process that favors growth and historical advance. Thus, conceptually the requirements for hope are at the heart of this Christology.

Beardslee has also shown that belief in hope is not simply an abstract possibility: The patterns of hope are grounded in the basic biological and human phenomena of sex and creativeness.[3] All life is naturally oriented toward the future in hope, and this pattern of hope can be readily expanded into a historical hope that undergirds responsible social action.

While Beardslee's perceptive analysis provides grounds for hope that historical hope can survive, it does not justify complacency. Beardslee knows that there are other factors in the world that have in most cultures prevented the development of historical hope and that now in our culture undermine it. In the broad sweep of history we discover that hope, which has been so central to our culture, is a rare and fragile blossom requiring a very special soil and weather. The most important factors that threaten it are (1) the impermanence and ambiguity of all historical achievement and (2) death. This chapter treats the first of these threats. The threat of death to historical hope is the subject of the next chapter.

Even those who believe that the future is open, who have concerns beyond narrowly selfish ones, and who discern processes making for good, do not always find historical hope possible. One main obstacle is the ambiguity of all historical events. Part of the time we can ignore this ambiguity. Ordinarily when we see a chance to achieve a cherished historical goal—peace, prosperity, or justice—we do not ask after the further consequences of success. It is sufficient that the bombs will stop falling, children will cease to be hungry, or blacks or women will be treated equitably. But the wider question does not disappear. We realize that every historical achievement has consequences for evil as well as for good. The heroism and self-sacrifice sometimes present in war can be succeeded in peace by ennui and self-indulgence. Prosperity can hasten ecological collapse entailing far greater suffering than that which it eases. Those who achieve justice by great struggle for themselves become the harshest enemies of extending justice to others.

If we look for historical progress instead in the increase of knowledge, natural science, and technology, the ambiguity is even more forcefully borne in upon us. The knowledge explosion has led to fragmentation of thought, so that the wisdom for whose sake knowledge is sought has become rarer than ever. The success of science through its objectivizing methods and concepts has led to a vision of reality that alienates human beings from themselves and their world. The achievements of technology threaten the continuance of life on the planet while making the value of that life questionable, as people feel themselves more and more servants or victims of their own machines.

Even the visions of hope so hopefully presented in the preceding chapters fall victim in the end to this ambiguity. Viewed from our perspective as future possibilities, they may inspire us to act. But even now we can discern that in radically going beyond our present world, much of present value will be forever lost, just as in the move from hunting and gathering societies to agrarian, or from agrarian to urban, a high price was paid. We know also that every opportunity for great good is also an opportunity for great evil, that new advances in consciousness produce not only creative energy but also power that can be perversely used.

Furthermore, even if results are attained in which the good is felt clearly to outweigh the evil, they do not last. Attained values grow stale. The perpetuation of valuable states of affairs has diminishing value and becomes in the long run a negative value. Most valuable states cannot last long, but even in those that do the value disappears. The value is more in the achieving than in the achievement, yet if the achievement is not valuable, the achieving loses its value.

Reflection of these ambiguities in the larger course of history leads back finally to the recognition that they are rooted in time itself. In Whitehead's words, time is perpetual perishing. No sooner has any event occurred than it has gone. Its value lies in its immediacy of enjoyment, but that enjoyment is lost in the instant it is attained. Not only can one not cross the same river twice, but the one who considers crossing is not the same in the two instances. What is lost is not merely some experience of an enduring subject who survives. What is lost is the subject itself along with its experience. In such a world the extinction of craving or desire appears much more appropriate than the endless and fruitless effort to attain personal and historical goals.

Jesus' response to the problem of ambiguity was the Kingdom of Heaven. This response presupposed that the historical situation was not unambiguously evil, for it contained elements that would be carried into the new age. Further, God was seen as already present in the world even apart from what was soon coming. His past creative work was visible. He cared about the grass in the field and the fall of a sparrow. Existing structures of authority were recognized as having a legitimate place in the order of things. But the world was not unambiguously good. Not only did individuals commit evil acts, but the cumulative power of sin had distorted the creative work of God. There were powers of darkness that contested the field with God. The reasonable expectation of one who lived for the Kingdom was persecution from the world as well as joy in the new community.

But this ambiguity did not undermine the worthwhileness of effort. These efforts might have ambiguous consequences from a general point of view, but insofar as they were directed from and toward the coming Kingdom they had an unambiguous validity as well. To witness to the Kingdom by word or by the cup of cold water to the thirsty neighbor might lead to suffering for oneself and even for others, but it was not thereby rendered questionable in its value. All such acts belonged to the Kingdom already and would be fulfilled in it.

The problem now is that our relation to this rhetoric, and through it to the hope it expressed and confirmed, is broken. We do not anticipate an imminent coming of a new order or a new age in which the ambiguities of our world will be superseded. If historical hope is to be maintained in the face of ever-heightening awareness of historical ambiguity, a different conceptuality is required. Yet unless that conceptuality is somehow homologous with the New Testament one, it will not serve. If what is unambiguous is found disconnected with history, it will provide no hope in history. If it is found in history, as with religious nationalism, then that element of history is absolutized. From the point of view of the Christian, idolatry has been committed. If it is identified with the whole of history, then ethical judgment is withdrawn. Hope gives way to the affirmation of whatever is.

No one has wrestled more sensitively with the problem of establishing meaning in history than has Whitehead. His own doctrine of perpetual perishing, which was sketched above, drove him to the fullest awareness of how easily the sense of the worthwhileness of historical action, action that has to do with the particularities of things, is undercut. His recourse, like that of the New Testament, was to seek the answer in God.

Whitehead's thought of God centered in the Logos, which he called the Primordial Nature. The understanding of the Logos in this book has been governed by Whitehead's brilliant analysis. But when Whitehead confronted the ultimate evil of perpetual perishing as it undermines all sense of meaning and importance in worldly events, he looked for the answer not in the Logos but in God's Consequent Nature. He identified the latter with the Kingdom of Heaven.

Whitehead saw the problem as one of permanence and of a fluency that involves perpetual perishing. In our world the attainment of value and the renewal of zest require continuous fluency, whereas permanence applies to the lifeless and value-less forms, or "eternal objects." But there is no reason, he thinks, of any ultimate metaphysical generality, why this must be so. There could also be a permanence that is enriched by inclusion of novel immediacies.[4]

Whitehead does not introduce this permanence in an ad hoc way merely because it is not metaphysically impossible. Instead, it follows from the development of his understanding of God. God for him is first the Logos, the principle of the relevance to the process of the forms of definiteness which make actuality possible. But Whitehead believes that all effective things are actual, and all actual things receive from as well as act upon others. To become is to synthesize other entities and to contribute oneself for synthesis by others. God is not an exception to this principle. He not only functions in the becoming of other entities but also is constituted as a synthesis of their contributions. The divine feelings of the world are woven upon the Logos, which is the primordial envisagement of all possibilities. In this inclusion of the world in God, the world is completed and becomes everlasting.

God's reception of these creaturely events in the Kingdom of Heaven is not merely passive any more than is the reception of the past in other actual entities. They are synthesized into a new whole. But whereas in the world the synthesis depends on extreme selectivity, so that most of what is offered is rejected, such limitation is not present in the Kingdom. God's aim is so inclusive that he can receive and synthesize into good what in worldly occasions would be mutually destructive elements, or elements incompatible with their limited aims. Even experiences whose intentions are evil or whose consequences in the world are destructive can be taken up into the Kingdom as contributions to its everlasting and growing harmony.

This does not mean that all human actions contribute equally to the Kingdom. They differ in their contribution according to their intrinsic value, their richness, or their own immediacy.

They differ also indirectly according to the possibilities for future occasions that they contribute or eliminate. The fact that God can find some value in whatever occurs and can give to it some place in the growing harmony does not reduce the importance of what is contributed to him. It increases it. How I act matters not only for the brief moment of the occurrence and the somewhat longer period of its discernible effects in the environment. It matters also and primarily because forever-more it alters the quality of the harmony that is the Kingdom of Heaven, contributing more or less according to my free decision.

Whitehead's doctrine of the Kingdom of Heaven is obviously different from that of the New Testament, but it is remarkably homologous. In both instances we live in an ambiguous world, but in that world we can make our decisions either exclusively in the light of foreseeable consequences in the world, where everything is ambiguous, or in terms of an unambiguous good. This good in both instances is assured. In the New Testament the Kingdom of Heaven will come, no matter what we do. For Whitehead it will preserve and redeem our actions, no matter what they are. But in both cases the content of the unambig-uous good is dependent on our free decisions. Who participates in the Kingdom proclaimed by Jesus, and how, depends on present decision. What values will be contributed to the Kingdom, for Whitehead, depends upon us. In both cases there is a relationship of continuity and completion between what will be and what is, rather than one of discontinuous reward or punishment. For Jesus one prepares for the coming age by living from it now. The Kingdom of Heaven for Whitehead redeems just that action which we now perform in whatever way that action allows.

In both cases the primary implications of the expectation are to reinforce and undergird as important those actions which would also appear as good from more general considerations. The ethics of the New Testament is an extreme one, but it does not ordinarily violate the intuitions of those whose ethical sensitivity derives from worldly considerations alone. It carries some of their ethical principles farther than they would allow, and, especially, it subordinates self-interest to other concerns to a greater degree than can elsewhere be found. But the conse-quences of its practice are generally recognized as good even from a purely worldly point of view. Similarly, the awareness that what we do contributes to the Kingdom in Whitehead's sense heightens the value and importance of doing what, in general, we would recognize in any case to be beneficial. It is not an awareness from which we would derive eccentric principles of right and wrong. But it does encourage a more intense consideration of the wider consequences of our actions for others, since these too will everlastingly matter. In this respect it can lead to something of the New Testament's extremeness. Indeed, it presupposes that we are capable of finding our greatest satisfaction in the assurance that we contribute beyond ourselves, utlimately to the Kingdom itself.

Finally, both the New Testament doctrine and Whitehead's doctrine lead to an emphasis upon the inner condition of the person that a purely worldly ethic usually lacks. The new age expected in the New Testament requires an inner purity and wholeness as much as an outer and social virtue. In the Christian tradition, why we act as we do has been as important as the act itself. Similarly, what we contribute to the Kingdom in Whitehead's vision is not what is publicly visible but rather our states of immediate feeling, anticipation, and decision. The way we constitute those states and the influence we have on those states in others is, therefore, the primary matter. The external appearances are secondary.

Some images of the Kingdom of Heaven have been bound up with specific sociopolitical programs. This is true of neither that of Jesus nor that of Whitehead. Indeed, the sense of history in both Jesus and Whitehead prevents any such identification. For Jesus, history must be transformed by the Kingdom in order that justice will reign. From Whitehead's process perspective, the requirements of different times and places vary, and all need the undergirding of the Kingdom. But Jesus' vision of the Kingdom has inspired reforms and revolutions throughout Christian history, and Whitehead was by no means indifferent to the particular demands of our socioeconomic and political situation. Belief in the Kingdom relativizes all specific images of historical hope, but it undergirds the importance of forming appropriate and relevant images and acting upon them. For both, the vision of the Kingdom brings the present injustice and misery of society to vivid light and supports the claims of the weak and powerless.

In these ways the meaning for historical hope of the two concepts is similar. Both find the unambiguous good that sustains hope in the face of historical ambiguity to be beyond history but confirmatory of the worth of effort within history to realize what can there be realized. They both ensure the meaning of historical action by grounding that meaning outside of history.

Despite his occasional use of Christian language, such as the Kingdom of Heaven, Whitehead did not regard himself as a theologian or even, necessarily, as a Christian. Indeed, at times he spoke harshly of both theology and the church. Still it is far from artificial to claim him, too, in his envisioning of hope, as a servant of Christ.

Whitehead knew he followed "the lure for feeling, the eternal urge of desire," [5] which he called the Primordial Nature of God, and which in this book is called the Logos. He understood his own thought to be a creative transformation of the philosophical tradition, which in turn should be creatively transformed in the ongoing history of thought. In this sense there is no question but that Whitehead in his most imaginative thought serves—and intends to serve—the process of creative transformation, which we recognize to be Christ. Furthermore, Whitehead himself recognizes that his conceptuality is in fundamental respects a twentieth-century enfleshment of the vision of Jesus. That vision, like Whitehead's, "dwells upon the tender elements of the world, which slowly and in quietness operate by love; and it finds purpose in the immediacy of a kingdom not of this world." [6] No other recent philosopher has embodied so fully the effect of the encounter with Jesus. The Christian is not wrong in claiming Whitehead's image of hope for Christ.

CHAPTER 15

The Resurrection of the Dead

In the preceding chapter the Kingdom of Heaven was offered in Whiteheadian form as the response to the threat of imperma- nence and ambiguity. The other great New Testament image is resurrection as the answer to the question posed by death, the last and most powerful enemy of hope.

The death that is in view is not simply or even primarily one's own. This is a serious issue, indeed, but historical hope can be sustained regardless of one's personal end. The problem for hope is rather the death of others and finally the death of all, the planetary death that must come eventually and that threatens imminently. Can historical occurrence have meaning in the face of that death? Even the belief that each momentary event is preserved in its immediacy does not fully answer this question. When death is not intensely considered, as is sometimes the case among youth, historical hope can flourish. But when death insists upon attention, the response profoundly affects the possibility of historical hope. How people understand what happens at death deeply influences how they understand what is important in life.

Four general views are representative: merging with undif- ferentiated being, metempsychosis (the transmigration of souls), extinction, and renewed personal existence beyond death. Neither the pantheistic idea of merging into the all nor metempsychosis has been associated with strong historical interest. The former tends to disparage concern for differen- tiated particulars and distinctions of better and worse in favor of a vision of being to which they are secondary.[1] It minimizes the openness of the future and sees no directional movement with which one can identify. The latter is usually associated with a static view of nature and society from which the individual gradually works for release through long eons of time. Adaptation of one of these views to a historical vision may be possible,[2] but if we seek a way of conceiving death that can support such a vision, we will do better to consider the other two.

For modern, secular people, the new common sense is that death is quite simply the end; that death is extinction. The body merges into the earth as it decays, but it is no longer common to recognize any psyche that could merge with being much less one that could migrate to another body or be awakened in resurrection. Furthermore, it is widely held that just this view of death is the one most supportive of historical meaning. It forces all attention and energy to be directed to the here and now and removes every excuse for present injustice in terms of future or otherworldly remedies.

The understanding of death as extinction can function in this way especially for those who have absorbed basic Judeo-Christian-humanistic values before undertaking to root out of themselves every vestige of anticipation of personal completion or existence beyond death. But when values are derived instead from this view of death itself, the precariousness of the historical orientation again becomes clear. If historical existence is known to have no wider context, historical movements themselves can become ultimate and, in the name of such movements, acts of appalling ruthlessness can be justified. Furthermore, living toward extinction can lead to a heightened individualism in which concern for others and for ongoing processes of history beyond one's death is diminished or undercut. Again, when we view others without qualification as what they are from birth to death, the sense of their immeasurable intrinsic worth, inculcated by Judaism, Christianity, and post-Christian humanism, is left without grounds. In a time when the greatest global problem has become excessive human population, this loss of the sense of individual worth, independent of social usefulness, can have frightening consequences. Finally, when one knows oneself to be just that which one is in the process toward death, the dimension of mind and spirit through which meaning, order, and morality are sought often appears incongruous or absurd. The reality appears to be biological life and death, and all else, including all history, is seen as an excrescence. Insofar as the claim to strengthen and purify the orientation to history has been the basis of the present dominance of the view of death as extinction, a fraud has been perpetrated upon us. It was not such a view that produced the requisite historical hope, and although it can accompany such hope, its own inner tendency does not support it.

The now precarious victory of historical hope in the West was associated with Christ as the risen one. Resurrection meant that men and women had a more than historical destiny that gave meaning to the historical one. Our question is whether resurrection in this sense can function in our time to ground historical hope. Beliefs about resurrection long antedated Jesus, and occasionally such beliefs are still found independently of his influence. But today, apart from the resurrection of Jesus, there is little power in this expectation.

Christ as the risen Jesus is understood in a number of ways. Sometimes it is held that Jesus rose into the spirit, so that Christ becomes faith and word. Bultmann taught that Jesus rose into the kerygma, so that Christ is identical with proclamation. Sometimes these views are read back into the New Testament as the deeper meaning of the texts, but other scholars insist that the Christ into whom Jesus rose has a more personal continuity with him than any of these theories allow.[3] In this view these theories testify to the unwillingness or inability of modern scholars to grapple with what the early Christians understood by the resurrection.

To gain perspective on this question of who the resurrected Christ was understood to be in early Christianity and how we should today come to terms with the resurrection, we will consider a debate in recent scholarship. The two major critical approaches are those of the post-Bultmannians on the one hand and the Pannenberg circle on the other. Willi Marxsen published a book *The Resurrection of Jesus of Nazareth*,[4] in which he ably presents the position of the post-Bultmannians. Ulrich Wilckens, the leading New Testament scholar of the Pannenberg circle, dealt at some length with Jesus' resurrection in *God's Revelation*.[5] Juxtaposition of their arguments will clarify the issues with which any attempt to ground historical hope in Christ must deal.

Marxsen makes a sharp distinction between the fundamental meaning or intent of a statement and the conceptuality in which it is couched. This distinction expresses the existentialist judgment that life, decision, or existence is prior and primary and that opinions about facts or philosophical ideas are secondary. Marxsen believes that in calling for decision or evoking faith a wide variety of opinions and conceptualities can be affirmed. For the Christian the evocation of faith is important, whereas the beliefs that may be associated with it are not.

Marxsen amasses considerable evidence that in the New Testament no consistent conceptuality was employed in the Christian proclamation about Jesus. One could speak of God revealing his son, of Jesus appearing, of seeing Jesus, or of Jesus' exaltation. All these ideas functioned to affirm faith in Jesus, but we cannot reconstruct the factual events on which they are based. The critical effort to do so leads back to the fact that Peter was the first to believe and that Paul had a somewhat independent experience. Both understood their experiences as being elicited by something outside themselves rather than as purely subjective decisions. We cannot get behind that understanding to just what their experiences were like. *A fortiori* we cannot argue from these experiences of the living Jesus to a resurrection as a supposed preceding event.

Marxsen does not deny that the tradition of a resurrection of Jesus was among the early Christian traditions and came to dominance among them. He does not question that the Gospel writers and Paul believed various versions of this tradition to be factually true. His point is that this was simply their interpretation of facts which we are free to interpret otherwise today. Information about these facts was not their major interest. We can share their fundamental concern, their faith, without committing ourselves to any one theory as to the events.

Indeed, faith in its distinctively Christian form is said to be better served by absence of factual demonstration of Jesus' resurrection. Marxsen writes: "If we believed the *witnesses* of the event which was Jesus' challenge, it would then be a counsel of wisdom for us as well. It would be hard enough to put it into practice in our lives; but we should be (merely) stupid if we did not do so. If we believed the witnesses of the event forming

Jesus' legitimation, this belief would not be succeeded in our lives by a *second and different* faith (a trusting commitment to Jesus' challenge). Jesus' challenge would then, indeed, still remain a challenge; but only because it is so difficult in this world to practice what he demanded. If we meet the challenge, it is not because we are making a venture but because Jesus is legitimated and we must therefore fulfill his demand." [6]

Hence, according to Marxsen, there is no need or even desirability that Christians today affirm the resurrection of Jesus. We can continue to share in the primitive affirmation that "Jesus is risen." But we can equally well use other language, such as "the cause of Jesus continues." [7] What happened after the crucifixion was that "God endorsed Jesus *as the person that he was*: during his earthly lifetime Jesus pronounced the forgiveness of sins to men in the name of God. He demanded that they commit their lives entirely to God, that they should really take no thought for the morrow. He demanded of them that they should put themselves entirely at the service of their neighbour. He demanded of them that they risk their lives—and that meant giving up any attempt to assert themselves. He demanded of them that they work for peace even where it was dangerous, humanly speaking, because it could mean relinquishing one's own rights. And he promised people that in fulfilling this demand they would find true life, life with God." [8]

To those who object that Christian faith has to do with assurance of salvation beyond this life Marxsen replies that no concept of such salvation is required. There is no conceptual consistency in the New Testament. The idea of the resurrection of the dead employed by Paul is simply part of his general philosophy rather than expressive of his Christian faith. The faith to which the Christian is called involves an attitude of hope and confidence in God, but it does not require any concept of what will happen after death.

The problem with this is that decisions and modes of existence are not ιs independent of conceptualities and opinions about facts as Marxsen's formulation implies and presupposes. He asserts that "whatever conclusions we may arrive at in the course of these lectures about the resurrection, they must on no account be based on the touchstone of our experience or of present-day scientific knowledge." [9] Yet in fact his radical

separation of faith from opinions and concepts is unquestionably drawn from modern philosophy, if not from Marxsen's own
experience or understanding of the implications of science. It
cannot be otherwise. Historians cannot separate themselves
from their own ideas about the nature of events when they
reconstruct the past. But just for that reason their ideas must
be subjected to critical scrutiny. Historians must not simply
assume them, as Marxsen tends to do. Unless Marxsen would
claim that the sharp distinction between unimportant fact and
all-important meaning or response is itself the view of the early
Christian tradition, he must acknowledge that he imports it
from our very different age.

It is noteworthy that those who most vigorously deny that
fact and significance can be separated in the understanding of
New Testament writers are those who reject this separation in
the modern experience as well. The argument has been pursued
with special vigor by Pannenberg. For him meanings are
ingredient in facts, and facts are ingredient in meanings.
Among New Testament scholars Ulrich Wilckens has worked
out the implications of this conviction most fully.

Whereas Marxsen indicates that a factual belief about Jesus'
resurrection was not essential to early Christianity, Wilckens
holds that apart from belief that Jesus rose there would have
been no Christianity. "Jesus expressly replaced the authority of
the law of Moses by the authority of his own word." [10] His
claim was that the truth of his message would be vindicated by
the arrival of the Kingdom. His death on the cross appeared to
shatter his claim. "For *Jewish* thinking and Jewish faith the
question of the truth of Jesus' claim would have been decided
negatively for ever if nothing else had happened." [11]

This implies that some Jews did believe that something else
had happened. This "something" could not be the rise of faith
as such or the continuation of the cause. It had to be an event
that vindicated Jesus' claim and thus warranted faith in that
claim, as well as the activity of continuing the cause. "It follows
that at no place of the New Testament story is historical
research so legitimate and necessary—in the interest of the
New Testament itself—as here in regard to the events after the
death of Jesus. . . . Whatever the power of the early christian
preaching of the resurrection, and however convincing the faith
of the first christians—we would still be betraying the message

of Jesus at its very heart if we were to rest theologically satisfied with the mere effects of the resurrection—if we were to argue along the lines that the risen Jesus could prove himself to be risen only by imparting to men, in a wonderful and powerful way, when and where he desired, the language to proclaim him and the experience of believing in him." [12]

Wilckens then proceeds to summarize his own conclusions, based on taking Paul's account in I Cor., ch. 15, as the clue, as follows: "We know only from Paul himself, who names himself here as the last witness (1 Cor. 15:8) what he thought of the 'vision' that he had experienced. As in Judaism, he was often granted, in the manner of a definite tradition of visions of God, a single short insight into the hidden upper region of the approaching eschatological events, and in this context—i.e., not somewhere on earth but in heaven, not in the immediate present but in the future of the last times—he saw Jesus as him whom God had raised and led into eternal life (Gal. 1:15). We may assume that the other witnesses named, Jews as they were, experienced and interpreted what happened to them, the 'appearance' of the resurrected Jesus, in a similar manner." [13]

Wilckens recognizes that the New Testament tells nothing of the resurrection as such, and he has no more interest than Marxsen in reconstructing the event. He believes that the stories of the empty tomb represent an independent and reliable tradition, but he does not insist on this or use it as a basis for grounding faith in the resurrection.[14] Hence, it might seem that the difference between the two New Testament scholars is not, after all, so great. Both believe something happened. Both believe that what happened was a vindication of Jesus by God. Neither thinks that the event narrowly called the resurrection can be known. The kind of vision affirmed by Wilckens is by no means excluded by Marxsen. Marxsen raises many skeptical questions about the tradition of the number of distinct appearances, which Wilckens assumes to be reliable, but nothing substantially hinges on this.[15] Wilckens' view that "the consequences of Jesus' resurrection are that in which its truth displays itself," [16] and that these consequences are the forward movement of the church, is not far from Marxsen's interpretation of resurrection as meaning that the cause of Jesus continues.

Nevertheless, there is a real and profound difference.[17] This difference arises from opposing judgments as to what was the message of Jesus that was vindicated by God. For Marxsen this message was a call to discipleship whose validity is unaffected by opinions as to facts. For Wilckens it was the Kingdom of God as an event. According to him, one misunderstands the "commandments of Jesus if one takes them simply as 'ethics,' distinct from their essential place in his preaching of the kingdom. . . . The humanity of the commandments . . . is true only where it is based on the truth of the kingdom of God; and it has meaning only for him who is able to recognise the significance of the love of one's neighbour in the love of God, which is powerful enough to give the whole destiny of the world its meaning. . . . Only if it is true—and will show itself in reality as true—that love has the last word, can it be meaningful for me, the individual man, and therefore totally persuasive and committing for me to offer my life without stint for love, as Jesus demanded. Brotherly love in his sense is not altruism or self-sacrifice; but it receives its power and its courage for full self-commitment from the sure trust that God will lead the lover to his perfection in salvation." [18]

Thus in Wilckens' view the effect of the message of Jesus in his own time depended on the confirmation that love would have the last word in the coming Kingdom of God. That belief could be vindicated only if Jesus' death was not the end. The vision of Jesus as the center of God's eschatological reality vindicated the claim of Jesus to be announcing that reality. Thereby the life for which he called was grounded.

The last quotation from Wilckens shows that his interpretation of the early Christian situation is closely connected with his general interpretation of the human situation. Whereas Marxsen experiences the demand of Jesus as a possibility for decision independent of what one may believe about the past or the future, Wilckens finds Jesus' call arbitrary or unfounded apart from the promise with which it was originally associated. It is because of what God will do that we are called to be what Jesus' message requires. Our expectation of what will happen in the end profoundly determines what is appropriate for us now.

Thus the deeper difference between Marxsen and Wilckens— as they express respectively the sensibility of existential theology and of theology of hope—is the structure of the relation of present and future. Both are concerned with both, but for

Marxsen hope is grounded in present experience. Faith as venturesome response to the challenge of Jesus' message produces hope as the assurance that God will keep us "safe." [19] For Wilckens, only assurance that love rules the future can provide the context of response to Jesus' challenge. Hence, we can live as Christians now only on the basis of what Marxsen dismisses as facts and concepts about what has happened and what will happen.

Expressed in other terms, Marxsen affirms a realized eschatology whereas Wilckens sees the eschaton as future. That means for Marxsen that if we speak of resurrection at all, we should identify it with victorious faith that is self-vindicating. For Wilckens, resurrection is the metaphor in which the future fulfillment of the believer is best grasped. Faith as present experience does not vindicate itself.

It is ironic but understandable that the scholar who disparages the resurrection is the advocate of an ungrounded faith, and the scholar who affirms its reality and importance appeals to reason. It is ironic because until recently faith was associated with acceptance as true of the whole structure of Biblical and traditional affirmations. It is understandable because the appeal to faith has now become a way whereby all questions of fact or theory are set aside as ultimately unimportant. Faith as a mode of being is held to be a possibility wherever Jesus' message (or the message about him) is proclaimed, independent of the opinions, convictions, or ideas of the hearers. It arises by decision or an "act of God." Ordinary psychological, sociological, and historical explanations of faith are held to be finally irrelevant. Hence, faith is not threatened by even the most rigid reductionism.

Wilckens and the other members of the Pannenberg circle share the perspective of this book in rejecting this kind of faith. They are interested in an attitude of trust, but trust arises in relation to definite opinions and convictions, especially about the future, and is threatened by others The relation between opinions and attitudes is an intelligible one, explicable in fully rational terms, although not excluding an element of decision. Hence, the effects upon attitudes of the picture of past, present, and future generated by reductionism must be seriously considered before that picture is accepted. Anyone concerned for human values will seek alternatives. This search leads to the reconsideration of the tradition that produced and sustained these values, and for Pannenberg and his associates it leads especially to the resurrection of Jesus as the central event in Christian history. The critical appropriation of this tradition, apart from any leap of faith, requires a rich speculative critique and the rejection of many features of contemporary common sense as shaped especially by reductionism.

In relation to the specific problem of historical hope, for Marxsen there is no question of seeking in Christ its grounds. Hope is grounded in faith, which has and needs no grounds. The relation of Christian beliefs to cultural phenomena such as historical hope does not come into consideration. The believer has hope, since hope belongs to the structure of faith. Whether historical hope as a cultural phenomenon waxes or wanes is irrelevant to faith. Hence, for Marxsen, any attempt to ground historical hope in particular facts of the past or particular expectations about the future is perverse. It displays a lack of the faith that is the only significant ground of hope.

For Marxsen, therefore, as for the post-Bultmannians generally, the New Testament doctrine of the resurrection of the dead appears as a problem for demythologizing. It does not call for investigation into the historical events occasioning it. Because he knows the concept of resurrection is so bound up with notions of an objective event, Marxsen almost rejects it rather than reinterpret it. However, one could say that for Marxsen, Jesus rises into the ongoing of his cause. Hope is neither justified nor explained thereby. One who in despair asks for grounds of hope is told to have faith. One is not shown hope-supporting aspects of history.

When this kind of faith is rejected, this response to the problem of a cultural hopelessness that dooms the Christian vision of reality and the Christian structure of existence is not possible. In the face of universal death, either the structure of hope must be reduced to triviality and become irrelevant to history, or the conviction must arise that in Christ this sting of death has been removed, that expectancy and anticipation can be renewed even in the face of death.

For Pannenberg and others like him this is *the* issue. He knows that there can be no simple appeal to the supposed fact of Jesus' resurrection to prove anything about the destiny of the world or of believers. The experiences of Peter and Paul cannot

be taken in isolation from their whole tradition. These could
have been experiences of the risen Lord only where some such
idea of rising already existed. We too can believe that Jesus
rose from the dead only if we find ourselves in a viable
contemporary tradition in which such a notion makes sense.
Jesus' appearances assured the disciples of the coming of the
new age only because they stood in a tradition in which the idea
of that new age was already present. Similarly, Jesus' resurrection can be relevant to us only if we are genuinely open to the
idea that we, too, might be resurrected. If we can understand
our own "resurrection" only as the present triumph of faith over
doubt, then, as Marxsen shows, the only relevant resurrection
of Jesus took place during his earthly life.

Pannenberg has devoted much of his remarkable erudition
and intellectual power to reversing this dominant modern
situation, which is represented by Marxsen. He has argued that
the contemporary social sciences implicitly display human
beings as oriented to the future in an unlimited and therefore
all-inclusive, or final, sense. He has argued philosophically that
since event and meaning cannot be separated, the reality of
every event lies in its consequences, and, hence, nothing is
definite until the end. He has argued anthropologically that all
life is lived by anticipation and that in principle this anticipation
is directed toward a final outcome.[20] And, finally, he has
stressed that the modern understanding of the unity of the body
and soul precludes the interpretation of this outcome in non-
physical terms. He shows that our situation is in this way
analogous to the Jewish one of Jesus' day and that for us also
the question of destiny can best be discussed by use of the
metaphor "resurrection." Thus the idea of resurrection, Jesus'
and ours, is highly relevant.

The question of what is relevant is not identical with that of
what is credible. Even if historians found the resurrection
stories relevant, few would believe them to be true. Not only
does the dominant world view fail to ask consciously the
questions to which Jesus' resurrection might be relevant, but
also it excludes the occurrence of the resurrection from the
sphere of possibility.

Against the dominant tendency of historians to deny the
possibility of resurrections, Pannenberg has argued that the
principle of analogy must not be used so as to deny the oc-

currence of novel and unique events. Furthermore, he has shown that modern research in parapsychology indicates a range of possibilities which have previously been dismissed by most historians. He has then shown that when historians approach the New Testament with an open mind, the use of critical methods vindicates the reliability of the traditions of the resurrection appearances.[21]

In the next chapter we will consider more critically the strengths and remaining difficulties with Pannenberg's position. For the present we can note that he helped to recover for theology the belief that Jesus' resurrection from the dead provides grounds for the needed hope for fulfilled personal existence beyond this life. In Pannenberg's own thought, the image of that fulfilled existence is changing and developing, but it is consistently an image of hope grounded in a comprehensive vision of history centering in the resurrection of Jesus.

CHAPTER 16

The Unity of Hope

In the four preceding chapters hope has been approached in four ways. Soleri offers us a vision of the plumbing for the City of God, that is, of the physical context within which a hopeful future can be lived. I have proposed that through inward encounter with Buddhism, Christian existence may transcend its individualism toward a community of perfect love. These are images of what might happen in the ongoing course of history. Whitehead offers a way of understanding the Kingdom of Heaven as the transcendent answer to the inevitable victory of perpetual perishing in the world. Pannenberg reaffirms the Biblical doctrine of resurrection as the answer to the question of death.

Placing these four images side by side can provide a place for theology to begin its more difficult work. Considering the first two together as forms of historical hope, each of the three types of approaches is felt by those who are most fully involved as adequate in itself. Those who live by effective images of fulfillment in history are often unshaken by either ambiguity or death. Those who are convinced that in the Kingdom of Heaven all that we are is transformed into everlastingness find that they can live without images of hope in history and in indifference to resurrection after death. Those who are assured of consummation in a final resurrection of the dead can sometimes accept the lack of images of hope in history with equanimity and are unmoved by the transiency and ambiguity of life.

This is to say that each of the answers to the need for hope understands itself as a complete and adequate answer. Within each answer the symbols of the others can receive a full and satisfactory interpretation. For example, there is no difficulty, when hope in history is alive, to employ the images of resurrection and Kingdom. The structure of experience with Christ which is bound up with hope in history is that of dying and rising. Each moment, as soon as it has realized itself, perishes or dies. The new moment truly lives only as it finds some novel possibility that is its own, appropriate to its unique situation, and worthy of realization in its own right. Living from our past instead is not a real option. If we seek life by clinging to past realizations, we do not live at all. It is only a question of the pace of death. The one who holds to the past and repeats it does not enliven the past but only joins it in death. However, the one who turns from the past in openness to the new finds the past restored and vitalized. The new possibility allows for the appropriation of the past in its continuing immediacy whereas the attempt to hold on to it or to repeat it does not. It is when we think new thoughts that our past thinking remains a vital contributing element, not when we endlessly repeat ourselves or try to defend what we thought in the past. Thus it is by dying that we live; only through accepting death do we experience resurrection.

Even clearer is the possibility of speaking of the Kingdom as the possible future world that is envisioned and which, through the envisionment, is already effectively present. Soleri himself speaks of the new community that his arcologies would make possible as the "City of God." The image of the Kingdom lies immediately at hand.

Similarly, advocates of the transcendent grounding of historical meaning likewise have no difficulty assimilating particular historical hopes when they wish to do so. Furthermore, advocates of the Kingdom image can assimilate the image of resurrection, and the reverse is equally true. The former understand that our experiences perish continually in the world only to rise immediately to fulfillment in the Kingdom. The latter understand that the final resurrection of the dead constitutes the realization of the Kingdom.

When these chapters on hope are presented successively, as if they were supplementary, a certain distortion is introduced. As they function in the present scene, they are in competition, each often sharply critical of the illusions of the others. It may be objected that instead of presenting all, my theological responsibility was to choose one and to make clear its Christian adequacy and appropriateness. It may be charged that the Christian images of historical and suprahistorical hope belong together and should not be divided into four types as has been done above.

The response could be that in our despairing age it is better to breathe what life we can into several images than to worry about their mutual coherence. Also, through much of Christian history, images of the Kingdom of Heaven, the immortality of the soul, and the resurrection of the body have lived together with their tensions unresolved. But these answers do not suffice. A multiplicity of unresolved images tends to reduce the persuasiveness of all. Indeed, none of these images is persuasive to the modern mind, which has learned to live with much more limited hopes or with no hope at all. Having abandoned the illusions of its past hopes, it does not even hope for hope. Indeed, the proposal of hope is troubling; for it would call forth energies that have been quiescent and would give seriousness to purposes that have been relativized and ridiculed. Christian faith is more acceptable when it describes the past and analyzes the present than when it projects images of hope into the future.

Still, to abandon the struggle for hope is not an option for the Christian. It is faithless to Christ and produces a situation in which his call is silenced. If we cannot hope, we must at least hope for hope. That means we must continue to work for images of hope that convince us—if not the modern mind.

In addition, in the 1960's we saw the surfacing of a post-modern mind for which new forms of hope are of crucial importance. This mind rejects Christianity not so much because it offers incredible images of hope as because its spokesmen do little more than mirror the barrenness of the modern mind. The post-modern mind finds far more attractive the bold affirmations of the tradition than the carefully qualified ones characteristic of our day. It sometimes finds power in Christian words to generate new images for its own use, but it expects little help from the church. Christians can share in shaping this post-modern mind only if we live more deeply into our images and dare to offer them seriously in the public marketplace.

The one option that remains, therefore, is to work with and

through the existing images of hope, hoping that, ultimately through the creative transformation of each, they will become one complex, satisfactory, and convincing image. The remainder of this chapter is devoted not to completing this project but to initiating it.

To bring into complementarity, if not full unity, the two partial images of hope in history—the City of God and perfection in love—is not difficult. Indeed, something very like the unity of these images is already present in the thought of Teilhard de Chardin. Soleri sees his arcologies as concretizations of the vision of Teilhard, who summed up his understanding of the world process in the affirmation: "That if the universe, regarded sidereally, is in process of spatial expansion (from the infinitesimal to the immense), in the same way and still more clearly it presents itself to us, physicochemically, as in process of organic *involution* upon itself (from the extremely simple to the extremely complex)—and, moreover, this particular involution 'of complexity' is experimentally bound up with a correlative increase in interiorization, that is to say in the psyche of consciousness." [1]

What Teilhard calls involution upon itself, Soleri calls implosion and miniaturization. He agrees that it leads to a correlative increase in interiorization or consciousness. He understands his arcologies as providing the physical structure that will make the city an instrument of involution and thus of interiorization as well. Teilhard's vision is that the involution of the human species upon itself through ever-increasing intensity of interconnections will produce a new interpersonal and transpersonal unity.

Soleri shares this vision, and, like Teilhard, he employs organic metaphors to describe the new social unity that is to constitute the next stage of evolutionary development for the human species. These organic metaphors point to more intimate, mutually participating relations. Our present highly individualized mode of existence must be transcended.

The Buddhist-Christian existence imaged in the chapter on the perfection of love provides one way of thinking of such relations and their resultant unity. It shows how such an evolutionary emergent is ontologically possible and would appropriately fulfill existing drives within Christian existence. It points also toward the transcendence of cultural pluralism

desired by both Teilhard and Soleri by indicating how the
internal development of Buddhism may lead in a similar direction. Thus the perfection of love gives more content and
specificity to Soleri's vision of a new kind of humanity. At the
same time, the radical alteration of spatial relations proposed by
Soleri may prove the only context in which a Buddhist-Christian
existence could emerge. The two images of this-worldly hope—
the City of God and perfection of love—are mutually complementary.

The reconciliation of the images of the Kingdom of Heaven
and the resurrection of the dead as developed by Whitehead and
Pannenberg respectively is not as easy. Yet, the initial appearance of conflict can be largely overcome by pressing more
deeply into both images, developing them, and distinguishing
what is essential from what is not. We will proceed by critical
development first of Whitehead and then of Pannenberg.

There are four major points at which Whitehead's understanding of the Kingdom appears inadequate from the point of
view of the advocates of resurrection. (1) Preservation seems to
be of entities in their objectivity rather than of their own
subjectivity. (2) Only individual events or experiences are
saved, not persons. (3) The state of being in the Kingdom
appears as static, passive completeness. (4) There appears to be
only a trivial relation between the Kingdom as a universal,
cosmological reality and the event of Jesus with which it is
bound up in Christian imagination. These limitations do characterize some of the systematizations of Whitehead's thought, but
his own language struggled to say more and to go beyond them.

1. Whitehead's doctrine of perishing and objectification has
been misunderstood. In objectifying a past occasion, a new
experience does not simply present its object to itself in terms of
forms the object exemplified. Instead, it feels the subjective
feelings of the datum occasion. It feels these feelings in their
immediacy. The subjective form of the new occasion has its
own immediacy, but what is felt has its immediacy as well.
There is a flow of feeling from object to subject. Elements of the
past are thus genuinely preserved and renewed in the present.

The problem is that in the world only a few of the feelings of
any occasion are conjointly preserved in their immediacy in

succeeding ones. "The present fact has not the past fact with it in any full immediacy." [2] Feelings are necessarily abstracted from the occasion in its unity as a subject. The self-worth of that occasion is lost in this process, and very rapidly all but a few of the feelings fade from distinctive reenactment in the world. Hence, this preservation of immediacy does not solve the problem of perpetual perishing.

The Kingdom preserves the immediacy in the same way, only without abstracting from the full unity of subjects. Whereas in the world this unity is fragmented as soon as the occasion is complete, in the Kingdom the subject is preserved as subject with its immediacy. The Kingdom is a manyness of such complete occasions. "It is as much a multiplicity as it is a unity," [3] for it is God's "reception of the multiple freedom of actuality into the harmony of his own actualization." [4]

2. It is objected that even if the Kingdom preserves the perished world in its immediacy, what is retained are individual events and not persons. But this is not Whitehead's intention; for he believes that in the preservation of occasions their relations are included. Particularly the kind of succession that constitutes personal unity in the world characterizes the same occasions in the Kingdom. In the world the unity is imperfect because the past rapidly fades, but the past occasions in the Kingdom retain their wholeness and are united in their wholeness with their successors. "An enduring personality in the temporal world is a route of occasions in which the successors with some peculiar completeness sum up their predecessors. The correlate fact in God's nature is an even more complete unity in a chain of elements for which succession does not mean loss of immediate unison." [5] Clearly, Whitehead means that persons as persons inhabit the Kingdom.

Yet these persons are not to be conceived as closed within themselves. Lewis S. Ford and Marjorie Suchocki have imaginatively developed Whitehead's vision of the Kingdom. They observe: "There can be no clearly defined 'border' of the personality; what obtains is more likely a center of personality which then extends and flows to others in the giving and receiving which is the Harmony of God. This is fitting, for the temporal purpose of personality was primarily suited to the greater intensity of feeling made possible by the complex structure of personality. This intensity now having been achieved, it may now be put at the disposal of its ultimate purpose—the enrichment of the whole. In the process the narrow confines of the self have been lost, but not its subjective reaction to the universe as a way of experiencing that whole." [6]

To the extent that the narrow confines of self are lost, those who can conceive no fulfillment that is not that of the personally identical individual will find Whitehead's vision of hope unsatisfactory. But it is doubtful that an eternal self-identity can be truly envisioned as fulfillment. What is reasonably required is the participation in redemption of the human actuality, not that this be conceived in the categories of individualism. This reasonable requirement is met by Whitehead's vision in harmony with that of the perfection of love developed in Chapter 13.

3. Whitehead's language suggests that he does not intend to view the Kingdom as mere preservation of fixed occasions. At the very least, he stresses that the Kingdom is the inclusion of "every actuality for what it can be in such a perfected system— its sufferings, its sorrows, its failures, its triumphs, its immediacies of joy—woven by rightness of feeling into the harmony of the universal feeling." [7] In the Kingdom we are "transformed selves, purged into conformation with the final absolute wisdom." [8] This weaving goes on everlastingly as novel temporal occasions join in the unison of immediacy of all the occasions in the Kingdom. Thus the occasion in God contributes to the Kingdom in which creative advance is combined with the retention of immediacy. Furthermore, the occasions in God are not mere means to God's blessedness, for "being a means is not disjoined from the function of being an end. The sense of worth beyond itself is immediately enjoyed as an overpowering element in the individual self-attainment." [9] As Ford and Suchocki envision, perhaps "in God the occasion experiences an enlarged and enlarging world, which contains new occasions as they come into being" and "each occasion would experience the consequences of its own actions." [10]

4. Finally, it is objected, the Kingdom of Heaven in Whitehead seems to be removed from any inward connection with Jesus Christ. This would be so to abstract from its original meaning

as to render use of the language questionable and to separate it from Christian hope. Hence, we must consider whether this abstraction is as complete as it seems, and whether Christian reflection upon what Whitehead means by the Kingdom can bring it into closer relation with Christ as the resurrected Jesus.

First, it is certain that Whitehead's own thought about the Kingdom is deeply influenced by Jesus. His use of the term was a conscious identification with Jesus' language. The homologous character of the Kingdom in Whitehead with the Kingdom in Jesus' message, described in Chapter 14, is not a mere coincidence. Whitehead intends to be presenting in the context of his cosmology just that reality to which Jesus witnessed in the context of a quite different conceptuality.[11]

Second, transformation of the structure of existence in the Kingdom is in the direction of the structure of Jesus' existence. Events and persons as they exist in the Kingdom are open to each other and above all to God. The opposition between their aim and that of the Logos, which characterized them in the world, is overcome. They become what God can make of them. They exist from and for him. In a profound sense they are Christified.

Third, Jesus himself exists in the Kingdom. This follows necessarily from Whitehead's doctrine, but since he makes nothing of it, it appears initially to be trivial. Yet it need not be. When Whitehead describes the experience of the Kingdom in this life as the love of God providentially flowing into the world, the experience to which he points is one that has been effective in human history because of Jesus. The belief that the Kingdom can be understood in terms of Christ as the resurrected Jesus has opened people to its providential power. The vision of Christ in the Kingdom that Wilckens attributes to Paul and other early Christians can be understood in terms of how Jesus lives on in the Kingdom of Heaven. The anticipatory union with him that is one way of understanding Christian faith may in fact be realized in the unison of becoming with him in the Kingdom of Heaven that Whitehead's vision requires. Of course, the unison of becoming with him is only part of the unison of becoming of the entire "multiplicity of actual components"[12] that make up the Kingdom. But if it is Jesus' message that makes the Kingdom real for us in anticipation, and if it is the structure of Jesus' existence that foreshadows what existence in the Kingdom is to be, then the notion that unity with the resurrected Jesus is of peculiar importance for the blessedness of the Kingdom is not as farfetched as it may initially seem.

Whether in the end this subjective, personal, dynamic, Christian way of conceiving the Kingdom can be fully clarified and justified within Whitehead's conceptuality remains to be seen. Insofar as this can be done, his image of the Kingdom progressively merges toward the image of the resurrection of the dead that is offered by Pannenberg. That image, too, can be clarified and developed so as to reduce the remaining barriers to its unity with other images.

Pannenberg's image of the resurrection of the dead affirms that in the new age there will be a community of personal subjects with Christ in God. In this way it clearly affirms what was felt as lacking in Whitehead's vision of the Kingdom. But it, too, poses apparent problems. (1) Although there is a new blessed reality, all that led up to this reality seems to be unredeemed. History seems to be depreciated. (2) Because it posits resurrection at the temporal end of history and even of cosmic process, it seems to conflict with our sense that history may end soon in an explosion or plague and that the cosmos may continue forever. (3) By positing the bodiliness of the resurrected persons, it raises numerous questions of intelligibility and it confirms the excessive sense of private individuality and separateness that has too long characterized Christians.

1. Pannenberg's doctrine of resurrection is by no means guilty of depreciating historical occurrence. Far from positing resurrection as an otherworldly event that could reduce the importance of what occurs in history, he sees it precisely as giving meaning and reality to history. All that has occurred is included in its actual meaning in the End.

Pannenberg believes that events cannot be abstracted from their actual consequences and interpretations. An event is not what it is in itself but what it is in its actual context and in terms of the future it anticipates. The subsequent course of events changes the meaning of an event, and its actuality is bound up with that meaning. Only when its consequences are complete is it settled what it means and therefore what it is. The resurrec-

tion is that completion of the consequences which makes the
event for the first time truly what it is. The resurrection is thus
the summing up of all history.

Furthermore, the resurrection sums up all history by completing its unity in God. This is viewed as the consummation of
a process taking place through all history. The idea of the
Kingdom of Heaven as the resurrection of the dead "far exceeds
everything that could be achieved by human efforts. . . . And
yet that idea provides an appropriate criterion for measuring
the degree of achievement in social and political efforts and
changes." [13] Pannenberg is hereby enabled to use his image of
hope specifically to appraise occurrences in history.

2. Although Pannenberg's language and arguments have
sometimes seemed to point to a resurrection at the temporal end
of history, he is fully aware of the inadequacy of such a
simplistic view. He sees that such a view is not that of Jewish
apocalypticism, where "the events that are to be revealed in the
end-time already pre-exist in heaven." [14] The New Testament
symbolism carries on this fusion of future and present. "All this
means that the eschatological future in some way is already
present, although in secrecy and mystery." [15] What is religiously essential to the symbol of the resurrection of the dead is
that all human individuals who have ever lived participate and
that the rule be that of God. But "a general resurrection of the
dead would obviously be an event which as an event would be
out of comparison with any other event. How then can it be
imagined to be a member of the same sequence with events of
the ordinary kind?" [16] "The eschatological future is identical
with the eternal essence of things. . . . The essence of things is
not to be conceived as something non-temporal: but it depends
on the temporal process and will be decided only by its
outcome." [17]

Whitehead shares the concern that all human beings who
have ever lived share in the eschatological fulfillment, and
although he does not prefer the language of "rule," he clearly
sees the fulfillment as given and ordered by God. As long as the
"general resurrection of the dead" is not an event at the
temporal end, nothing forbids its interpretation in Whiteheadian
terms in which "the eschatological future in some way is

already present." Pannenberg may not be fully satisfied with
Whitehead's formulations, but the earlier appearance of contradiction has vanished.

3. Pannenberg's language about resurrection has often
stressed the bodily character of the resurrected person. Here
there seems to be a strict conflict with Whitehead; for the events
of which Whitehead's Kingdom is composed appear to be quite
different from the bodies on which Pannenberg insists. In this
respect it seems that Pannenberg narrows unnecessarily, for
philosophical reasons, the acceptable images of resurrection,[18]
insisting upon the unity of body and soul understood in terms of
our modern common sense.[19] He is correct that there are
features of contemporary thought that favor this doctrine, and it
corresponds with dominant New Testament images, but the
Bible is far less rigid here than Pannenberg appears to be. Both
the ideas of bodily resurrection and those of separated life after
death by the soul were developed independently of Judaism and
Christianity, and both were adopted and adapted by them.
Their contrast is commonly exaggerated, and when confronted
by modern skepticism, their differences in existential import are
comparatively minor. Even in the New Testament the idea of
some distinction and even separability of soul from body is
present.[20]

Furthermore, the resurrection of Jesus is not unequivocal
support of the traditional view of the resurrection of the body.
Marxsen and Wilckens agree that the idea of resurrection in the
sense of coming forth from the tomb is an inference drawn
primarily from the appearances of Jesus. In Wilckens' account,
these appearances were glimpses of the eschatological future of
God, in which Jesus was seen as playing a central role. Paul's
vision supported his expectation of resurrection of the body
rather than some other form of fulfillment, but the vision as
understood by Wilckens does not entail this doctrine. Furthermore, Paul's own idea of a spiritual body qualifies the usual
distinctions between resurrection of the body and separate life
for the soul.

Pannenberg describes the appearances of the risen Jesus as
nonhallucinatory visions.[21] For one who takes parapsychologi-
cal phenomena seriously, that is a plausible account. It implies

that Jesus was really present as the cause of the appearances
but that the sensory content of the visions was contributed by
the psychic activity of the percipient. This is to be distinguished
from a dream or hallucination in which only the psychic activity
of the percipient is involved and any external cause must be
sought in the more remote past.

Even if this theory is correct, however, Jesus' appearances
would not give evidence for resurrection of the body any more
than for a new life of the soul. They support the idea of the
presence of the resurrected Jesus in some form, but they give no
evidence for the presence of the body since, by hypothesis, the
visual image of the body is contributed by the perceiver.
Analogous experiences in our time, those in which a living
person has a vivid visual experience of a close friend or a
relative who has recently died, are not taken as evidence that
the body of the deceased has been revivified or transformed.

The point of these criticisms is to say that the stress on the
bodiliness of what is resurrected, in a conventional sense of
bodiliness, creates unnecessary difficulties for the understanding of resurrection and is not required by the Bible. Pannenberg
himself seems to be moving away from it. He has always
emphasized that the body that rises is not qualitatively the same
as the one that dies, for what is sown in corruption is raised
incorruptible. The body is transformed. The language of resurrection of the body is in any case metaphorical and doxological.
Furthermore, in recent writings he has recognized that bodies in
the ordinary sense are not ontologically primary. He finds in
Einstein that "the definitive turning point from a conception of
natural forces to a field of energy as e.g. in the case of an electric
or magnetic field means to conceive of energy as the primary
reality that transcends the body through which it may manifest
itself—a reality that we no longer need to attribute to a body as
its subject." [22] Clearly, when the body is subordinated to a field
of energy, the apparent opposition to Whitehead's vision fades
away.

Pannenberg states that "Teilhard de Chardin did not yet fully
appreciate this radical change of the concept of natural force
from a property of bodies to an independent reality that only
manifests itself in the genesis and movement of bodies." [23] But
Teilhard did provide an image that adjusts the idea of the body

Concerns of philosophy of nature

to the field of energy and thus can help us preserve the image of the resurrection of the body in its unity with that of the Kingdom of Heaven.

Teilhard wrote: "Hitherto the prevailing view has been that the body (that is to say, the matter that is incommunicably attached to each soul) is a fragment of the universe, a piece completely detached from the rest and handed over to a spirit that informs it. . . . In the future we shall say that the body is the very Universality of things, in as much as they are centered on an animating Spirit, in as much as they influence that spirit, and are themselves influenced and sustained in it. . . . My own body is not these cells or those cells that belong *exclusively* to me: it is *what,* in these cells *and* in the rest of the world feels my influence and reacts against me. *My* matter is not a *part* of the universe that I possess *totaliter:* it is the *totality* of the Universe possessed by me *partialiter.*" [24]

If my body is, in Teilhard's language, "everything in the universe which in any way enters my experience, my constitution," then the question of the resurrection of this body or the constitution of a new private body does not arise. The whole sphere of the resurrected is the body in which each would participate more fully than in this life. Finally we will be joined with one another in a single body. Pannenberg's stress that the eschatological End is unity is well served by this image of the resurrected body. Through this understanding, the image of resurrection and that of Kingdom of Heaven as it can be developed from Whitehead almost merge.

Teilhard's understanding of body also brings the conjoint image of Kingdom and resurrection into closer union with the idea of the City of God that includes community perfected in love. In that community there is a progressive realization of the sharing of a common body in a way facilitated by the new intensity of interconnectedness in the three-dimensional city. Thus the new existence in the City of God on earth would foreshadow its fulfillment in transformation through resurrection into the Kingdom of Heaven.

The image of new existence in the City of God can thus merge with the image of new life in the Kingdom of Heaven and find in that its completion. There is also in Whitehead the suggestion of a reverse movement that carries still farther the unification of the images of hope. Whitehead writes: "The Kingdom of Heaven is with us today. The action of the fourth phase [of the cosmic process] is the love of God for the world. It is the particular providence for particular occasions. What is done in the world is transformed into a reality in heaven, and the reality in heaven passes back into the world." [25]

This means that the line between the transcendent Kingdom of Heaven and history is not as rigid as it might seem. The reality of the Kingdom enters into the reality of the world. Anticipation of the Kingdom not only grounds meaning and gives content to hope, it also shapes the images of hope. The vision of the City of God to be realized in history participates in the nature of the Kingdom that is already being realized in heaven.

As is all too characteristic of Christian images of hope, only humanity is clearly in view in the four presentations that have been made in the four preceding chapters. That anthropocentric focus somewhat distorts the images themselves, for they are all far more sensitive to the inclusive creation than is the dominant form of hope theology.[26] Although Soleri concentrates on the human city, he envisions a city that will allow the processes of nature to continue on the planet less disturbed by human manipulation. Although the Buddhist-Christian synthesis concentrates on a new form of human existence, that existence must involve relations to the totality of reality and not only among human beings. Although Whitehead's Kingdom of Heaven concentrates on the saving of human values, it comprises the saving also of the values of all creatures. Although Pannenberg concentrates on the resurrection of the human dead, he writes that "genuine Christian hope means a fascinating vision of a new life . . . even for the natural world." [27]

Today it becomes urgent that this heretofore subordinated motif in Christian images of hope be brought forward to prominence. The whole planet groans in travail. Human beings are cocreatures with all the rest, participating in the destiny of the biosphere. Images of hope for human beings alone betray an exaggerated estimate of the separability of our species from the rest of creation and of God's exclusive preoccupation with us. They also betray an unchristian indifference to our fellow creatures that has been all too characteristic of us and has appalled such sensitive critics as Schopenhauer.

Emil Fackenheim tells a Hasidic story that, in its depicting of a Jewish image of Christ or Messiah, highlights the inadequacy of our exclusively anthropocentric Christian images: "A Hasidic rabbi who had moved to Palestine to be right on the spot in case the Messiah should arrive in his lifetime once heard the sound of a trumpet from the Mount of Olives (the traditional sign for the arrival of the Messiah). What had happened was that a prankster had gone up there and thought he would pull a practical joke. So the rabbi immediately rushed to the window, opened the window to see the redeemed world, and what did he see? A driver beating his donkey. And he said, 'I don't have to see anything else. So long as people still beat their donkeys, the world is not redeemed.' " [28]

Part Three began with a chapter on "Christ as the Image of Hope." The four following chapters were intended to flesh out that hope. In this chapter the potential unity of the images they offered has been adumbrated as one immanent/transcendent, personal/communal, human/cosmic hope. In conclusion, we will consider whether in fact this unity is one with the Christ to which it intends to give more concreteness.

It is apparent that it is Christ who gives the hope. Images of hope arise only through creative transformation, and in the two instances where commitment to Christ was not explicit on the part of the proponent of the image—Soleri and Whitehead—we have seen that the commitment is implicit. The images of hope have arisen in Jesus' field of force through openness to the present working of the Logos. Furthermore, what is hoped for is the continuing work of Christ; for the one Christ who transforms events in history also transforms the events of history by the resurrection into the Kingdom of Heaven.

But this still does not answer the final question. Is the content of the hope also Christ? To answer that, we recall that Christ is the Logos insofar as the Logos is incarnate. Is the content of the hope the completion or consummation of incarnation? What would that mean?

Our clue to the meaning of perfect incarnation is to be found in Jesus. In him the Logos was fully and normatively incarnate. That incarnation was not simply an intensification of the presence of the Logos in all people. It was a distinctive structure of existence in which Jesus' selfhood was coconstituted by the incarnation of the Logos; that is to say, Jesus was Christ. If the content of our hope is Christ, then it is the hope that Christ be perfectly formed in us, that he become one with our very selves, that we too become Christ. The images of the City of God, the Kingdom of Heaven, and the resurrection of the dead—are they images of this perfect incarnation of the Logos?

In none of these images has a personal existence been described in which Christ coconstituted selfhood. Yet the discussion has led repeatedly in that direction. Perfection of love breaks down the boundaries of the private self. One becomes open to others as one is open to one's own past and future. One constitutes oneself out of the wider past and toward the wider future. The aim of the Logos for each of us is always toward an inclusive future that allows us to encompass an inclusive past. Insofar as through love that inclusiveness is attained, the tension between personal purposes and the claim of the Logos declines. As self and Logos draw together, the Logos becomes more fully incarnate. The direction is toward the structure of existence already realized in Jesus.

Likewise in the Kingdom in Whitehead's vision, whereas personal unity is retained, it is also transcended. There is unison of becoming with an ever-enlarging whole. The need for personal identity over against others falls away. The Kingdom has its own encompassing unity, participation in which is blessedness. Here, too, the tension between the claim of the immanent Logos and one's inherited personal aims is overcome. Christ is realized in each.

In considering the problem of bodiliness of the resurrected state, I introduced the vision of Teilhard, who sees that our bodies are the totality of that with which we are united. Hence, our bodies are not bits of matter that separate us from one another but the inclusive whole through which we are drawn into a new unity. In this unity the tension between our individual wills and the presence of the Logos must diminish. The fulfillment of this movement in the coconstitution of our selfhood by our personal past and the Logos would be that perfection of incarnation already attained in Jesus.

All our images of hope converge also in this—that they point toward a transcendence of separating individuality in a fuller community with other people and with all things. In this community the tensions between self and Christ decline, and in a final consummation they would disappear. This is the movement of incarnation. Christ is the name of our hope.

POSTSCRIPT

The Trinity
and Sexist Language

Christology has always been bound up with the Trinity, but there has never been a fully satisfactory formulation, and what would seem to be a technically orthodox imagery has not fastened itself upon the mind of the church. The problem is as follows: The Biblical language clearly identifies the Father with God. There is also the Son whom he sends into the world and the Spirit of God that works redemptively in the Christian community. When the question was asked in the early church whether the divine in Jesus belonged to the sphere of God or to that of a creature, the church correctly insisted that it belonged with God. The Logos that was incarnate was God's Logos and not something else. Still the dominant imagery associated the Father with God himself in his full Godhead, whereas the Logos was God in a particular mode of his being. The analogous question about the Spirit received the same answer. The imagery was then of one God who expressed himself through Logos, or Son, and Spirit. In art, the Trinity could be portrayed as one man with two hands.

Having determined that there is only one *ousia* in God so that Son and Spirit share in the *ousia* of the Father himself, the church felt it necessary to find a way to express its sense that nevertheless Son and Spirit are not simply identical with the Father. The intention would be properly served if it could have been explained how the two hands belong to deity but are not identical with God as a whole—without, of course, the spatial associations. The actual image was of the Son as God in one mode of his activity and the Spirit as God in another mode, whereas the Father was quite simply God. Unfortunately, the church employed a language that obscured this. In its correct effort to say that there is a difference and that the difference is not just one of the name but an actual difference within God, it chose the word *hypostasis*. Previously it had been rightly asserted that God was a single *hypostasis*. But now the word was used to designate the difference. This would have done no harm if it had been asserted that the Father was a *hypostasis* and the Son and Spirit were two modes of his activity in himself and toward the world. It would have done only moderate harm if Son and Spirit had been declared two *hypostaseis* in which the one Father actualized himself. Either way, the real distinction of Father, Son, and Spirit would have been preserved, and the meaning of *hypostasis* could have been adjusted to fit. But by using *hypostasis* both of the Father and of the Son and Spirit, serious confusion was introduced. The apparent implication conflicted with the actual images dominant in the church.

When we pray to the Father in the Lord's Prayer, we do not pray to a *hypostasis* or person who is one of three who jointly, equally, and in the same sense constitute God. We pray, quite simply, to God. When we speak of the Son or the Spirit, we continue to have more specific aspects or activities of God in mind. The liturgy and art of the church refuse to accommodate themselves to the parallelism of the three that the creed seems to assert, and even the creeds give a certain precedence to the Father as the one who begat the Son and from whom the Spirit proceeds. New Testament imagery is too strong for this to be abandoned.

The church has rightly affirmed a trinity. It has rightly said that Father, Son, and Spirit all refer to God himself. It has rightly said that still the meanings of the three names differ. But its final step of forcing almost parallel conceptuality upon the three misrepresented the Biblical imagery and the actual thought of the church. It has tended to turn reflection on the Trinity from serious effort to understand how what is known as Son and experienced as Spirit is to be affirmed as truly God to speculative discussions of how three *hypostaseis* can have one *ousia* without ceasing to be three *hypostaseis*. This kind of Trinitarianism has become more of an obstacle to Christology than an aid.

The relation of Son and Spirit to Father is better seen as like the relation between my thinking and my feeling to myself. I include my thinking and my feeling. They have no existence apart from me. But that does not mean that I could first exist and then begin to feel and think. I am the unity of my feeling and thinking. In this trinity my feeling and thinking are more or less parallel, but to think of me as a third parallel entity is seriously misleading. To do this undercuts the correct implication of lack of parallelism that is contained in the "begetting" and "proceeding" language of the creed. The only solution is to assert that the term *hypostasis* is not used univocally of the Father on the one hand, here analogous to the self, and of the Son and Spirit on the other, here analogous to thinking and feeling as distinct though inseparable activities of the one self.

There is another respect in which the images are not quite parallel. It is in much less serious tension with the official formulation. The term "Son" functions as equivalent both to Logos and to Christ. Logos refers primarily to the Son in his transcendence. The Logos is that which became flesh. The term "Logos" is better than "Son," when the Trinity is under consideration. "Christ" refers to the Son in his immanence or incarnation. The term "Christ" is better than "Son" when Jesus is under consideration. Jesus is Christ, because he is the incarnation of the Logos. "Spirit" also refers to an aspect of God that is both transcendent and immanent, but the New Testament imagery and the piety of the church, when they give meaning to the Spirit at all, stress its immanence. Spirit is thus analogous to Christ rather than to Son.

Unfortunately, the church has not established any clear connection between Spirit and another image that could serve to focus attention on the Spirit as it is in God in distinction from its immanence in us. Or if it seems better to keep the term "Spirit" as analogous to Son, in view of the long history of the Trinitarian formula, we lack other terms analogous to Logos and Christ to guide thought about its transcendent/immanent character. In either event, one step toward a solution would be to identify Spirit in its transcendent character as the resurrection of the dead or the Kingdom of Heaven. The justification is that the Spirit is regarded in Christianity as an eschatological phenomenon; it points to the End to which we move. That End is God as the resurrection or Kingdom. The immanent presence of the Spirit now is anticipatory of that End, assuring us of it and uniting us with it. The Trinity can then be God, his Logos, and his Kingdom. The Logos is present with us as Christ; the Kingdom, as Spirit.

Much of the book explains the justification for this way of thinking of Logos and Christ, and it is in any case in clear continuity with the tradition of Christian usage. The identification of the Kingdom as one "person" of the Trinity requires more explanation. It follows, however, from the usage of both Whitehead and Pannenberg. For both men the Kingdom is God. Whitehead calls it the Consequent Nature of God to distinguish it from the Primordial Nature, which has been identified as the Logos. For Pannenberg, God, as the Power of the Future, is that which will be in the resurrection of the dead. This is the Kingdom of God proclaimed by Jesus. Whitehead does not explicitly establish a relation between the Kingdom and the Spirit, but his comments about the immanence of the Kingdom are suggestive. It is experienced as "the great companion—the fellow sufferer who understands," and it is "the particular providence for particular occasions." [1] It is also an occasion's "sense of worth beyond itself as an overpowering element in the individual self-attainment." [2] The way in which the End is already effectively present can be understood as producing the fruits of which the New Testament speaks.

Before deciding to accept the understanding of Spirit in terms of particular providence and the special experiences to which Paul directs us, we need to attend to Pannenberg's criticism. He points out that Spirit in the New Testament should be understood against the background of its use in the Old Testament. It should not be limited to the sphere of Christian faith and cut off as something special and supernatural from God's wider work in the world. Particularly it should be remembered that, in the Old Testament, Spirit is understood as "the origin of all life." [3] One should speak of Spirit not when something wholly distinct occurs but when what occurs everywhere is perfected. "The ordinary life is not life in the full sense of the word because it is perishable" whereas "true life . . persists in communication with its spiritual source." [4]

This book has followed John 1:4 in identifying the Logos as the principle of life. To identify Spirit also as the source of life, then, seems to be redundant. But to recognize that all creative novelty (and, therefore, all life) aims toward the Kingdom and gains a sense of worth through its anticipation of the Kingdom is to recognize with Pannenberg the presence of the Spirit as that by virtue of which true, unending life becomes effective in time. What happens in the distinctive Christian experience of Spirit is new life as the perfection of biological and psychological life.

The Christological and Trinitarian positions put forward in this book are very much in process. Such deep changes are needed in our habitual formulations and thought patterns for Christ and Spirit to again be real for us that any attempt here and now to fix their meaning is doomed to failure. All the preceding chapters have the character of tentative explorations and proposals rather than well-established conclusions. Nowhere is the unfinished character of this work more apparent than in the confrontation with the urgent issue of gender in our thought of God.

The heightened consciousness produced by women has forced us to recognize that the masculine character of all the persons in the traditional formulation of the Trinity is not a mere technical matter of language. The language is appropriate to the actual images. God and all the persons of the Trinity have been experienced as masculine. Important aspects of original Christian teaching have been distorted by this sexism, which is connected with the one-sidedness of the dominant thought of God that has been treated in the book.

In this book I have spoken chiefly of God, Logos, and Kingdom. I have referred both to the Logos and to the Kingdom as "it." One could take the further step of substituting "deity," "Godhead," or "the divine unity" for God. This too could then be referred to in the neuter. However, neuterization is a high price to pay for neutrality, and in any case it would not suffice. The Logos is indissolubly bound up with Christ, and because Jesus was Christ, Christ must be referred to as "he."

A better solution would be to recognize that Logos is masculine in connotation and then bring out the feminine aspect of deity under Kingdom or resurrection. Since the term "Kingdom" is still too masculine, "Realm" can be substituted. In the actual account provided in Chapter 14, it is the receptive, empathetic, suffering, redemptive, preservative aspect of God, whereas Logos is order, novelty, call, demand, agent, transformer, and principle of restlessness. Hence, traditionally feminine characteristics are dominant in the Kingdom. Currently, the received polarity of feminine and masculine is under a reconsideration that may affect language about deity as well, but at least it should be recognized that in Whitehead's vision it is the "feminine" aspect of God that is final, inclusive, and fully actual.

There would still remain the problem of naming the unity of God. "Father" will not do, and our best chance is to allow our images to develop freely. One possibility would be to make use of the Christian identification of God as love. Whitehead in *Adventures of Ideas* identifies the Logos with the divine *erōs* of Plato. The Logos is also, and more inclusively, *agapē*. In *Process and Reality* compassion is the dominant note in the Kingdom. The unity of *agapē* and compassion might then be named Grace. The sexist connotations would be overcome.

An equally promising way ahead lies in the pluralism that we are to affirm in Christ. That pluralism involves the interiorization of images from other traditions. In some of these the masculine and the feminine are in better balance. Their novelty for us allows them to be appropriated in abstraction from their full connotations in their own traditions, in all of which they have been employed for sexist purposes. Perhaps in time, for example, we can merge the image of Logos with that of the Yin and the image of the Kingdom with that of the Yang. In such a merger the images of Yin and Yang would be greatly enriched and transformed, but in their turn, they could purify the Christian imagination of the divine from its masculine sexism. Perhaps a suitable nonsexist image could then be found for the unity of the Yin and the Yang.

These proposals are made not to fasten new language on Christian use but to suggest how free we rightly are to reimage the Trinity. Once we realize that we are dealing with images and not with things, we can allow for the interaction of our words with the meanings they bring. We can test these in terms of their appropriateness to our tradition and its current needs. We can use them and then pass them by as they cease to serve or guide us. In this way the Christian understanding of the Trinity can become what it should always have been, a way of affirming our liberty in Christ.

NOTES

PREFACE

1. Thomas J. J. Altizer, "Dialectical vs. Di-Polar Theology" in *Process Studies*, Vol. 1, No. 1 (Spring 1971), pp. 29–37.
2. William A. Beardslee, *A House for Hope: A Study in Process and Biblical Thought* (The Westminster Press, 1972), Ch. VIII.

INTRODUCTION

1. David L. Miller, *The New Polytheism: Rebirth of the Gods and Goddesses* (Harper & Row, Publishers, Inc., 1974).
2. Paul Tillich, *Systematic Theology*, Vol. I (The University of Chicago Press, 1951), pp. 47–48.
3. *Ibid.*, p. 49.
4. André Malraux, *The Voices of Silence*, tr. by Stuart Gilbert (Doubleday & Company, Inc., 1953), and *The Metamorphosis of the Gods*, tr. by Stuart Gilbert (Doubleday & Company, Inc., 1960).
5. The view that even those we call insane are *merely* deluded is now effectively challenged. Cf. R. D. Laing, *The Politics of Experience* (Random House, Inc., 1967).
6. Ryusei Takeda and John B. Cobb, Jr., "Mosha-Dharma and Prehension: Nagarjuna and Whitehead Compared," in *Process Studies*, Vol. 4, No. 1 (Spring 1974), pp. 26–36.
7. This was my own attempt to solve the problem of what is essential to Christianity. See John B. Cobb, Jr., *The Structure of Christian Existence* (The Westminster Press, 1967).

CHAPTER 1
CHRIST AS CREATIVE TRANSFORMATION IN ART

1. André Malraux, *The Voices of Silence*, p. 607.
2. *Ibid.*, p. 608.
3. *Ibid.*, p. 609.
4. André Malraux, *The Metamorphosis of the Gods*, p. 185.
5. Malraux, *The Voices of Silence*, p. 228.
6. Malraux, *The Metamorphosis of the Gods*, p. 200.
7. *Ibid.*, p. 213.
8. *Ibid.*, pp. 217–218.
9. *Ibid.*, p. 295.
10. *Ibid.*, p. 351.
11. Malraux, *The Voices of Silence*, p. 243.
12. *Ibid.*, p. 217.
13. *Ibid.*, p. 243.
14. *Ibid.*, p. 217.
15. Malraux, *The Metamorphosis of the Gods*, p. 285.
16. *Ibid.*, p. 316.
17. *Ibid.*, p. 366.
18. *Ibid.*, p. 312.
19. Malraux, *The Voices of Silence*, p. 470.
20. *Ibid.*, p. 427.
21. *Ibid.*, pp. 435–437.
22. *Ibid.*, pp. 471–473.
23. *Ibid.*, p. 91.
24. *Ibid.*, p. 640.
25. *Ibid.*, p. 603.
26. *Ibid.*, p. 616.
27. *Ibid.*, p. 601.
28. *Ibid.*
29. *Ibid.*, p. 600.
30. *Ibid.*, p. 608.
31. *Ibid.*, p. 605.
32. *Ibid.*, p. 334.
33. *Ibid.*, p. 102.
34. *Ibid.*, p. 113.
35. *Ibid.*, p. 604.
36. *Ibid.*, p. 605.
37. *Ibid.*, p. 334.
38. The French edition of *The Voices of Silence* appeared in 1951.
39. Malraux, *The Voices of Silence*, p. 604.
40. *Ibid.*
41. *Ibid.*, p. 603.

CHAPTER 2
CHRIST AS CREATIVE TRANSFORMATION IN THEOLOGY

1. Nicolas Berdyaev, *The Beginning and the End*, tr. by R. M. French (Peter Smith Publisher, Inc., 1970), pp. 173–174.

2. John W. Dixon, Jr., *Nature and Grace in Art* (University of North Carolina Press, 1964), pp. 191–192.

3. Cf. Lord Herbert of Cherbury.

4. Friedrich Schleiermacher, *The Christian Faith*, tr. by H. R. Mackintosh and J. S. Stewart from the second German edition (Edinburgh: T. & T. Clark, 1948), p. 32.

5. *Ibid.*, p. 34.

6. G. W. F. Hegel, *Lectures on the Philosophy of History*, tr. from the 3d German edition by J Sibler (London: George Bell & Sons, 1894), p. 58.

7. *Ibid.*

8. Schleiermacher, *The Christian Faith*, p. 33.

9. Arthur Schopenhauer, "The Christian System," in Bailey Sanders (ed.), *Religion and Other Essays* (London: Swan, Sonnenschein & Co., 1890), p. 114.

10. Rudolf Otto's most influential book is *The Idea of the Holy*.

11. Cf. Rudolf Otto's *The Kingdom of God and the Son of Man*.

12. Ernst Troeltsch, *Christian Thought: Its History and Application*, ed. by Baron F. von Hügel (Meridian Books, Inc., 1957), p. 52.

13. H. Richard Niebuhr, *The Meaning of Revelation* (The Macmillan Company, 1955), especially Ch. 1.

14. *Ibid.*, p. 28.

15. Richard Rubenstein, *My Brother Paul* (Harper & Row, Publishers, Inc., 1972), p. 21.

16. *Ibid.*, p. 86. Note that Freud is himself critically judged in terms of this theory, e.g., p. 162.

17. *Ibid.*, p. 21.

18. *Ibid.*, p. 173.

19. *Ibid.*, p. 60.

20. Jaroslav Pelikan, *The Christian Tradition: A History of the Development of Doctrine*, Vol. I, *The Emergence of the Catholic Tradition (100–600)* (The University of Chicago Press, 1971), p. 229.

21. Adolf von Harnack, *What Is Christianity?* tr. by Thomas Bailey Saunders (Putnam, 1901), p. 55. The gospel can also be summarized under the heads "the kingdom of God and its coming," and "the higher righteousness and the commandment of love."

22. Dietrich Bonhoeffer, *Prisoner for God: Letters and Papers from Prison* (The Macmillan Company, 1954), p. 179.

23. Masao Abe, "Buddhist Nirvana: Its Significance in Contempo-

rary Thought and Life," in *The Ecumenical Review,* Vol. 25 (April 1973), p. 163.

24. *Ibid.,* p. 162.

CHAPTER 3
CREATIVE TRANSFORMATION AS THE LOGOS

1. Alfred North Whitehead's doctrine is developed in his *Science and the Modern World* (The Macmillan Company, 1925), *Religion in the Making* (The Macmillan Company, 1926), and *Process and Reality* (The Macmillan Company, 1929), where the term "initial aim" actually appears. I have attempted to give a systematic account of Whitehead's view in Chs. 3 and 4 of *A Christian Natural Theology: Based on the Thought of Alfred North Whitehead* (The Westminster Press, 1965).

2. Cf. Karl Barth, *Church Dogmatics,* I/1, tr. by G. T. Thompson (Charles Scribner's Sons, 1936), pp. 41 f. Heinrich Barth's essay, "Philosophie, Theologie, und Existenz," was published in the journal *Zwischen den Zeiten* in 1932.

3. Berdyaev, *The Beginning and the End,* p. 174.

4. Whitehead, *Religion in the Making,* p. 156.

5. Tillich, *Systematic Theology,* Vol. I, p. 205, and John Macquarrie, *Principles of Christian Theology* (Charles Scribner's Sons, 1966), pp. 98 ff.

6. Cf. Paul Tillich, *Biblical Religion and the Search for Ultimate Reality* (The University of Chicago Press, 1955).

CHAPTER 4
THE LOGOS AS CHRIST

1. Cf. Emil Brunner, in *Zwischen den Zeiten,* 1932, p. 527n.: "True reason—i.e., reason determined by God's Word—is nothing else but faith: the receiving of the divine Word."

2. Alfred North Whitehead, *The Function of Reason* (Beacon Press, Inc., 1967), p. 66.

CHAPTER 5
JESUS' WORDS AND CHRIST

1. Lynn White, Jr., "Cultural Climates and Technological Advance in the Middle Ages," in Lynn White (ed.), *Viator: Medieval and Renaissance Studies* (University of California Press, 1971), Vol. II, pp. 200–201.

2. Milan Machoveč, *Jesus für Atheisten,* tr. into German by Paul Kruntorad (Stuttgart: Kreuz-Verlag, 1972), pp. 102–103.

3. Albert Schweitzer, *The Quest of the Historical Jesus,* tr. by William Montgomery with an introduction by James M. Robinson (The Macmillan Company, 1968), p. 402.

4. Norman Perrin, *Rediscovering the Teaching of Jesus* (Harper & Row, Publishers, Inc., 1967).

5. Ernest Cadman Colwell, *Jesus and the Gospel* (Oxford University Press, 1963).

6. See note 2, above.

7. Machoveč, *Jesus für Atheisten,* p. 99.

8. *Ibid.,* p. 101.

9. Colwell, *Jesus and the Gospel,* p. 73.

10. Rudolf Bultmann, *Jesus and the Word,* tr. by Louise Pettibone Smith and Erminie Huntress Lantero (Charles Scribner's Sons, 1934), p. 110.

11. *Ibid.,* pp. 110–111.

12. Machoveč, *Jesus für Atheisten,* p. 131.

13. Colwell, *Jesus and the Gospel,* p. 56.

14. *Ibid.,* pp. 44–47.

15. Bultmann, *Jesus and the Word,* p. 155.

16. *Ibid.,* p. 199. This generalization fails to do justice to the recognition by some Jews of intimations of grace for Gentiles.

17. Perrin, *Rediscovering the Teaching of Jesus,* p. 94.

18. *Ibid.,* p. 41.

19. Colwell, *Jesus and the Gospel,* p. 56.

20. *Ibid.,* pp. 47–48.

21. Machoveč, *Jesus für Atheisten,* p. 108.

22. Perrin, *Rediscovering the Teaching of Jesus,* p. 204.

23. *Ibid.*

24. Machoveč, *Jesus für Atheisten,* p. 108.

25. Bultmann, *Jesus and the Word,* p. 189.

26. *Ibid.*

27. Perrin, *Rediscovering the Teaching of Jesus,* p. 141.

28. Machoveč, *Jesus für Atheisten,* p. 104.

29. Colwell, *Jesus and the Gospel,* p. 39.

30. *Ibid.,* p. 56.

31. Whitehead, *Religion in the Making,* p. 56.

32. This is not to imply that Nader has in fact displayed pride or Ehrlichman humility!

33. Jesus' parables have recently been analyzed into two types along these lines. See Norman O. Perrin, "Wisdom and Apocalyptic in the Message of Jesus," *Society of Biblical Literature Seminar Papers,* 1972, Vol. II; John Dominic Crossan, "The Servant Parables of Jesus," *Society of Biblical Literature Seminar Papers,* 1973, Vol. II.

CHAPTER 6
LIFE IN CHRIST

1. Albert Schweitzer, *The Mysticism of Paul the Apostle,* tr. by William Montgomery (Adam & Charles Black, 1931), p. 17.
2. Rudolf Bultmann, *Theology of the New Testament,* Vol. I, tr. by Kendrick Grobel (Charles Scribner's Sons, 1951), p. 328.
3. Walter Grundmann, "The Christ-Statements of the New Testament," in Gerhard Kittel and Gerhard Friedrich (eds.), *Theological Dictionary of the New Testament,* tr. and ed. by Geoffrey Bromiley (Wm. B. Eerdmans Publishing Company, 1964–1974), Vol. IX, p. 550.
4. *Ibid.,* p. 551.
5. Schweitzer, *The Mysticism of Paul the Apostle,* p. 18.
6. *Ibid.,* p. 367.
7. Bultmann, *Theology of the New Testament,* Vol. I, p. 328.

CHAPTER 7
FROM JESUS' WORK TO JESUS' PERSON

1. Justin Martyr, *Dialogue with Trypho,* VIII, tr. by M. Dods and G. Reith, Ante-Nicene Christian Library, Vol. II (T. & T. Clark, 1867), p. 96.
2. William Telfer (ed.), *Cyril of Jerusalem and Nemesius of Emesa,* The Library of Christian Classics, Vol. IV (The Westminster Press, 1955), p. 127.
3. *Ibid.,* p. 135.
4. Hans von Campenhausen, *The Fathers of the Greek Church,* tr. by Stanley Godman (Pantheon Books, 1959), p. 144.
5. Cf. Jaroslav Pelikan (ed.), *The Preaching of Chrysostom* (Fortress Press, 1969).
6. Irenaeus, *Against Heresies,* V, ch. 1, tr. by Edward Rochie Hardy, in Cyril C. Richardson (ed.), *Early Christian Fathers,* The Library of Christian Classics, Vol. I (The Westminster Press, 1953), p. 385.
7. *Ibid.,* p. 386.
8. Athanasius, *On the Incarnation of the Word,* in Edward Rochie Hardy (ed.), *Christology of the Later Fathers,* The Library of Christian Classics, Vol. III (The Westminster Press, 1954), p. 62.
9. *Ibid.,* p. 63.
10. *Ibid.*
11. Cyril of Alexandria, from *De incarn. unigen.* in Henry Bettenson (ed.), *The Later Christian Fathers* (Oxford University Press, 1970), p. 263.
12. Machoveč, *Jesus für Atheisten,* p. 91.
13. *Ibid.,* p. 93.

14. Bultmann, *Jesus and the Word*, pp. 216–217.

15. Rudolf Bultmann, "The Primitive Christian Kerygma," in Carl E. Braaten and Roy A. Harrisville (eds.), *The Historical Jesus and the Kerygmatic Christ* (Abingdon Press, 1964), p. 23.

16. Perrin, *Rediscovering the Teaching of Jesus*, pp. 97–98.

17. *Ibid.*, p. 98.

18. *Ibid.*, p. 118.

19. *Ibid.*, p. 122.

20. *Ibid.*, p. 140.

21. *Ibid.*, p. 82.

22. *Ibid.*, p. 67.

23. Colwell, *Jesus and the Gospel*, p. 37.

24. *Ibid.*, p. 33.

25. *Ibid.*, p. 37.

26. *Ibid.*, p. 42.

27. *Ibid.*, p. 38.

CHAPTER 8
Jesus' Person as Christ

1. Ernst Fuchs, *Studies of the Historical Jesus*, tr. by Andrew Scobie (Alec R. Allenson, Inc., 1964), p. 22.

2. Machoveč, *Jesus für Atheisten*, p. 93.

3. *Ibid.*, p. 119.

4. This theory is congenial to the proposal of Piet Schoonenberg that we think of an "enhypostasia of God's Word or only Son in the human Jesus" instead of the more traditional view of the enhypostasia of the humanity of Jesus in the person of the Logos (*The Christ*, tr. by Della Couling [Herder & Herder, Inc., 1971], p. 87).

CHAPTER 9
The Christ of the Creeds

1. Cf., for example, the beginning of the reconstruction of early Christian history in terms of trajectories rather than of successive periods in James M. Robinson and Helmut Koester, *Trajectories Through Early Christianity* (Fortress Press, 1971).

2. Reginald Fuller, *The Foundations of New Testament Christology* (Charles Scribner's Sons, 1965), p. 243. The diagrams that follow are reproduced from this book by permission of Charles Scribner's Sons.

3. *Ibid.*, p. 244.

4. *Ibid.*, pp. 245–246.

5. There were occasional exceptions to this identification of the Son and the Logos, e.g., Marcellus of Ancyra. Cf. Pelikan, *The Christian*

Tradition: A History of the Development of Doctrine, Vol. I, *The Emergence of the Catholic Tradition (100–600),* pp. 207–208.

6. Sabellius' own position is not precisely known and was probably not so simple. Cf. Pelikan, *The Christian Tradition,* Vol. I, p. 179.

7. Origen is not consistent on this point, and he sometimes speaks of the Logos as created. Cf. Pelikan, *The Christian Tradition,* Vol. I, p. 191; Origen, *On First Principles,* ed. by G. W. Butterworth (Harper & Row, Publishers, Inc., 1966), p. 314.

8. Pelikan distinguishes a third that identified "three states in the history of the person of Christ: Only divine before the incarnation . . . , both divine and human during his kenosis . . . , and still completely man and completely God in his exaltation" (*The Christian Tradition,* Vol. I, p. 256). He traces this doctrine from Hilary to Augustine and the Tome of Leo that placed its mark so decisively in Chalcedon. However, Pelikan recognizes its lack of conceptual rigor.

9. Pelikan points out that eucharistic thought supported the doctrine that the natural or creaturely was transformed into the divine rather than supplemented by it. This accorded with Alexandrian Christology and was in tension with that of Antioch. (Cf. Pelikan, *The Christian Tradition,* Vol. I, pp. 236 ff.)

10. Eutyches is the key figure. For his statement and defense of his position, see Robert Ferm (ed.), *Readings in the History of Christian Thought* (Holt, Rinehart & Winston, Inc., 1964), pp. 169–170.

11. Adolf von Harnack, *History of Dogma,* Vol. IV, tr. from the 3d German edition by Neil Buchanan (Dover Publications, Inc., 1961), pp. 264–265.

CHAPTER 10
CHRIST AND THE CREEDS

1. Cf. Morton Smith, *Clement of Alexandria and a Secret Gospel of Mark* (Harvard University Press, 1972).

2. Emil Brunner, *The Christian Doctrine of God,* tr. by Olive Wyon (The Westminster Press, 1950), pp. 227–228.

3. Schoonenberg, *The Christ,* p. 75.

4. *Ibid.,* p. 87.

5. Alfred North Whitehead, *Adventures of Ideas* (The Macmillan Company, 1933), pp. 214–215.

6. *Ibid.,* p. 216.

CHAPTER 11
CHRIST AS THE IMAGE OF HOPE

1. Augustine, *The City of God,* XIV, ch. 25.

2. Pierre Teilhard de Chardin, *Science and Christ* (Harper & Row,

Publishers, Inc., 1968), pp. 212–213. I am indebted to Bernard Lee for calling my attention to this and certain other important passages in Teilhard. Cf. Bernard Lee, *The Becoming of the Church* (Paulist Press, 1974).

3. Cf. Walter H. Capps, "Mapping the Hope Movement," in Walter H. Capps (ed.), *The Future of Hope* (Fortress Press, 1970). Capps ably shows the centrality of Bloch's work for what he calls the "hope movement" (i.e., besides that movement's rootage in Christian tradition) and for recent ecumenical theology. He also shows how the earlier influence of Teilhard de Chardin and various forms of process philosophy provided a congenial context within which the theology of hope could win its way, although these did not directly inspire it.

4. Cf. William Irwin Thompson, *Passages About Earth: An Exploration of the New Planetary Culture* (Harper & Row, Publishers, Inc., 1973), esp. Chs. 5–7.

5. Ernst Bloch, "Man as Possibility" in Capps (ed.), *The Future of Hope*, p. 63.

6. *Ibid.*

7. *Ibid.*, p. 64.

8. *Ibid.*

9. Cf. Henry Nelson Wieman, *The Source of Human Good* (The University of Chicago Press, 1946), Ch. 3.

10. Cf. Cobb, *The Structure of Christian Existence.*

11. The close connection of Christ and hope for a better future can be recognized also by the Buddhist. Buddhism overcomes hope in this sense instead of seeking to ground it.

12. Jane Dillenberger, *Style and Content in Christian Art* (Abingdon Press, 1965), p. 200.

13. Jane Dillenberger, *Secular Art with Sacred Themes* (Abingdon Press, 1969).

CHAPTER 12
THE CITY OF GOD

1. Alfred Heller (ed.), *The California Tomorrow Plan* (William Kaufmann, Inc., 1972).

2. Cf. George R. Stewart, *Earth Abides* (Hermes Publications, 1974).

3. Warren Johnson, "Paths Out of the Corner," *IDOC International*, North American Edition, Oct. 1972.

4. The Arcological commitment has not been published in a book. It is used in Soleri's slide showings and on pieces of literature such as the 1973 Arcosanti calendar.

5. Paolo Soleri, *Arcology: The City in the Image of Man* (The MIT Press, 1969), p. 12.

6. Paolo Soleri, *Forum*, April 1974. *Forum* is an extended newsletter of the International Center for Integrative Studies.

CHAPTER 13
THE PERFECTION OF LOVE

1. Cobb, *The Structure of Christian Existence*, Ch. 12.

2. Note that most Buddhists deny that Buddhism *is* a pluralism, a monism, or a nihilism. Cf. Kenneth K. Inada, "Some Basic Misconceptions of Buddhism," *International Philosophical Quarterly*, Vol. 9, No. 1 (March 1969), pp. 101–119.

3. The possibility of this kind of development in Buddhism has been discussed in some detail by David Griffin, "Buddhist Thought and Whitehead's Philosophy," *International Philosophical Quarterly*, Vol. 14, No. 3 (Sept. 1974), pp. 261–284.

4. Jean-Paul Sartre, *The Transcendence of the Ego: An Existentialist Theory of Consciousness*, tr. by Forrest Williams and Robert Kirkpatrick (The Noonday Press, 1957).

5. Martin Heidegger, *Being and Time*, tr. by John Macquarrie and Edward Robinson (Harper & Row, Publishers, Inc., 1962), sec. 26.

6. Jean-Paul Sartre, *No Exit*, tr. by Paul Bowles (Samuel French, Inc., 1958), p. 52.

7. Whitehead, *Adventures of Ideas*, p. 368.

8. Buddhist leaders do, of course, recognize limitations just as Christians do, but at somewhat different points. Masao Abe writes: "Up to the present time it seems that Buddhism has not wrestled with this problem [of man's social life and history] successfully. Only rarely has Buddhism even raised a basic question about it. The time has come for it to ask whether and how the problem of ethics and history can be solved from the standpoint of *jinen*, which is entirely non-dichotomous. In order to be able to answer this basic question, Buddhism must break through its traditional patterns of thought and rethink the whole matter from the depth of its genuine spirit." ("Buddhism and Christianity as a Problem Today, Part II," *Japanese Religions*, Vol. 3, No. 3 [Autumn 1963], pp. 30–31.)

CHAPTER 14
THE KINGDOM OF HEAVEN

1. Beardslee, *A House for Hope*, p. 119.

2. *Ibid.*, pp. 118–119.

3. *Ibid.*, Chs. 1 and 2.

4. Whitehead, *Process and Reality*, pp. 517 and 527.

5. *Ibid.*, p. 522.

6. *Ibid.*, p. 520.

CHAPTER 15
THE RESURRECTION OF THE DEAD

1. This view has recently been beautifully put forward by Richard Taylor in *With Heart and Mind* (St. Martin's Press, 1973).

2. The astonishingly popular *Jonathan Livingston Seagull* expresses such partial Christianization and even historicization of metempsychosis.

3. It is significant that in our century, despite the dominance of existentialist tendencies, all the major renewals of emphasis on Jesus' personal resurrection have been strongly oriented to history: e.g., Pierre Teilhard de Chardin, Wolfhart Pannenberg, and Jürgen Moltmann.

4. Willi Marxsen, *The Resurrection of Jesus of Nazareth*, tr. by Margaret Kohl (Fortress Press, 1970).

5. Ulrich Wilckens, *God's Revelation: A Way Through the New Testament*, tr. by William Glen-Doepel (The Westminster Press, 1970). Wilckens has also published a more detailed and strictly historical study of resurrection: *Auferstehung: das biblische Auferstehungszeugnis historisch untersucht und erklärt* (Stuttgart: Kreuz-Verlag, 1970).

6. Marxsen, *The Resurrection of Jesus of Nazareth*, pp. 151–152.

7. *Ibid.*, p. 141.

8. *Ibid.*, p. 125.

9. *Ibid.*, p. 21.

10. Wilckens, *God's Revelation*, p. 29.

11. *Ibid.*, pp. 42–43. Cf. Wilckens, *Auferstehung*, p. 168: "Without this experience [of the resurrection of Jesus] Christianity would doubtless not have arisen."

12. Wilckens, *God's Revelation*, pp. 44–45. Cf. Wilckens, *Auferstehung*, pp. 168–169: "All the religio-ethical, world-changing élan, that has indwelt Christianity until now, is grounded in the truth of what the New Testament proclaims as the act of God in Jesus."

13. Wilckens, *God's Revelation*, p. 47.

14. Wilckens holds that the historical kernel of the empty tomb tradition is the story of the women finding the grave empty on Sunday morning. But "the story serves as the expression of faith in Jesus' resurrection, not to awaken it" (Wilckens, *Auferstehung*, p. 151).

15. In *Auferstehung*, Wilckens definitely defends only the appearance to James in addition to the appearances to Peter and Paul accepted by Marxsen (*The Resurrection of Jesus of Nazareth*, p. 147).

16. Wilckens, *Auferstehung*, p. 156.

17. Wilckens explicitly criticizes Marxsen's "wanting to recognize in the New Testament talk of Jesus' resurrection merely a means of

expressing the experience of faith, which can be just as well replaced by other forms of interpretation" (*Auferstehung*, p. 157).

18. Wilckens, *God's Revelation*, pp. 32–33.

19. Marxsen, *The Resurrection of Jesus of Nazareth*, p. 188.

20. Cf. especially Wolfhart Pannenberg, *What Is Man?* tr. by Duane Priebe (Fortress Press, 1970).

21. Wolfhart Pannenberg, *Jesus—God and Man*, tr. by Lewis L. Wilkins and Duane A. Priebe (The Westminster Press, 1968), pp. 88–92. Pannenberg also affirms the empty tomb tradition as providing accurate historical information, but does not insist upon this (pp. 100–102).

CHAPTER 16
THE UNITY OF HOPE

1. Pierre Teilhard de Chardin, *The Phenomenon of Man*, tr. by Bernard Wall with an introduction by Julian Huxley (Harper & Brothers, 1959), p. 300.

2. Whitehead, *Process and Reality*, p. 517.

3. *Ibid.*

4. *Ibid.*, p. 530.

5. *Ibid.*, p. 531.

6. Lewis S. Ford and Marjorie Suchocki, in an unpublished essay entitled, "A Whiteheadian Reflection on Immortality," p. 16.

7. Whitehead, *Process and Reality*, p. 525.

8. *Ibid.*, p. 527.

9. *Ibid.*, p. 531.

10. Ford and Suchocki, "A Whiteheadian Reflection on Immortality," pp. 14–15.

11. Cf. Whitehead, *Process and Reality*, pp. 520–521.

12. *Ibid.*, p. 531.

13. Wolfhart Pannenberg, "Future and Unity," in Ewert H. Cousins (ed.), *Hope and the Future of Man* (Fortress Press, 1972), p. 65.

14. *Ibid.*, p. 71.

15. *Ibid.*, p. 72.

16. *Ibid.*, p. 71.

17. *Ibid.*, p. 72.

18. Leslie Weatherhead is typical of the best popular writers on this subject. Cf. his *The Christian Agnostic* (Abingdon Press, 1965), pp. 253–339. Also Teilhard's image of Omega should not be excluded as a legitimate expression of Christian hope. Cf. Teilhard de Chardin, *The Phenomenon of Man*.

19. Pannenberg, *Jesus—God and Man*, pp. 86–88.

20. In his article on *ruach* in Palestinian Judaism, in *Theological Dictionary of the New Testament*, Vol. VI, p. 379, Erik Sjöberg points

out that "the Pharisees believed both in the immortality of the soul and also in the resurrection."

21. Pannenberg, *Jesus—God and Man*, pp. 94–99.

22. Wolfhart Pannenberg, "The Doctrine of the Spirit and the Task of a Theology of Nature," *Theology*, Jan. 1972, p. 15.

23. *Ibid.*

24. Teilhard de Chardin, *Science and Christ*, pp. 12–13, quoted from Lee, *The Becoming of the Church*, p. 133.

25. Whitehead, *Process and Reality*, p. 532.

26. Jürgen Moltmann, for example, explicitly contrasts the theology of hope with that of Teilhard as oriented to history rather than nature. Cf. Walter H. Capps (ed.), *The Future of Hope*, p. 71.

27. Wolfhart Pannenberg et al., *Spirit, Faith, and Church* (The Westminster Press, 1970), p. 28.

28. Emil L. Fackenheim, "The Commandment to Hope: A Response to Contemporary Jewish Experience," in Capps (ed.), *The Future of Hope*, p. 80.

POSTSCRIPT
THE TRINITY AND SEXIST LANGUAGE

1. Whitehead, *Process and Reality*, p. 532.

2. *Ibid.*, p. 531.

3. Pannenberg, "The Doctrine of the Spirit and the Task of a Theology of Nature," *Theology*, January 1972, p. 9.

4. *Ibid.*, p. 10.

INDEX